-81

Lawrence E. Thompson
(814) 873-6696

DIVINE HEALING OF THE BODY

BOOKS BY J. SIDLOW BAXTER

DIVINE HEALING OF THE BODY

J. SIDLOW BAXTER

ZONDERVAN
PUBLISHING HOUSE   OF THE ZONDERVAN CORPORATION
GRAND RAPIDS, MICHIGAN 49506

Library of Congress Cataloging in Publication Data

Baxter, James Sidlow.
  Divine healing of the body.
    1. Faith-cure. I. Title.
BT732.B35   615'.852   78-15096
ISBN 0-310-20720-7

Printed in the United States of America

Contents

Preface

Dear reader, the chapters which comprise this book were written not only with keen eagerness but with prayerful studiousness. Therefore this is not a book for superficial skimming. It is meant not only to interest but to challenge and to contribute constructively to one's thinking on an important subject.

All too many who may be attracted by such a title as *Divine Healing of the Body* seek nothing more than exciting confirmations and illustrations of miracle healing. It is publications of that sort which, unfortunately, many people "go for." They desire the lighter, pleasantly plausible, quickly stimulating rather than the painstaking and scriptural. Consequently, there is much mere emotionalism through the holding of exciting ideas on threadbare evidence.

With a subject like *Divine Healing of the Body*, there is need to inquire carefully, What saith the Scripture? Otherwise some of us might hug a phantom, thinking it is Scriptural truth, only to experience later, in case of illness, heart-rending delusion. So I ask you to read the following pages carefully and prayerfully, with your Bible at hand—for that Book of Books must ever be our decisive court of appeal. Whether you do or do not find yourself agreeing with all that is here written, dig into it open-mindedly, asking God Himself to guide you as you think into the matter of *Divine Healing of the Body*.

J.S.B.

Acknowledgments

Let me here make grateful acknowledgment of valued cooperation by the following. My thanks to Logos International, Plainfield, New Jersey, for allowing me to quote from H. Richard Casdorph's book *The Miracles* (1976); also to the Kathryn Kuhlman Foundation, Pittsburgh, Pennsylvania, for generous permission to use lengthy excerpts from the following three books: *Never Too Late* (1975), *Captain LeVrier* (1973), and *How Big is God?* (1974). The above permissions have meant much in my documenting parts of this present thesis.

Perhaps, also, I should acknowledge valuable appropriations from the late A. J. Gordon's *The Ministry of Healing;* also from the learned Benjamin B. Warfield's *Counterfeit Miracles* (1918; reprint ed., Edinburgh: Banner of Truth Trust, 1976); also Johann Neander's ten-volume *A General History of the Christian Religion and Church.* These works of those three departed worthies are now, of course, in the public domain. Also, in one place I have appreciatively appropriated some valuable paragraphs from the *British Encyclopedia* (1933 ed.). In the earlier and historical part of my treatise I have been glad to avail myself a time or two of Earle E. Cairns's *Christianity Through the Centuries* (Grand Rapids: Zondervan Publishing House, 1954), a masterly history of the Christian church which I recommend to all.

Last, but opposite of least, let me thank my treasured wife, who has typed (sometimes more than once) the manuscripts of all but one of the twenty-one volumes which it has been my privilege to issue. How glad I am that *she*, my dearest, is *not* in the "public domain"!

J.S.B.

Editor's note: Mrs. Ethel Baxter passed away during the time the manuscript was being edited for publication.

PART ONE

Divine Healing Through the Centuries

Is the Testimony Reliable?

A Royal Proclamation

KING NEBUCHADNEZZAR

> To the peoples, nations and men of every
> language who live in all the world:
> May you prosper greatly.

It is my pleasure to tell you about the miraculous signs and wonders
which the Most High God has performed for me.

> How great are his signs,
> how mighty his wonders!
> His kingdom is an eternal kingdom;
> his dominion endures from generation
> to generation.

A messenger, a holy one, coming down from heaven, said: You will be
driven away from people and will live with wild animals: you will eat
grass like cattle and be drenched with the dew of heaven. Seven times
will pass by for you until you acknowledge that the Most High is
sovereign over the kingdoms of men and gives them to anyone He wishes.
At the end of that time, I, Nebuchadnezzar, raised my eyes toward
heaven, *and my sanity was restored.* At the same time that my sanity was
restored, my honor and splendor were returned to me for the glory of my
kingdom. My advisers and nobles sought me out, and I was restored to
my throne, and became even greater than before. Now I, Nebuchadnezzar, praise and exalt and glorify

> The King of Heaven

because everything He does is right, and all his ways are just. And those
who walk in pride He is able to humble.

(Dan. 4:1-4, NIV)

> Praise, my soul, the KING OF HEAVEN,
> To his feet thy tribute bring;
> Ransomed, HEALED, restored, forgiven,
> Who, like thee, his praise should sing?
> Praise Him! Praise Him!
> Praise the everlasting King!

—Henry F. Lyte

CHAPTER ONE

Introduction

Until the long-looked-for Millennium sheds its golden transformations over our world, the subject of these pages will always be poignantly up to date for the big, sore reason that bodily sickness will not stop. One of the ironies of this present so-called age of enlightenment is that the discovery of new remedies seems tantalizingly outpaced by the incidence of new maladies.

Sooner or later sickness of one sort or another "gets" almost every one of us. Few of us sit in the rocking chair and gently pass into the Beyond on the last, placid sigh of a contentedly tired old age. With the far larger majority there is a painful and sometimes protracted struggle before the bird breaks free from the cage. Some who naively assume that they never need bother their heads about the matter are suddenly felled at one blow by the cancer brigand. Others find themselves impaled in the long-drawn-out martyrdom of multiple sclerosis. Others slowly but surely find themselves doddering to the grave in some disintegrating disease which baffles the ablest medical science. Thousands who go bouncing through years of rosy hope find themselves sitting with stark surprise and blanched faces in a doctor's consulting room, scarcely believing their ears as he sadly says, "Sorry, but there's really no hope." The scourge of sickness swings unceasingly, plowing ten million backs (and hearts) every day.

Christian believers have no exemption from this general lot of mankind. They are not immune from the inexorable laws of physical cause and effect in the present permitted scheme of things. Although their new birth by the Holy Spirit brings them a regenerated new *spiritual* life, they are still part of Adam's fallen humanity so far as their *bodies* are concerned; and they therefore inherit, with all others, the distressing physical legacies of the Fall. Because of the clean and temperate life which they lead, they *do* escape many of the self-inflicted disorders which the vicious living incur; but except for that, they are inseparably part and parcel of the racial travail.

What is more, the undergoing of sickness and suffering is often a more sensitively painful problem to Christian believers than to others because it seems cruelly, even exasperatingly, to clash with what they have been brought to believe about God. Inasmuch as everything which happens is viewed by the Christian as being related to the will of God, dire sickness wrings from the heart a groan echoing Calvary's "My God . . . why?" This is a different kind of "why" from that of the unregenerate who suffer in dull, spiritual ignorance.

Not a few Christians, knowing the Scriptures and the many healings recorded in them, are set wondering, *Why are there not healings now?* They and others find themselves vaguely but pleadingly groping after either healing or answer. Still others have loved ones who are laid low, crippled, suffering, languishing; and they too ask about divine healing as they see human doctoring unable to cure. Some of them are startled by reports of direct divine healings in crowded meetings; but they also glean that there are many dud healings and that in many instances there is no healing at all. What are they to believe? *Is* there hope of miracle healing? Does God's Word, the Bible, give ground for such hope? Who will tell them the sure truth?

It is with such thoughts in mind that I prayerfully approach these present studies, in addition to which there is a further stimulant, namely, that the subject has a resurrected prominence again today, accompanied by new developments which seem decidedly significant.

About the time our twentieth century came in, the churches of Europe and America were surprised, perhaps I should say shaken, by certain new theological and spiritual emphases. Destructive new theological concepts came in from the German schools of rationalistic Bible criticism and far too quickly infiltrated the whole of Christendom. In extreme contrast to that, perhaps the most startling new spiritual feature was the reassertive emphasis on the Holy Spirit's activities in the Church, particularly in supernatural healings. Here in America, early in the nineteen hundreds, R. A. Torrey wrote these words in his book *Divine Healing:*

> The subject of Divine Healing is awakening an unusual interest in all parts of our country at the present time. Much is being said in favour of it, even by persons who have been opposed to the doctrine in times past; much is being said against it on every hand.
> Everywhere there is a most extraordinary interest in the subject. People are flocking by the thousands and tens of thousands in different cities to adventurers and adventuresses who oftentimes not only rob them of their gold but of that which is far more precious than gold. . . . There have been, to my personal knowledge, some very sad tragedies, insanity, death and shipwreck of faith arising from this pitiable business.[1]

If the upsurge of interest was such at that time, it is equally so, if not more so, today (though, hopefully, not with the same degree of charlatanism or hucksterism). After a short intervening ebb, occasioned seemingly by World Wars I and II, there is a flood tide of fascinated new inquiry into the subject. Once again, also, there are the protagonists and the antagonists. There are the "all-for-its" and the "won't-have-its." Some see only those Scriptures which *support* divine healing for the body. Others see only those Scriptures which ostensibly *disallow* its applicability to today. However, whether the pros or the cons have the ascendancy, the fact is that the subject is excitingly in vogue again, enlivened by peculiarities which do not seem to have appeared hitherto.

I cannot even remotely hope to please every reader by the searchings and findings in this chain of studies. Some, especially those who are linked up with modern charismatic groups, will be disappointed that I do not speak out at once in glowing endorsement of their teachings on healing. Others, who disapprove of the usual charismatic emphases as being extravagantly sensory, will be sorry that I do not clamp down on "all that sort of stuff." So I take a calculated risk in issuing these chapters! I feel rather like some ancient mariner edging through the Strait of Messina, with the whirlpool Charybdis on the port side and the jagged rock Scylla to starboard. My reassurance is that in my Bible I have a safe chart and compass; also (as I believe) I have a safe-guiding Hand from heaven on the helm. My one purpose is to "get through" with something Scripturally sound and worthwhile on a vital but vexed subject.

I have mentioned the certain new theological emphases which came from the late second half of the nineteenth century into the twentieth. Let me here say a word about the strong new theological emphasis, for it bears on our present studies. During my youth, when I lived in Lancashire, England, the German-originated Higher Criticism, or "new biblical scholarship," or "theological rationalism," or "modernism," had so stampeded through the officialdoms and pulpits of our main Protestant denominations that belief in miracles had been ousted by a supposedly superior knowledge. The intellectual snobbery of the modernists was such that at the faintest sniff or suggestion of a bodily healing by divine miracle, they would tilt their noses up in supercilious scorn. No longer was it left to atheists and skeptics to doubt or deny the miracles recorded in the Bible; it was now the fashion for Christian leaders, theological professors, and ordained ministers to desupernaturalize them.

As the straight-hitting Sir Robert Anderson wrote during that period, "The only thing distinctive about the infidelity of our own times is that it has assumed the dress and language of religion. Among its teachers are doctors of divinity and professors in Christian universities and colleges." As for healing *miracles* in this twentieth century: Nonsense! Miracles do not happen in an age of science, in a world of inexorable law, of inflexible cause and effect. The generally accepted thesis was "The reign of law is absolute and universal; therefore, a miracle is an impossibility." It sounded so scientific and final, but we might well have written over it the old lines from Hamlet:

> There are more things in heaven and earth, Horatio,
> Than are dreamt of in your philosophy.[2]

Today there is a marked change. That conceited desupernaturalizing of the Bible has been just about knocked to pieces by the spade of the archeologist and by scholarly rebuttals from giants of a truer biblical scholarship. Albeit, the *effects* of that modernism, or liberalism, still persist in our less-evangelical denominations, perpetuating the same *attitudes* toward the miraculous. To the educated natural man, even though a church member, miracles are an irritation. Both the secular scientist and the religious rationalist still try to disallow the factuality of a miracle because they are jealous of anything which man himself cannot perform or explain. Alongside that, the idea prevailing among most of our "churchy" ministers and congregations is that miracles are just "not proper" in decent Christian circles: the Lord's doings must be respectably dressed in natural cause and effect lest He should break out of bounds and work surprises which would bring discredit on the Faith!

So far as people in general are concerned, strangely enough (such are the unpredictable alternations of history) there is a swing of the pendulum to the opposite extreme; for nowadays not only is there belief in the supernatural, but everywhere there is *superstition*. That is always what happens when public belief in the supernatural drifts away from its true moorings in the Bible. At the present juncture there is popular reaction against both religious and philosophical rationalism, but there is not a corresponding return to the Bible. Even among Evangelicals there tends to be a gullible emotionalism, a feverish running after the exciting, the demonstrative, the miraculous. For every ten people today who do not believe in miracles, there are a hundred who *do* — and often on insufficient grounds. Kathryn Kuhlman's ensign, under which thousands recently have marched, was *I Believe in Miracles*. Whatever else she may or may not have been, the recently deceased Kathryn was a sign of the times. She represented the latest mood, reaction, searching, and longing among multitudes of eager Evangelicals: "Yes, yes, we want to know the truth about divine healing of the body."

Well, those are the two attitudes going side by side in our present-day mix-up. Meanwhile, I am sure that very many among us are wanting to get our feet on solid rock, wanting to know whether the true answer to miracle healing is yes or no.

What, then, is the balanced truth about healing? Far abler pens than mine have written on the subject, but perhaps a point has now been reached where an up-to-the-moment resurvey of the data might be helpful. So under that conviction I find myself asking two questions mainly. (1) What are the Biblical bases on which the teachers of direct divine healing rest their case? (2) What clear proofs of such healings can be furnished?

However, before we can respond to these two questions adequately we need to see the subject as a whole in its historical perspective. Divine healings of the body (or at least reports of such) are not a phenomenon of the twentieth century only. They have occurred, either actually or purportedly, from Apostolic days right down to the present hour. All amply validated divine healings today, if such there are, must be viewed as the latest link in a long chain stretching through the centuries; and from this chain we must not sever them, or else we shall be the more liable to reach wrong or uncertain conclusions.

The Term "Divine Healing"

Another preparatory necessity is that we make clear our terms. The four most usual in connection with our subject are (1) "divine healing," (2) "miracle healing," (3) "faith healing," and (4) "supernatural healing." Each of these is used ambiguously by one group or another, with attendant confusion or sometimes hurtful delusion. Take this recent comment of an evangelical minister: "Certainly I believe in divine healing. In answer to prayer God often heals through medical skill, which is just as truly divine healing as by any other means." In the first statement "divine healing" ostensibly means direct intervention from God whereas the second statement refers to healing through professional doctoring.

Christian Science, so-called, has laid claim to many divine healings; yet no such healings can truthfully be called *divine*, i.e., from God, for Christian Science rejects outright the idea of a personal God. On that score alone it cannot be either Biblical or Christian for if there is one thing emphasized more than another in Biblical revelation, it is that God is a *personal* Being.

It would almost appear as though Mrs. Eddy believed in a personal God when she wrote in the *Christian Science Journal*, "The words I have written on Christian Science contain absolute Truth. . . . I was a scribe under orders, and who can refrain from transcribing what God indites?"[3] Yet in *Science and Health* she stated that God "is not a person, God is Principle" and also that God "is Love, and Love is Principle, not person."[4] Warfield observed that "the whole foundation of Mrs. Eddy's theory and practice alike was denial of the personality of God."[5] That has been true of her successors ever since. A writer in the *Christian Science Sentinel* for September 25, 1907, representatively said, "Principle and not personality is the only foundation upon which we can build safely."[6]

Let it be clearly understood that in these present studies, when we speak of "divine healing," we always mean healing by direct intervention of the one and only true God, the living and *personal* God revealed in Holy Writ and crowningly so in our Lord Jesus Christ.

"Miracle Healing"

From an evangelical standpoint, one of the worthiest books written on divine healing is the saintly A. J. Gordon's *The Ministry of Healing*, issued in the 1870s. In it he defined a miracle as "the immediate action of God, as distinguished from his mediate action through natural laws."[7] Later (1918) the learned Benjamin B. Warfield, critically surveying Gordon's book, endorsed that definition of a miracle and added that "no definition could be clearer or better."[8] Yet with all respect to those two exegetical specialists, surely that definition is faulty; for a miracle is *not* always an "action of God." Miracles can be wrought by Satan and demons. Pharaoh's magicians wrought miracles in competition with Moses, but were *they* "of God"? Deuteronomy 13:1-2 warns against false prophets who perform "signs and *wonders*" (Heb. *mopēt* = miracles as in 29:3, emphasis mine). In Revelation 13:13 the Antichrist "makes fire come down from heaven" and deceives men by other "sign miracles." Again, in chapter 16 we see "the spirits of demons, working miracles" (v. 14). Yet again, in chapter 19 the "false prophet" is said to work "miracles" which deceive men (v. 20).

When Nicodemus came to our Lord by night, he said, "Rabbi, we know that thou art a teacher come from God: for no man can do these miracles that thou doest, except God be with him" (John 3:2). As a syllogism it was logically correct. (1) Every one who works miracles is sent of God. (2) This man works miracles. (3) Therefore He is sent of God. But the major premise is wrong; i.e., every one who works miracles is sent of God. In fact, the Pharisees attributed our Lord's miracles to Satan; and doubtless miracles by Satan were well in evidence, for instance, as seen in the magical arts and wonders of Simon Magus in Acts 8.

That miracles have happened at different times during the church's history seems well established, but have these all been *divine* miracles? Also, that miracles have happened at Lourdes is said to be "abundantly proved"; but is there equal evidence that these have all been *divine* miracles? Still more recently, miracles of healing are reported and apparently documented among occult groups. Would any of us, or even the occultists themselves, call *those* "divine" healings? I would state plainly, therefore, that in these present studies the expression "miracle healing" will *not* uniformly mean a *divine* healing. It may *sometimes* mean so; but in each instance the context will have to indicate whether the healing is divine or otherwise.

"Faith Healing"

Until recently the term "faith healing" has been widely used, though at present it is applied more cautiously, even suspiciously, and rightly so; for there are modern faith healings which are neither divine nor even physiologically supernormal. So let me underscore that by "faith healings" I mean healings which are effected *through* faith, not merely *by* faith. Bodily healings which come *through* Christian prayer and faith come from God whereas healings which are wrought *by* faith are no more than the reflex effect of faith itself upon mind and body. We may amplify this by adding that "faith healings" in the sense of their coming directly from God *through* faith are healings without the use of *means* (sometimes despite means) whereas cures which are achieved by faith itself, or by any other mental effort, are just as *non*-miraculously produced by means as if they were the result of the surgeon's knife or of a specific drug. And it would tend towards clearness if such healings were always classified as being neither more nor less than *psychotherapeutic* healings.

Admittedly, in these days astonishing physical results are obtained by the intensified action of faith itself; yet such "faith healings" are by no means new even though some of the techniques are. It has been truly observed that faith healing is the oldest form of healing in the world. Today it appears in new forms corresponding with scientific advance and new psychological patterns which have developed since Sigmund Freud. We have "mental healing," as in Christian Science, which treats disease as an illusion and aims at curing it by transferring from the practitioner to the sick person "the discovery that he is well." There is "magnetic healing" in the form of hypnotism or mesmerism, alias animal magnetism. There is spiritualistic healing, so-called, practiced by spiritist mediums. There is "spiritual healing" engaged in by groups who are theistic but not Christianly so. Rightly do they say, "The power which alone can heal is of God"; but it is by the faith of the healer (rather than of the sufferer) that there is induced an "influx of spiritual life" which brings health in place of sickness.

Also, of course, there are now the more-or-less evangelical charismatic groups who ostensibly effect cures through group mind-and-prayer focus. So far as I have ascertained, the healings associated with those groups are usually of the more gradual kind, which (to my own mind at least) makes a doubt-provoking contrast with the instantaneous miracles of our Lord and his Apostles. I do not wish unkindly to prejudge, but that kind of "faith healing" seems to me rather like an approximation to Christianized telepathy.

In all these naturalistic species of "faith healing," a most potent factor is *suggestion*. We make no charge of insincerity in its use. If it can be an agent bringing relief to sufferers in mind and body, we can be truly grateful. Not only faith healers but psychiatrists and physicians know today, more than ever before, the healing effect which can be produced by a suggestion powerfully gripping a human mind. The crucial differential which I would forcefully note again here is between healings which come *through* faith (i.e., from God) and those which are induced *by* faith (i.e., by the effect of faith itself). If and when we use the phrase "faith healing" in these present studies, we shall mean healings which come *through* faith from *God* unless otherwise indicated.

Benjamin B. Warfield called attention to the fact that apparently all so-called faith cures are confined to the realm of *functional* as distinct from *organic* diseases and from limb or bone fractures requiring osteoclasis or other surgery. He quoted Sir William Osler as telling in a few direct words why Mrs. Eddy went to a dentist: "Potent as is the influence of mind on body and many as are the miracle-like cures which may be worked, all are in *functional* disorders; and we know only too well that nowadays the prayer of faith neither sets a broken thigh nor checks an epidemic of typhoid fever."[9]

Luther T. Townsend issued this challenge to the Christian Scientists:

> If you or the president of your college, or your entire college of doctors, will put into place a real case of hip or ankle dislocation, without resorting to ordinary manipulation or without touching it, I will give you a thousand dollars. Or if you or your president or your entire college, will give sight to one of the inmates of the South Boston Asylum for the Blind, that sightless person having been born blind, I will give you two thousand dollars.[10]

The dollars were in no jeopardy. The challenge was evasively bypassed. "The drawing of a tooth is not a great thing," noted Warfield, "but Mrs. Eddy's Science was not equal to it. . . . She employed the good office of a dentist to obtain relief, and even availed herself of his 'painless method' to guard herself from suffering in the process. . . . Mrs. Eddy had no Lord to pray to. . . . Let us be thankful she at least had a dentist."[11] We remember, too, that she later had to wear glasses, evidently unable either by faith or mind to heal her ocular defect.

We are not alone in thinking that faith healing is limited to *functional* ailments only. Warfield referred to some comments of the greatly esteemed English physician A. T. Schofield. After visiting a faith-healing home, he reported that he was unable to find there any cure of a "truly organic disease. The bulk at any rate of the cases benefited are clearly mental, nervous, and hysterical."[12] J. M. Charcot, another physician, wrote to the same effect: "The domain of faith-healing is limited."[13] It is confined, he said, to that area alone where "the power which the mind has over the body" is enough to account for the cure. Nor can it ever "pass these bounds," he added, for it is "powerless against natural laws. For example, no instance can be found amongst the records sacred to so-called miraculous cures where the faith-cure has availed to restore an amputated limb."

It should be noted, though, that in the foregoing quotations (as in other critiques which might be cited), there is again no distinction made between healings *through* faith (i.e., from God) and healings *by* faith (i.e., purely natural). In the strictly Christian sense, faith healings are solely those which come through faith directly from God Himself; they are so genuinely miraculous that they simply cannot be naturalized.

Warfield's threefold conclusion was (1) miraculous healings *through* faith (i.e., from God) do not happen today; (2) on critical investigation, those which are *said* to be miracle healings can be explained naturalistically; and (3) whether they claim to be miracle healings or not, they are limited to functional disorders as distinct from organic disease. Is he right? I believe that on all three counts he is wrong, as will come up for consideration later.

"Supernatural Healing"

We could wish that all preachers and writers on our special subject were more precise and perspicuous in their use of the term "supernatural healings." In the final analysis, of course, *all* healing is from God. A famous French surgeon Ambroise Paré, who died in 1590, now known as "the first of the moderns," had a saying: "I apply the dressing, but God heals the wound."[14] It may have seemed truer then than now, for until about fifty years ago all a doctor could do was to put the patient into as conducive a state as possible to enable the body to cure itself. There were scarcely any specific drugs apart from quinine for malaria, iron for anemia, and digitalis for certain types of heart disease. How different today, with all the sophisticated surgical instruments and the more than two thousand specific drugs—all discovered since Paul Ehrlich demonstrated arsphenamine (about 1900) as a specific for syphilis and Sir Alexander Fleming (in 1928) discovered the antibiotic penicillin! Yet only a few months ago a distinguished otologist in California remarked to me, "I never perform an operation without looking to God for help and healing. As I see it, fundamentally all healing is a miracle."

It always rings a responding bell in my heart when I hear a modern medic speak like that. I fully agree with him: Fundamentally, all healing is a miracle. Why *should* diseased or injured human bodies so often heal *themselves,* even when helped by careful treatment? Why doesn't the disease or injury persist deterioratingly until life is quenched by death? Bodily self-healing is indeed a miracle. Yet such use of the word "miracle" in that connection is none-the-less misleading. As with some other words (e.g., "perfect"), there is both an exact use and a hyperbolic use.

The unfolding of the golden daffodil from its drab-looking bulb is a miracle. The metamorphosis from egg, larva, caterpillar, chrysalis to gay-winged butterfly is a miracle. That big-scale annual resurrection which we call Spring is a miracle. That field of harvest gold from a few bags of tiny seeds is a miracle. The lily of the valley "down here" and the suspension of that Alpha star "out there" are equally miracles. In that same sense all life on this planet, both sentient and nonsentient, is a miracle. Yet all these are only "miracle" hyperbolically, not in the *exact* sense; for they are all brought about by the operation of second causes in the realm of natural law.

However seemingly abnormal an occurrence may be, if on careful examination it can be accounted for by the operation of natural cause-and-effect, it is *not* a miracle in the exact sense. Nothing is truly miracle which is not truly *supernatural.* It must be even more than superhuman and preternatural; it must be nothing less than *supernatural,* i.e., beyond all possible explanation in terms of natural law or human science.

Therefore, when we speak about "supernatural healing," we mean scientifically inexplicable miracle. We may not always mean divine healing, for supernatural is not synonymous with divine. Satan and his auxiliary angels and demon accomplices are supernatural beings, and they can perform supernatural works; so supernatural is not necessarily divine. That intellectual British prime minister of Victorian times, William Ewart Gladstone, in replying to the skeptic philosopher Hume, wrote, "Now, unless we know all the laws of nature, Hume's contention [against the admissibility of miracles] is of no avail; for the alleged miracle may come under some law not yet known to us." But the right honorable statesman was wrong. For if an alleged miracle can be explained by *any* natural law,

whether a known law or "some law *not* yet known to us," it ceases to
be a miracle. A true miracle, whether wrought by God Himself or by
some lesser but supernatural being, is a *direct* act from that sphere
which is *above* the "natural laws" operating in the physical creation.

So, then, let us sum up these prior clarifications. (1) By "divine
healing" we mean bodily healing *directly* communicated by the one
true God. (2) By "miracle healing" we mean healing which is
demonstrably beyond all naturalistic explanation. (3) By "faith
healing" we mean solely that healing which comes *through* faith
directly from God unless otherwise stated. (4) By "supernatural
healing" we mean healings directly effected either by God Himself
(by far the more often) or by supernatural spirit intelligences.

What a story is that of the Christian Church. Is there anywhere a
comparable romance of truth stranger than fiction—unless it be that
of the nation Israel? What a contiguity of opposites—of heavenly
minded exploit and carnal drama, of noble adventure and ignoble
lapses, of orthodoxy and heterodoxy, of selfless spirituality and
clerical avarice, of heroic martyrdoms and surreptitious maneuver-
ing, of triumph and tragedy, of periodic decline and surprise resurgence!

In broad outline the history of organized Christianity may be said
to run in three periods: (1) the *early* period, i.e., roughly the first five
centuries A.D., (2) the *midway* or mainly medieval period, i.e., A.D. 500
to 1600; (3) the *later* period, i.e., from about 1600 down to the
present.

The first of these three periods is often referred to as the *patristic*
because in it the early "Fathers" of the Church wrote, exhorted,
championed, defended, and hammered the Christian facts and faith
into basically standard doctrine. The patristic era may be sub-
divided into ante-Nicene and post-Nicene: (1) the period preceding
the Council of Nicea, which gave us the Nicene Creed in A.D. 325, and
(2) the period following that event and going down to the Fall of
imperial Rome in 476.

Already, toward the end of the fourth century, those earliest
Christian writers of outstanding influence in the pre-Nicene centuries had become known as the Fathers. Their very antiquity now
tends to surround them with an aura of sanctity. Yet some of the very
greatest Fathers in the Church's early period came during the post-
Nicene centuries: Athanasius (296-373), Basil of Caesarea (329-

379), Gregory of Nazianzus (330-389), Gregory of Nyssa (330-395), Ambrose (339-397), Augustine (354-430), Chrysostom (345-407), Jerome (345-419).

True to form, in elevating tradition to a practically equal authority with the Bible, the Roman Catholic Church views the Fathers as infallible, at least where they exhibit unanimity. We evangelical Protestants will allow them no such inerrancy, though we accord them the special respect which properly belongs to them, recognizing the unique value of their testimony. As a matter of fact, even among the ante-Nicene Fathers, who are the nearest link back to the Apostles themselves, there is considerable disagreement. As H. L. Ellison of England said in *Baker's Dictionary of Theology,* "It is a striking fact that whenever we turn to Ante-Nicene exegesis for light on more difficult New Testament passages, we find the most divergent views."[15] We therefore cannot allow those venerated worthies any infallibility in whatever they may tell us about divine healings of human bodies in those now misty yesterdays.

Perhaps it is well to be reminded that our inquiry into the occurrence of supernatural healings is only one part of a larger subject, namely, miracles. Apart from anything else, the necessity to economize in page-space will limit us strictly to miracles of *healing,* and even so our treatment must be as brief as clearness will allow. So, then, we shall first consult the testimony of the patristic period, or, roughly the first five centuries A.D.

NOTES

[1]R. A. Torrey, *Divine Healing* (Grand Rapids: Baker Book House, reprint 1974), p. 12.

[2]*Hamlet,* I, v, 206-7.

[3]*Christian Science Journal,* January 1901: quoted in B. B. Warfield, *Counterfeit Miracles* (1918; reprint ed., Edinburgh: Banner of Truth Trust, 1976), p. 319, n. 32.

[4]*Science and Health, With Key to the Scriptures,* ed. 1875, ed. 1881, and *No and Yes,* 1906.

[5]Warfield, *Miracles,* p. 320, n. 41.

[6]*Christian Science Sentinel,* 25 September 1907.

[7]A. J. Gordon, *The Ministry of Healing.*

[8]Warfield, *Miracles,* p. 161.

[9]*The Treatment of Disease,* 1909: quoted in Warfield, *Miracles,* p. 229.

[10]*Faith Work, Christian Science and Other Cures:* quoted in Warfield, *Miracles,* pp. 227-28.

[11]Warfield, *Miracles,* p. 230.

[12]*A Study of Faith-Healing,* 1872: quoted in Warfield, *Miracles,* p. 309, n. 43.

[13]*The New Review,* vol. 8, p. 19: quoted in Warfield, *Miracles,* p. 309, n. 44.

[14]"Je le pansay et Dieu le guarit"

[15]Everett F. Harrison, ed., *Dictionary of Theology* (Grand Rapids: Baker Book House, 1960).

The Patristic Period

To sum up: an examination of the passages in apostolic literature which treat of spiritual gifts inevitably brings us to the conclusion that the life of the early church was characterized by glowing enthusiasm, simple faith, and intensity of joy and wonder, all resulting from the consciousness of the power of the Holy Spirit; also that this phase of Spirit-effected ministries and service was temporary, as such "tides of the Spirit" have since often proved, and gave way to a more rigid and disciplined Church Order, in which the official tended more and more to supersede the charismatic ministries.[1]

—R. Martin Pope

CHAPTER TWO

The Patristic Period

I have before me the ten closely written volumes of the German Jewish scholar Johann August Wilhelm Neander: *A General History of the Christian Religion and Church*.[2] It covers from the first century A.D. to the beginning of the fifteenth. So far as I am aware, a more encyclopedic history of the Christian church, covering that long period, has never been written by any other man. I quote from it the more confidently because, along with the learned Neander's penetrating insight into the mutual relation of historical phenomena, there is a determined fidelity to the true facts and real meanings.

After an ample description and analysis of the old Roman world—religiously, philosophically, intellectually, socially—into which Christianity at first came, Neander points out that over against wide disillusionment with the old religions (among the upper classes) and with the fake miracles of hoodwinking magicians (among the lower classes), the *genuine* miracles of physical healing and demon expulsion wrought by the Christians were peculiarly appropriate and convincing. The "striking facts" of such indubitable healings were necessary at that time, says Neander, to bring people out of their entanglement with pseudo-philosophies and deceptive arts so as to "render them capable of higher spiritual impressions." He adds, "To this end served those supernatural operations which proceeded from the new, creative power of Christianity, and which were destined to accompany it until it had blended itself completely into the natural process of human development."

Neander draws an interesting picture of those days and the part which miracle healings played.

> Let us bring before our minds some of those cases in all their vivid connection with the character and spirit of the times. A Christian meets with some unhappy individual sunk in heathenish superstition, who, diseased in body and soul, had in vain hoped to get relief in the temple of Esculapius [i.e., Asclepius, the god of medical art, with temples in widespread cities] where so many in those days sought a cure for their diseases, in dreams sent from the god of health [see the Orations of Aristides]. To no purpose also had he tried the various incantations and amulets of pagan priests and dealers in enchantments. The Christian bids him to look no longer for help from impotent and lifeless idols, or from demoniacal powers, but to betake himself to that Almighty God who alone can help. He [God] hears the prayers of all who invoke His aid in the name of Him by whom He has redeemed the world from sin. The Christian employs no magic formulas, no amulets, but, simply calling upon God through Christ, he lays his hand on the sick man's head, in faithful reliance on his Saviour. The sick man is *healed;* and the cure of his body leads to that of his soul.

Neander refers to the prevalence of demon possession—both imagined and real—at that time and then comments:

> There was no want, either among Pagans or Jews, of pretenders who by various methods—perfuming with incense, embrocations, medicinal herbs, amulets, adjurations expressed in strange enigmatical formulas—set themselves to expel those demoniacal powers. In any case, if they produced any effect, it was only to drive out one devil by means of another. . . . What great credit these pretended exorcists obtained at the date we may judge from the "thanksgiving" which the Emperor Marcus Aurelius offers to the gods because he had learned from a wise instructor not to trust in any of the tales about the incantations and exorcisms of magicians and wonder-workers.
>
> It so happens that one who has vainly sought relief from such imposters falls in with a devout Christian. The latter recognizes here the power of darkness, and looks no farther for the cause of disease. But he is confident of this one thing, that the Redeemer has overcome the powers of darkness, and that in whatsoever form they may manifest themselves they must yield to Him. In this confidence he prays and bears witness of Him who by His sufferings has triumphed over the gates of hell; and his prayer, drawing down the powers of Heaven, works deeply and inwardly upon the distracted nature of the patient. Peace succeeds to the conflicts that had raged within. . . he is thoroughly and forever *healed*.

Such are the deductions drawn by Neander from the carefully considered data, but we must supplement them by quotations from some of the Fathers themselves.

Justin Martyr (100-165)

In his first *Apology*, Justin Martyr wrote the following:

That the empire of spirits has been destroyed by Jesus you may even now convince yourselves by what is passing before your own eyes; for many of our people, of us Christians, have healed and *still continue to heal* in every part of the world; and even in your city [Rome] numbers possessed of evil spirits [are healed] such as could not be healed by other exorcists, simply by adjuring them in the name of Jesus Christ, who was crucified under Pontius Pilate.

Irenaeus (c. 125-200)

Irenaeus in his *Adversus Haereses* (Book 1) tells us that often those who had been healed of demon-inflicted disorders thereby became believers and were added to the Church. He testifies also that through the laying on of hands maladies were healed. He even reports the raising of the dead, who afterward remained alive in the Church for many years. Moreover, with obvious confidence he appeals to these genuine supernatural attestations of Christianity as being in marked contrast to the juggling tricks resorted to by other would-be miracle workers. In Book 2: 4 he adds, "Wherefore also those who are in truth disciples, receiving grace from Him, do in His Name perform miracles so as to promote the welfare of others, according to the gift which each has received from Him"; and *"others still heal the sick* by laying their hands upon them, and they are made whole."

Back in 1882 Dr. George W. Samson made a clever attempt to discount this testimony of the early Fathers as to divine healings in their days, ingeniously arguing that when they used the present tense it was merely the "historical present," a literary form of referring to things which had happened back in the Apostles' days *as though* they were still occurring. That argument, however, which was used in particular against Irenaeus, is a drowning man clutching at a straw, as some of our quotations will show. Who can read without prejudice such words as those just quoted ("others *still* heal the sick," etc.) without seeing that Irenaeus is clearly referring to his own day? If that is not enough, consider the following longer culling:

For some certainly and truly drive out devils, so that those who have been cleansed from evil spirits frequently both believe [in Christ] and join themselves to the Church. Others have foreknowledge of things to come; they see visions, and utter prophetic expressions. Others *still* heal the sick by laying their hands upon them, and they are made whole. Yea, moreover, as I have said, even the dead have been raised up, and remained among us for many years. And what shall I more say? It is not possible to name the number of the gifts which the church throughout the world has received from God in the name of Jesus Christ, who was crucified under Pontius Pilate, and which she exerts *day by day* for the benefit of the Gentiles, neither practicing deception upon any, nor taking any reward from them [for such miraculous interventions]. For as she has received freely from God, freely does she also minister [to others].

Nor does she perform anything by means of angelic invocations, or by incantations, or by any other wicked, curious art; but, directing her prayers to the Lord who made all things, in a pure, sincere and straightforward spirit, and calling upon the name of our Lord Jesus Christ, she has been accustomed to work miracles for the advantage of mankind, and not to lead them into error. . . . The name of our Lord Jesus Christ *even now* confers benefits, and *cures thoroughly* and effectually all who anywhere believe on Him.

Tertullian (c. 160-220)

Tertullian, one of the Western Fathers, spoke so as to ensure beyond doubt that he was referring to what had happened in *his own days* when he mentioned this particular incident: "Even Severns himself, the father of Antonine, was graciously mindful of the Christians. For he sought out the Christian Proculus surnamed Torpacion, the steward of Euhodias, and in gratitude for his once *having cured him* by anointing, he kept him in his palace till the day of his death."[3]

Or take the following from the same book and section: "For the clerk of one of them who was liable to be thrown upon the ground by an evil spirit was set free from his affliction, as was also the relative of another, and the little boy of a third. And how many men of rank, to say nothing of the common people, have been delivered from devils and *healed of disease.*"

Origen (c. 185-c. 254)

Another witness is Origen, most famous of the early Eastern Fathers. Let me quote Neander again:

In his defence of Christianity against Celsus he [Origen] cites cases from his own experience where he had been an *eye-witness of the fact* in which, simply by invocation of the name of God and of Jesus, after the preaching of His history, many were healed of grievous diseases and states of insanity which neither human skill nor demoniacal influence had been able to relieve. . . . He calls God to witness that nothing was further from his wish than to attempt to add to the glory of Christianity by false statement, yet he could relate many things seemingly incredible which he had himself witnessed.

Let me quote Origen himself, from his *Against Celsus.*

And some give evidence of having received, through their faith, a marvellous power, by the cures which they perform, invoking no other name over those who need their help than that of the God of all things, and of Jesus, along with mention of his history. For we too have seen many persons freed, by those means, from grievous calamities and from distractions of mind and from madness and from countless other ills which could not be cured either by men or devils.[4]

We could quote elsewhere from Origen, underscoring that he was indeed referring to healings in *his own days.*

Neander himself takes a cautious view of those supernatural healings and other evidential miracles. While not doubting either the sincerity or the creditability of such godly and scholarly witnesses, he believes that the reported healings and other supernatural interventions were to be regarded as very subordinate to the big *spiritual* miracle of Christianity and as being much more relevant to the original propagation of the Christian message than to later centuries after the Christian faith had become established throughout the civilized world. More upon that later, but now we turn to a couple of the post-Nicene Fathers.

Chrysostom (345-407)

Chrysostom, who because of his supernormal eloquence is known as the "golden mouthed," was also a giant in moral and spiritual stature. He was one of the Eastern Fathers and the greatest of the Antiochian school. He was and still is hailed as the greatest pulpit orator the Eastern church ever had. About six hundred and forty of his homilies are still extant, and conjoined to his verbal skill is his marked ability as an expositor. In his *Libra Contra Gentiles* he comments on our Lord's words in John 14:12: "He that believeth on Me, the works that I do shall he do also; and greater works than these shall he do, because I go unto my Father." Chrysostom refers to the miracles recorded in the Acts of the Apostles as fulfilling that promise spoken by our Lord, and then he adds:

But if anyone should assert that those were mere smoke and a fictitious wonder unworthy of credit, let us view *those of the present day,* which are calculated both to stop and put to shame the blaspheming mouth, and to check the unbridled tongue. For throughout our whole habitable world there is not a country or a nation or a city where these wonders are not commonly spoken of, which, if figments, would never have occasioned so much admiration. And you yourselves indeed could testify to this. For we have no need to receive confirmations from others of what we assert, seeing that you yourselves, our opponents, supply us therewith.

Augustine (354-430)

In his notable work *Christianity Through the Centuries,* Earle E. Cairns observes: "Between the Councils of Nicea (325) and Chalcedon (451) several of the most able Fathers of the Christian Church did their greatest work. They endeavored to study the Scriptures along more scientific lines in order to develop their theological meaning. Because of the sheer weight of his work and his influence upon the Church of his day, Augustine was the greatest of these fathers."[5] By all proportions Augustine is truly great. The brilliant, recently deceased T. R. Glover, one-time senior wrangler at Cambridge, England, gave it as his view (which seems shared by other scholars) that the greatest four figures in the history of the Christian Church are Paul, Augustine, Luther, and Wesley. But besides that, Augustine's witness to divine healings in his own days is the more to be heeded because it overlaps well into the *fifth* century. Unfortunately, along with candor there is a blemish of oblivious inconsistency in his testimony to those miracle healings, though it is not such as to impair its basic value, as we shall presently see.

Regrettably, too, by the time we reach Augustine's later years, in the third decade of the fifth century, we find an unhealthy change in the *climate* of the Church's early history. Let it be borne in mind that the dividing date between the pre-Nicene and post-Nicene Fathers is 325 A.D. Twelve years before that date, one of the topmost events in the story of Christianity had occurred. By the edict of Constantine in 313, the persecuted religion of the Nazarene had become an officially accepted religion of the Roman Empire. From then onward the hated and hunted became the hailed and haloed. Instead of barbaric hostility came civility and acclaim. Many a nation (e.g., Rome itself) which has climbed to greatness through obstructive adversity has rotted to ruin through seductive prosperity. Something like that now began to show itself in ecclesiastical Christendom. There ensued a change of attitude, outlook, and spiritual quality. Deterioration set in, slowly indeed at first but eating its way more and more corrosively as decades slipped away. Before Augustine passed from this earthly scene in 430, deep shadows of superstition were creeping over the organized Church, as is perceivable in his testimony to healing miracles.

Yes, that edict of Constantine, which seemed at the time like a golden dawn heralding the promised Millennium, may well evoke a sombre mixture of feelings. In big, bold lines it objectifies the old adage, Not all that glitters is gold. It need not, in itself, have incepted the downgrade which followed, but in point of fact it *did*. All too soon afterwards men's minds began to be diverted from our Lord Himself to the Church, not to the Church as a spiritual fellowship, but as mainly a visible institution. Gradually but surely came the drift from evangelical doctrines to ecclesiastical sacraments, from Biblical truths to clerical rites, from sane sanctity to vain superstitions. A. J. Gordon remarks on the grim irony that as "death and the grave" gradually became "the goal of the Christian's hope,"[6] instead of the visible return of our risen Lord, miracles of healing began to be alleged, not through the prayer of faith to a living Christ, but through contact with the bones of dead saints—ruefully reminding us of Dante's lines:

> Ah, Constantine! of how much ill the cause,
> Not thy conversion, but those rich domains
> Which the first Pope received of thee!

As the Church forgot that her citizenship is in heaven and began to establish herself in luxury and splendor on earth, the genuine charismata gradually gave place to sentimental simulations and gullibility. This, we repeat, did not happen like an avalanche. It came in with almost imperceptible beginnings. Then, once in, it spread as with the tentacles of a clinging parasite. By the time of Augustine's later years, it was gripping extensively; and we must make allowance for that as we now requisition the princely theologian's testimony. He gave us much more material than we can reproduce here, but what we select is impartial and representative.

In a masterly way, Augustine gives special distinction to the New Testament miracles (i.e., of our Lord and the Apostles, especially our Lord's bodily resurrection), calling them the "former" miracles and asserting that they were greater than those wrought among Christians *since* then—for a very good reason. Those "former" miracles, he says, were foundational to the Christian faith and vitally necessary to its first confirmation and propagation in the world. That, however, does not minimize either the fact or the power of the many miracles wrought more recently. Then he goes on to say the following in *The City of God:*

> Even now miracles are wrought in the name of Christ . . . but they are not so brilliant and conspicuous as to cause them to be published with such glory as accompanied the former [i.e., New Testament] miracles. For the canon of the sacred writings . . . causes those [the former] to be everywhere recited and to sink into the memory of all the congregations; whereas these modern miracles are scarcely known even to the whole population in the midst of which they are wrought . . . especially if the state [or area] is a large one.[7]

After further such comment Augustine gave examples in book 22, chapter 8, from which we pick the following.

First, he says, "The miracle which was wrought at Milan when I was there, and by which a blind man was restored to sight, could come to the knowledge of many; for not only is the city a large one, but also the emperor was there at the time, and the occurrence was witnessed by an immense concourse of people that had gathered to the bodies of the martyrs, Protasius and Gervasius."

Second, Augustine relates a miracle healing at Carthage, his account being too long to reproduce here but of which we give the substance. These are the words with which he introduced it: "Who but a very small number are aware of the cure which was wrought upon Innocentius, ex-advocate of the deputy prefecture, a cure wrought at Carthage, *in my presence, and under my own eyes?*" (emphasis mine). After torturously painful surgery to remove intestinal abcesses, further surgery was found necessary to deal with a remaining inflamed fistula. The surgeons were called; but examination revealed that in answer to fervent prayer beforehand, the malignancy had completely disappeared.

Again, Augustine tells about "a very devout woman of the highest rank in the state" who had "cancer in one of her breasts." The physician had apparently advised that it was beyond operation. In a dream the Lord told her to intercept the first woman who came up from the baptistry that Easter time and ask her to make the sign of Christ upon the growth. "She did so, and was immediately cured."

Augustine further tells of a doctor in Carthage who suffered severely from gout and who was suddenly healed in the very undergoing of baptism. So besides losing all the "extraordinary pain he was tortured with," never again did he have gout though he "lived a long time afterwards." Alongside that "an old comedian of Curubis [a town near Carthage] was cured at baptism, not only of paralysis but also of hernia."

Augustine goes on and on until he says, "What am I to do? I am so pressed by the promise of finishing this work that I cannot record all the miracles I know; and doubtless several of our adherents, when they read what I have narrated, will regret that I have omitted so many which they, as well as I, certainly know."

It is puzzling to some of us, admittedly, that many such healings occurred in connection with the monuments or relics of martyrs. It tends to make those healings seem far-fetched. Yet scholars who are most knowledgeable of those days may be inclined to think that perhaps our Lord was using the best (even though poor) means at hand to work with a people very different from ourselves in culture, outlook, and susceptibility. Also, it may be that some of those monuments were places where the true Word was still preached; and we may reasonably assume that despite the growing veneration of shrines and such, the faith which brought healing was not faith *in* those outward objects but faith *through* them to the living Lord Himself. This, too, should be added: the concomitants of those early century healings were scarcely stranger than in the case of some extraordinary miracle healings of recent date, as we shall see later.

In some quarters there seems to be a grudging overcautiousness lest we should admit the full weight of the testimony from the early Fathers. Bishop John Kaye, in his book on Justin Martyr, thus detracted from this early testimony: "He produces no particular instance of an exercise of miraculous power, and therefore affords us no opportunity of applying those tests by which the credibility of miracles must be tried."[8] Buy *why* did not Justin go into any "particular instance"? Obviously for the same reason that many of us today do not give detailed instances when we are writing general statements about which the truth is so widely known that we need not use space in unnecessary particularizing. If the statements Justin made had not been true, they would have been torn to shreds by critical opponents almost as soon as they were written. Also, we cannot but wonder what sure "tests" of credibility could be applied at this present late date. If Justin *had* given individual names and places, would they have been any more verifiable than those miracle healings which he said were well known to those to whom he wrote his "Apology," seeing that they had occurred in the very city where they lived (Rome)? If individuals had been named, wouldn't doubters have said, "We do not know who those persons were; so we do not know what value to place on their testimony"?

The same objection is made by several against the testimony of Irenaeus and with the same lack of good reason. For if his statements had been erroneous, hostile critics would soon have made sport of him, as he well knew. Furthermore, there is no evidence anywhere that the veracity of either Justin or Irenaeus as to those divine healings was ever impugned.

However, no such lack of specific instances can be charged against the post-Nicene testimony. We have seen how detailed some of Augustine's references are. Yet he too must needs be made to appear doubtful, though for a different reason. Benjamin B. Warfield complained, with some seeming justification, that the illustrious Father contradicted himself in his witness as to divine healings. Warfield called attention to Augustine's seeming disbelief that miracles any longer happened, quoting from Augustine's treatise *On the True Religion:*

> *We perceive* [said Augustine] that our ancestors, by that measure of faith by which the ascent is made from temporal things to eternal, obtained visible miracles (for thus only could they do it); and through them it has been brought about that these should no longer be necessary for their descendants. For when the Catholic Church had been diffused and established through the whole world, those miracles were no longer permitted to continue in our time, lest the mind should always seek visible things, and the human race should be chilled by the customariness of the very things whose novelty had inflamed them. [9]

Warfield also quotes several sentences to the same effect from Augustine's *On the Usefulness of Believing.*

Is there any solution to these apparent discrepancies in Augustine's testimony? I think there is. The two works from which Warfield quotes were written in A.D. 390 and 391 respectively, only four or five years after Augustine's conversion (at the age of 32), whereas his greatest work, *De Civitate Dei* (or, as popularly known, *The City of God*), in which he so amply relates widespread miracles of healing, was not completed until 427, when he was over seventy. To which we may add, that in his even later *Retractationes*, written shortly before his death, he actually corrected what he had immaturely said in those first two treatises. In fairness I should mention that our always careful Warfield admitted this. But let me quote Augustine himself.

> For I myself, when I wrote that book [*On the True Religion:* 390 A.D.]
> already knew that a blind man had been given his sight in Milan, by
> the bodies of the martyrs in that city; and certain other things which
> were done at that time in numbers sufficient to prevent our knowing
> them all or our enumerating all we knew.[10]

Then again, as already noted, by the time of Augustine's mature
manhood, the stream of Christian experience and practice had
become muddied with much which was spurious while the necessary
means for separating pretense from reality and sentimental veneration from vital belief were not readily at hand. We can well understand why many "miracles" now became suspect or disregarded.
Even so, we must not jump to the gratuitous conclusion that because
some were fakes *all* were false. On the contrary, as in many other
connections, the superstitious copies of the real were a negative
witness to the real.

The Remarkable Anthony (251–356)

Another pertinent factor is that we know from other sources that
genuinely divine miracle healings *were* still happening up to the time
of Augustine's conversion, i.e., during the period in which he is
incorrectly supposed to have presumed that they were no longer
numerous. There can be no doubt that Anthony, the so-called father
of monasticism, who was born in 251 and died at the age of 105, just
after Augustine's birth, was used remarkably as one of our Lord's
healers. He may have been comparatively illiterate, but he had an
intuitive spiritual wisdom, nurtured by long solitudes in communion
with God, which lifted him far above most of the elaborately educated churchmen of those times. In his earlier years, Anthony had a
badly distorted idea of Christian separation, so impairing his health
by rigorous asceticism that at one point he almost swooned away.
Later he saw his big mistake and realized more truly the kind of love
God desires from us, though he still rigidly adhered to a monastic
regimen.

During those many years, Anthony became famous for his holy
character, for his wise sayings, and for the frequent bodily healings
imparted through him by the risen Lord. Little did he ever want to
be called the father of monachism or to be known as a healer. Such
thoughts drove him into further withdrawal. Let me quote Neander
concerning Anthony:

> He could easily have acquired the fame of being a worker of
> miracles, since many, particularly of those who were thought to be

possessed of evil spirits, were indebted to his prayers and to the impression of tranquility and peace which went forth from him. . . . But he pointed those who applied to him for help, or had been indebted to him for it, away from himself to God and Christ. . . . They were to know that the power of *healing* belonged neither to him nor to any other man, but was the work of God alone, who wrought it when and for whom He pleased.[11]

Such was Anthony; but although he was a cynosure, he was not so because he was a vehicle of divine healing. There were others, not a few, through whom healings came, right on through those decades up to the time of Augustine.

We recall, for instance, the so-called prince of the ancient exegetes, Theodore of Mopsuestia (Cilicia), almost to the same year of birth and death a contemporary of Augustine. Christlieb had the following comment to make concerning him:

With regard to the continuance of miracles after the Apostolic age, we have testimonies not only from Tertullian and Origen, who tell us that many in their time were convinced, against their will, of the truths of Christianity by miraculous visions; but also much later, from Theodore of Mopsuestia. The latter says, "Many heathen amongst us are being *healed* by Christians from whatever sickness they have, so abundant are miracles in our midst."[12]

Evidence From the Donatists

There is another circumstance, too, which further tones away the dissonance between Augustine's earlier and later comments on miracle healings and again confirms that such healings were then occurring widely. Soon after becoming bishop of Hippo, Augustine wrote against the Donatists, who were schismatical but not heretical. Here is what he penned: "Neither do we ourselves affirm that men ought to believe us because . . . such wonderful instances of answers to prayers or *the healings of sick ones* have been witnessed on sacred spots in the whole world, which have been visited by members of our communion."

The point is that in mentioning *those* divine healings, Augustine was setting them off against similar healings which were claimed as credentials by the dissenting Donatists themselves; so we thus have a *double* testimony to the widespread continuance of miracle healings. Furthermore, his words show us that during those earlier years his mind was too occupied with the great doctrinal issues of Christianity for him to be overly concerned with physical healings. As he himself said, the vital test is fidelity to divine *truth*, not miracles. That, indeed, he held to the end. But as we have seen, Augustine *did* later revise his thinking about the reality and value of supernatural healings and admitted so. They *were* still happening—right on into the fifth century!

I do not wish unduly to labor this aspect of Augustine's witness to the prevalence of miraculous healings, or to overpress the witness of the early Fathers as a whole, but I *am* anxious that the full force of it shall come through; for it is of great preliminary importance. So let me bring just one more factor into play which has a fascinating bearing upon the subject. Over against those scholars who hesitate to accept without modification the testimony of the early Fathers to such widespread miracle healings in those early centuries, there has lately come new evidence that the Fathers were correct and were *not* exaggerating.

The Biggest Miracle of All

I refer first to the amazing *spread* of Christianity in the first three centuries A.D., both geographically and numerically. Talk about miracles! The whole thing was a miracle—a miracle of conversion and expansion beyond compare! There is reason enough now to see how we have been misled through the figures and percentages given to us by Gibbon in his *Decline and Fall of the Roman Empire* and by some Christian historians as well.

For too long, it now seems, church historians have so overstressed the modifying influence of paganism on early Christianity that they have considerably unfitted us to realize the overpowering impact of Christianity on paganism itself in that ancient Roman world. Christianity did not merely collide with paganism and conquer it, but it changed the whole intellectual, moral, political, and cultural environment. It is questionable whether the new Christian faith either absorbed or even became mentionably infected by pagan impurities until the setting in of those dangerously easy days after Constantine proclaimed Christianity an officially accepted religion of the Roman Empire. This much, at least, is now certainly established, for as James Orr put it, "The effects of Christianity on pagan society, both extensively and intensively, were greater than has been admitted." [13]

The historian Gibbon estimated the population of Rome at about one million and the Christians there at about fifty thousand, or one-twentieth of the total. The population of the whole empire Gibbon gives as about 120 million and the Christians as about six hundred thousand, or again about one-twentieth. [14] Church historians have more or less agreed with those figures, though lately some have tended to compute a higher percentage of Christians. Even so, the statement by ante-Nicene Father Tertullian, that in his time, about the beginning of the third century, the Christians in a single province were more numerous than the entire Roman army, has been dismissed as unthinkable inasmuch as it would make the number of Christians in the empire about nine million!

Taking it for granted that it was impossible for the new religion to have made such wide conquest in so short a time, the attitude of our church historians has been that which is expressed in Williston Walker's *History of the Christian Church*, namely, that at the time when the Edict of Milan (313) granted the Christians equal rights, they were "*but a fraction* of the population" anywhere. Yet the true indications, so it now seems, may well be that Tertullian's statement was quite conservative.

Both Keim, in his *Rom und das Christenthum*, and Canon Robertson, in his *History of the Church*, believe that the Christians were by then no less than *one-sixth* of the Empire population. James Orr mentions that Victor Schultze—"one of the best informed of recent investigators"—has it that they were no less than *"one fifth or even more."*[15]

The Amazing Catacombs

One factor tending to these higher estimates is the evidence supplied by the Catacombs—evidence long there but until recently perhaps not keenly enough appreciated. Those immense underground burial places were excavated in "the soft volcanic tufa," or porous rock, near the great roads "within a radius of about three miles around Rome." Based on careful measurement of six different Catacombs, the total length of the passages covers 587 geographical miles! Each Catacomb consists of galleries and chambers of from three to five stories. It has been calculated that there were nearly *four million* graves in them, spread over approximately ten generations, during about two to three centuries. Even the lowest estimate places them at about *two million* as a *minimum*.

Of course, the numbers were smaller in the early generations and larger in the later; but taking a middle point, say about A.D. 230 to 250, what do we find? Let me quote James Orr again. "In reality, unless the testimony of the Catacombs has been totally misread, they [the Christians] might have been anything between one-third and one half" the population of Rome.[16] If, as according to Gibbon, the population of Rome was about one million, then the proportion of Christians would be anything from three hundred thousand to half a million! And if we accept Gibbon's ratio, that roughly the same proportion of Christians existed throughout the empire as in Rome, then we get the astounding yet evident figure of between forty- and sixty-million Christian believers by the end of the third century. This despite the successive, widespread persecutions! No wonder the last of the imperial persecutions under Diocletian (A.D. 303) broke down and the frustrated emperor simply had to come to terms! Christians were honeycombing society and commerce everywhere. They were even in the royal palace, among officials and employees there, as well as in the Roman army; and popular feeling toward them had lost its early hostility now that Christian truth was more widely known.

Can we not see, at last, that the famous letter of Pliny to the Emperor Trajan was no exaggeration? For the benefit of any uninformed reader, may I recall the circumstances? Plinius Caecilius Secundus, usually referred to as "Pliny the younger" to distinguish him from his uncle, Plinius Secundus the elder, was a man of eminent literary gift and a close friend of the Emperor Trajan. The letter which we here mention was written from Bithynia, perhaps within a year or two after Pliny became governor there at about A.D. 110. From the reign of Trajan to that of Antoninus Pius (98 - 161) Christianity, although still officially frowned upon, was not as bitterly persecuted as it was again to be under later emperors. Under the so-called five good emperors (Nerva, Trajan, Hadrian, Antoninus Pius, Marcus Aurelius), or at any rate under the first four of the five (96 - 161), even though Christianity was legally banned and had no right to exist and often incurred severe penalties, there was some degree at least of tentative toleration. There had been outbreaks of imperial madness against the Christians since Nero; yet by the time Pliny wrote to the Emperor Trajan in A.D. 110 or 111 (only forty years or so after Nero), we can see how the Christians were multiplying! Note particularly the lines which we italicize in Pliny's letter:

PLINIUS CAECILIUS SECUNDUS
TO THE EMPEROR TRAJAN

It is my custom, my Lord, to refer to thee all questions concerning which I am in doubt; for who can better direct my hesitation or instruct my ignorance? I have never been present at judicial examinations of the Christians; therefore I am ignorant how and to what extent it is customary to punish or to search for them. And I have hesitated greatly as to whether any distinction should be made on the

ground of age, or whether the weak should be treated in the same way
as the strong; whether pardon should be granted to the penitent, or he
who has ever been a Christian should gain nothing by renouncing it;
whether the mere name [i.e., "Christian"], if unaccompanied with
crimes, or crimes associated with the name, should be punished.

Meanwhile, with those who have been brought before me as Christians, I have pursued the following course. I have asked them if they
were Christians; and if they have confessed, I have asked them a
second and third time, threatening them with punishment. If they
have persisted, I have commanded them to be led away to punishment. For I did not doubt that whatever it might be which they
confessed, at any rate pertinacious and inflexible obstinacy ought to
be punished. There have been others afflicted with like insanity who
as Roman citizens I have decided should be sent to Rome. In the
course of the proceedings, as commonly happens, the crime was
extended, and many varieties of cases appeared.

An anonymous document was published, containing the names of
many persons. Those who denied that they were or had been Christians I thought ought to be released when they had followed my
example in invoking the gods and offering incense and wine to thine
image—which I had for that purpose ordered brought with the
images of the gods; and when they had also cursed Christ—things
which they say that those who are truly Christians cannot be com-
pelled to do. Others, accused by an informer, first said that they were
Christians and afterward denied it, saying that they had indeed been
Christians, but had ceased to be, some three years, some several, and
one even twenty years before. All adored thine image and the statues
of the gods, and cursed Christ.

Moreover, they affirmed that this was the sum of their guilt or
error, that they had been accustomed to come together on a fixed day
before daylight and to sing responsively a song unto Christ as God;
and to bind themselves with an oath, not with a view to the commission of some crime, but, on the contrary, that they would not commit
theft, nor robbery, nor adultery, that they would not break faith, nor
refuse to restore a deposit when asked for it. When they had done
these things, their custom was to separate and to assemble again to
partake of a meal, common yet harmless (which is not the characteristic of a nefarious superstition); but this they had ceased to do after my
edict, in which according to thy demands I had prohibited frater-
nities. I therefore considered it the more necessary to examine, even
with the use of torture, two female slaves who were called deaconesses
(ministrae), in order to ascertain the truth. But I found nothing except
a superstition depraved and immoderate; and therefore, postponing
further enquiry, I have turned to thee for advice. For the matter seems
to me worth consulting about, especially on account of *the number of
persons involved. For many of every age and of every rank and of both sexes have
been already and will be brought to trial. For the contagion of this superstition has*

permeated not only the cities, but also the villages and even the country districts. Yet it can apparently be arrested and corrected. At any rate, it is certainly a fact that the temples, which were almost deserted, are now beginning to be frequented, and the sacred rites, which were for a long time interrupted, to be resumed, and fodder for the victims to be sold, for which previously hardly a purchaser was to be found. From which it is easy to gather how great a multitude of men may be reformed if there is given a chance for repentance.

THE EMPEROR TRAJAN'S REPLY
(Commonly called "Trajan's Rescript")

Thou hast followed the right course, my Secundus, in treating the cases of those who have been brought before thee as Christians. For no fixed rule can be laid down which shall be applicable in all cases. They are not to be searched for. If they are accused and convicted, they are to be punished; nevertheless with the proviso that he who denies that he is a Christian, and proves it by his act *(re ipsa)* i.e., by making supplication to our gods—although suspected in regard to the past, may by repentance obtain pardon. Anonymous accusations ought not to be admitted in any proceedings, for they are of most evil precedent, and are not in accord with our age.

(Observation: If such anti-Christian measures were everywhere in operation even during the milder reigns, how remarkable indeed that by the opening of the second century believers were everywhere so numerous and apparently multiplying!)

All this, of course, has a big bearing upon our subject of divine healings through the centuries and especially upon the witness of the early Christian Fathers as to the continuance of those healings during the second, third, fourth, and fifth centuries of our era. For how can we explain that rapid, victorious, sweeping expansion of the new Christian religion throughout the known world, despite imperial persecutions of such frequency and ferocity and magnitude, unless there were those accompanying, authenticating miracles which the early Fathers and others report?

Certainly, there have been powerful revivals of Christianity at different times and in different places during subsequent centuries, with little or no accompaniment of physical miracles; but not one of them has been on such a world-wide scale or against such ruthless opposition of world government. Nor has any such Christian resurgence since then been the victory of a strange novel religion, contradicted and opposed by a hostile world environment. All such subsequent revivals have been reawakenings of a Christianity already well known and nominally accepted even though neglected (rather than bitterly opposed) by the masses. What happened in those first two-and-a-half centuries has had no parallel since. Even

the great Protestant Reformation was not a collision of Christianity
with world paganism or anti-Christian religions but a liberating
reaction against a corrupted form of Christianity itself. Similarly, the
glorious Methodist revival in Britain, as also revival outbreaks on
the European mainland, occurred in areas where Christianity was
already acknowledged—even by unbelievers—as the national religion.

Moreover, even in some of *those* revivals, if reports are trustworthy, there have been attendant physical miracles, including supernatural *healings*. This is also true of similar Christian upsurges on
overseas mission fields (a consideration of which, however, must
here be postponed).

In Review

What, then, must we conclude? Can the testimony of those ante-
Nicene and post-Nicene Fathers as to the continuing prevalence of
miracle healings be accepted as honest, well informed, and reliable?
Surveying again their intellectual stature, sobriety, definiteness, and
unanimity, we believe the answer is yes, in which conviction we are
the more confirmed because the efforts to reduce that testimony are
feeble or forced. Surely, unless our minds are biased by some theory
against such miracles, the evidence is clear and ample. Nor am I
alone in so thinking. Some of the most competent weighers of evidence have recorded their convincedness. As A. J. Gordon says,
"The weight of these and like testimonies [of the Fathers] is so
generally acknowledged by Church historians that it seems little less
than hardihood for scholars to go on repeating the well-worn saying,
'The age of miracles ended with the Apostles.'"[17]

As it is so important to establish whether divine healings did or did
not continue *after* the days of the Apostles (for if they did *not*, we
might as well terminate these studies right here), perhaps, finally, I
should quote a few acknowledged authorities. Take first Neander's
carefully weighed comment:

> The Fathers, down at least to the middle of the third century, in
> language which bespeaks the consciousness of truth, and often before
> the pagans themselves, appeal to such extraordinary phenomena as
> conducing to the spread of the faith: and however *we* may be disposed
> to interpret the facts, we must still admit *the facts themselves* and their
> effects on the minds of men. It is therefore undeniable that even
> *subsequently* to the Apostolic age the spread of the Gospel was ad-
> vanced by such [miraculous] means.[18]

The historian Mosheim, in his *Historical Commentaries: Century II*, spoke thus of the second century A.D.:

> That those gifts of the Spirit which are commonly termed miraculous were liberally imparted . . . in the succeeding age . . . has, on the concurrent testimony of the ancient fathers, been hitherto universally credited throughout the Christian world . . . Only let it be considered that the writers on whose testimony we rely were all of them men of gravity and worth, who could feel no inclination to deceive; that they were in part philosophers; that in point of residence and country they were far separated from each other; that their report is not grounded on mere hearsay, but upon what they state themselves to have witnessed with their own eyes; that they call on God in the most solemn manner to attest its truth (vid. Origen contra Celsum, L.I. p. 35), and lastly that they themselves do not pretend to have possessed the power of working miracles, but merely attribute it to others; and let me ask what reason can there possibly be assigned that should induce us to withhold from them our implicit confidence?

But what of the *fourth* century? Mosheim added: "I cannot, on the other hand, assent to the opinion of those who maintain that in this [fourth] century miracles had entirely ceased."

Even a keen critic like A. Tholuck concedes the following: "Down into the third century we have credible testimonies of the persistence of the miraculous forces which were active in the first century."[19]

Marshall, translator of Cyprian, commented, "There are successive evidences of them [i.e., healings and other miracles] . . . down to the age of Constantine."[20]

Dodwell has it that though they "generally ceased with the conversion of the Roman Empire" in the third century, there are several strongly attested cases "up to the close of the fourth."[21]

Gerhard Uhlhorn wrote, "Witnesses who are above suspicion leave no room for doubt that the miraculous powers of the Apostolic age continued to operate at least into the third century."[22]

Similar confirmations might easily be added, but are they needed? We may not necessarily agree with the *viewpoint* of some whom we have quoted, i.e., their theory that divine healings and other sign miracles *ceased*, either gradually or more abruptly, after the third or fourth century. The one vital point at the moment is their decided *concurrence* as acknowledged authorities on the subject, that such charismata, or supernatural activities of the Holy Spirit, *did* continue plentifully for so long *after* the close of the apostolic interval.

Therefore, from the unimpeachable testimony of the ante-Nicene and post-Nicene Fathers, corroborated by collateral evidences such as we have mentioned and which have been accepted by many scholars of later times as trustworthy, I submit my first premise: *Divine healings of the body, along with other divine miracles, continued until well into the fifth century A.D.*

NOTES

[1]"Gifts," in *Dictionary of the Apostolic Church*, ed. Hastings, vol. 1, p. 451: quoted in B. B. Warfield, *Counterfeit Miracles* (1918; reprint ed., Edinburgh: Banner of Truth Trust, 1976), p. 235, n. 6.

[2]Johann August Wilhelm Neander, *A General History of the Christian Religion and Church*, 10 vols.

[3]Tertullian, *Ad Scapulam* 4.

[4]Origen, *Against Celsus* 3.24.

[5]Earle E. Cairns, *Christianity Through the Centuries* (Grand Rapids: Zondervan Publishing House, 1954), p. 151.

[6]A. J. Gordon, *The Ministry of Healing*.

[7]Augustine, *City of God*, book XXII, chapter 8.

[8]Justin Martyr, 1853, p. 121: quoted in Warfield, *Miracles*, p. 11.

[9]*On the True Religion* 25:47: quoted in Warfield, *Miracles*, pp. 40-41.

[10]*Retractationes* I.13.7: quoted in Warfield, *Miracles*, pp. 41-42.

[11]Neander, *History*.

[12]*Modern Doubt*.

[13]James Orr, *Neglected Factors in Early Church History*.

[14]Edward Gibbon, *The History of the Decline and Fall of the Roman Empire*.

[15]Orr, *Factors*.

[16]Orr, *Factors*.

[17]Gordon, *Healing*.

[18]Neander, *History*.

[19]"Ueber die Wunder der katholichen Kirche," in *Vermischte Schriften* (1839) 1:28: quoted in Warfield, *Miracles*, p. 237, n. 8.

[20]Warfield, *Miracles*, p. 7.

[21]Ibid.

[22]*Conflict of Christianity with Heathenism*, E.T., p. 169: quoted in Warfield, *Miracles*, p. 9.

The Midway Period

God never puts a man upon the stage that Satan does not immediately bring forward an ape [of him].

—F. L. Godet

Satan has ever been seeking to thwart God by imitation rather than by denial.

—A. J. Gordon

Many will say to me in that day, Lord, Lord, did we not prophesy by thy name, and by thy name cast out demons, and by thy name do many mighty works? And then will I profess unto them, I never knew you: depart from me, ye that work iniquity.

(Matthew 7:22-23, ASV)

And I saw coming out of the mouth of the dragon, and out of the mouth of the beast, and out of the mouth of the false prophet, three unclean spirits, as it were frogs: for they are spirits of demons, working signs.

(Revelation 16:13-14, ASV)

CHAPTER THREE

The Midway Period

Earle E. Cairns reminds us in *Christianity Through the Centuries* that the name "Middle Ages" originated with Christopher Keller (1634-1680).[1] To Keller the middle period ran from the Council of Nicea in 325 until the Fall of Constantinople in 1453. My own picture of it is rather from the Fall of Rome in 476 to the Protestant Reformation in the sixteenth century. In that stretch of the church's history, the earlier part—say 500 to 1000—is known as the "Dark Ages" because of its intellectual and spiritual stagnation. That, naturally, is our general Protestant view of it. Roman Catholic apologists doubtless would demur; for that era may seem to them more like the "golden age" of their church, sandwiched between repulsed paganism and recalcitrant Protestantism, when the Roman hierarchy had practically a totalitarian grip on emerging nations and peoples. Perhaps Thomas Hobbs expressed the view of most Evangelicals when he described the Roman church of that dark period as no other than "the ghost of the deceased Roman Empire, sitting crowned upon the grave thereof."

At the moment, our own particular interest in that midway area, roughly from 600 to 1600, is what it reveals pertaining to our inquiry into divine healings through the centuries.

Yet before we go into that, there is another matter which will be best dealt with at this point, for it decisively affects our thinking on all that follows. There are four different attitudes to reported divine healings and other miracles in the Church's history.

1. The direct divine healing of human bodies, along with other such "signs and wonders," ceased entirely with the end of the Apostolic age; and all such reported divine healings since then may be either dismissed as spurious or shown to be healings *not* by divine intervention.

2. Divine healings, along with other Christian miracles, belonged only to the *earliest* centuries of the Church. They ceased because they were no longer necessary as divine credentials of Christianity when once it had become widely established and officially accepted.

3. Divine healings faded out *gradually*, as the condition of the organized Church deteriorated, giving place eventually to the Dark Ages. Reported reappearings of such miracles since then are at best doubtful or may be explained as other than directly from God.

4. Direct divine healings have *never* ceased among true Christian believers, but have occurred from Apostolic days until now, though with intermissions, sometimes lengthy, for various reasons, mainly the condition of the professing Church.

Which of these four theories is true? They are sufficiently different from one another to mean that if any one of them is right, the other three are wrong.

The First Theory

The first theory is that divine miracles, including healings, *ceased with the Apostolic age.* It has surprised me to find how common this idea has been and still is. A. J. Gordon opens his book *The Ministry of Healing* with these words: "A call recently put forth in one of our religious journals, asking the opinion of ministers, teachers and theological professors on this point, was very largely answered; and the respondents were well nigh unanimous in the opinion that the age of miracles passed away with the Apostolic period."

In the early years of our century, some stir was caused by the late Sir Robert Anderson's *The Silence of God.* He was simply voicing the mind of British intelligentsia as a whole at that time when he wrote, "What may be called *evidential* miracles have no place in this Christian dispensation" (emphasis mine).[2] He himself was of like mind, as the following excerpts will confirm. "But though miraculous powers and prophetic gifts abounded in the Pentecostal Church, yet when the testimony passed out from the narrow sphere of Judaism and was confronted by the philosophy and civilization of the heathen world—at the very time in fact when, according to accepted theories, their voice was specially required—that voice [i.e., of miraculous powers] died away." "Ever since the days of the Apostles the silence of Heaven has been unbroken." "So long as the kingdom was being preached to Jews, miracles abounded; but when the Gospel appealed to the heathen world, miracles lost their prominence and soon entirely ceased."[3]

Sir Robert Anderson, who was not only a knighted Doctor of Laws, high in the legal profession, but also for years head of Britain's famous Scotland Yard, has always been one of my pen heroes. England never had a doughtier scribe on behalf of the evangelical faith. His writings have a verve, a lawyer-detective perceptiveness, incisiveness, and forcefulness which express what he was both personally and professionally. I am bound to add, however, with undiminished respect, that rather too often there is the tendency to overpress points with the sharp eagerness of a lawyer set on winning a "case"; there is a forcible overdogmatizing which leads to inconsistencies. The quotations here given from his masterly book are to show how firmly entrenched has been the idea that miracle healings ceased with the passing of the Apostles and also to indicate inconsistencies in the teaching of it even by ablest writers—on which more comment shortly. So let me add two more brief cullings. "The special testimony to the Jew having ceased [at the end of the Apostolic interval] the *purpose* for which miracles were given was accomplished" (emphasis mine).[4] "As Scripture plainly indicates, they [miracles] continued so long as the testimony was addressed to the Jew, but *ceased* when, the Jew being set aside, the Gospel went out to the Gentile world" (emphasis mine).[5]

Other well-known writers between then and now might be quoted as supporting this theory, that Christian miracles ceased with the passing of the Apostles; but we need refer only to one, for he most powerfully represents them all. I refer again to Benjamin B. Warfield and his brilliant treatise *Counterfeit Miracles*. Let me pay tribute to him: Professor of Didactic and Polemic Theology at Princeton Theological Seminary, he was one of the all-time masters among evangelical theologians. To any Biblically related subject which he handled, he brought an erudition, acumen, learning, and wide range of reference which betoken spacious scholarship. His *Counterfeit Miracles* lies right athwart our pathway here because the whole of it is written to champion the argument that Christian miracles disappeared along with the Apostles and to refute all other theories. In alliance with his massive learning is a dissective genius, also a cast-iron logic. He is most of all master when it comes to demolition of specious error. His is no mere rifle fire: in theological argument he is heavy artillery. It will be realized at once that his thesis is of utter concern to our present studies; for if Christian miracles really *did* cease with the Apostles, then of all the many, many healing and other miracles reported in the Church's history since then, *not one* was a genuine *divine* miracle.

First, let us see his position clearly. I quote from the 1976 reprint of *Counterfeit Miracles*. The italicized words here and there are my own and are simply to emphasize what should be especially noted.

> Everywhere, the Apostolic Church was marked out as itself a gift from God, by showing forth the possession of the Spirit in appropriate *works* of the Spirit—miracles of *healing* and miracles of power, miracles of knowledge, whether in the form of prophecy or of the discerning of spirits, miracles of speech, whether of the gift of tongues or of their interpretation. The Apostolic Church was characteristically a miracle-working church.
>
> How long did this state of things continue? It was the characterizing peculiarity of *specifically* the Apostolic Church, and it belonged *therefore* exclusively to the Apostolic age. . . . These gifts were not the possession of the primitive Church as such . . . they were *distinctively* the authentication of the Apostles. They were part of the credentials of the Apostles as the authoritative agents of God in founding the Church. Thir function [i.e, healing and other miracles] thus *confined* them to distinctively the Apostolic Church, and they *necessarily* passed away with it. . . .
>
> The possession of the charismata [i.e., the supernatural gifts of the Holy Spirit in the early church] was *confined* to the Apostolic age. . . .
>
> They [the miracle workings] were confined to the Apostolic age, and to a very narrow circle then.[6]

These three examples will be sufficient, for they are as clear as they are representative. Of course, if we demand strict logical precision, Warfield's use of the words "therefore," "confined," and "necessarily" (which we have italicized in the second paragraph) should be disqualified since they state as a conclusion what he had not yet proved. However, we overlook that in order to ask *why* Warfield held this theory. Here is the answer:

> The immediate end for which they [the miracle gifts] were given is not left doubtful, and that proves to be not directly the extension of the Church, but the *authentication of the Apostles* as messengers from God. This does not mean, of course, that only the Apostles appear in the New Testament as working miracles, or that they alone are repre-

sented as recipients of the charismata. But it does mean that the charismata belonged, in a true sense, to the Apostles, and constituted one of the signs of an Apostle.[7]

Merely incidentally we note the contradiction there. If, as Warfield says, the miracle powers were for the authentication of the Apostles rather than for the extension of the Church, then why was there any need for the authentication at all? Were the authenticating miracles only for the personal gratification of the Apostles themselves? If so, they were pragmatically purposeless. Or again, if they were not primarily for the extension of the Church, why are they continually mentioned in *connection* with the extension and development of the Church? Furthermore, if, as Warfield himself admitted, *others* in the New Testament as well as the Apostles similarly exercised the miraculous charismata, why did not those supernatural efflorescences similarly authenticate those others as Apostles? Also, how strange it seems that after Warfield has said so strongly (see first quotation) that those miracle gifts "were *distinctively* the authentification of the Apostles," he himself admits: (1) that they were *not* "distinctive" inasmuch as *others* had them; and (2) that they were only "*one* of the signs of an Apostle"! He did not say what the other signs were; but I cannot help thinking of Ephesians 4, which tells us that our ascended Lord gave the Apostles *themselves* for the upbuilding and growth of the *Church* (vv. 11-13). Albeit, these are mere comments by the way; though they are worthwhile as putting us on guard against further aberrancies in the theory that divine healing miracles ceased with the close of the Apostolic years. Let me bring just one more excerpt here. In the follow-up notes to his lectures, Warfield approvingly quotes B. F. Manire:

> The matter of imparting the Holy Ghost through the laying on of their hands, belonged exclusively, as it appears to me, to the Apostles, and therefore *passed away with them.* . . . Others besides the Apostles could . . . work miracles in confirmation of their testimony; but only the Apostles by the imposition of their own hands could impart the Holy Spirit to others in its wonder-working power.[8]

I by-pass the strange use of the neuter "its" for the Holy Spirit to remark on the still stranger feature, that "the Apostles by the imposition of their own hands could impart the Holy Spirit to others." Surely something wrong has crept in there! Not even the Apostles could communicate the Holy Spirit *Himself,* i.e., in regeneration or the "new birth." That is *never* effected through *any* intermediate agency. As for His communicating of supernatural gifts or activities or experiences through the Apostolic laying on hands, it is bad logic to argue that because a particular *one* abnormality "passed away" with the Apostles, *all* the charismata, or miracle gifts, did likewise! That is the fallacy of applying to the *whole* what is stated of only one part.

I too will be submitting, later on, that the interval covered by the Acts of the Apostles was an abnormal suspense period and that certain of the peculiar features in it passed away *with* it; but one needs to distinguish carefully as to what *did* and what did *not* "pass away" with it. What is more, even the imparting of the Holy Spirit's "gifts" through the laying on of hands was *not* (as the above quotation says) something which "belonged *exclusively*" to the Apostles. In Acts 13:1-3 it was the "prophets" and "teachers" at Antioch who "laid their hands" on Barnabas and Saul (not the Apostles); and what was *that* laying on of hands for, if not to *impart* some spiritual enduement? In 1 Timothy 4:14 Paul exhorts Timothy not to neglect "the charisma" given to him through the "laying on of hands by the *elderhood*" (literal Greek, emphasis mine). Barnabas was not an Apostle, but in Acts 14:3 "signs and wonders" were done by *his* hands as well as Paul's. In Hebrews 6:2 the "laying on of hands" is referred to as such a widespread practice that we simply cannot limit it to the hands of the Apostles; and what were those "laying on of hands" for, if not for some divine healing or enduing or imparting of *charismata?*

But it is time that we met head-on this theory that Christian miracles ended with the Apostolic epoch. Its first and decisive disqualification is that it has *no warrant in Scripture.* It is with diffidence arising from deep esteem that I differ with such a Mr. Valiant-for-the-Truth (in a Bunyan phrase) as B. B. Warfield. How much the modern evangelical cause owes to his pen! However, here is an *un*characteristic peculiarity in his *Counterfeit Miracles.* From beginning to end (230 pages), including his expansive "Notes" to the lectures (193 pages), nowhere does he even once adduce any Scripture to support his contention that divine healing and other Christian miracles ceased upon the demise of the Apostles and their generation. We cannot but ask *Why?*—and the answer is patent, namely, that there is *no* Scripture which can be cited either stating it or implying it.

Second, the theory unreasonably belittles and then rejects the whole *testimony of the early Fathers* on the matter. As already reflected, those pre-Nicene Fathers were the intellectual Christian giants of our earliest A.D. centuries. Every one of them was "head and shoulders" above his brethren. As might be expected, Warfield himself pens eloquent eulogy of them. Relative to the fourth century he says:

> Nor must we imagine that these marvels [healing and other miracles] are recounted only by obscure and otherwise unknown hero-worshippers, whose only claim to be remembered by posterity is that they were the over-enthusiastic admirers of the great ascetics of their time. They are rather the outstanding scholars, theologians, preachers, organizers of the age. It is Jerome, the leading Biblical scholar of his day. . . . Gregory of Nyssa, one of "the three great Cappadocians" . . . the incomparable Athanasius himself. . . . And the greatest preacher of the day, Chrysostom; the greatest ecclesiastic, Ambrose; and the greatest thinker, Augustine.[9]

Yet those are the "mighty men of valor" whose combined witness Warfield rejects as utterly mistaken! I say "*utterly* mistaken" because (let it be realized) if genuinely divine healings and other divine miracles ceased completely upon the removal of the Apostles (as the theory says), then *not one* of the many miracles recorded by Justin Martyr, Irenaeus, Tertullian, Origen, Chrysostom, Gregory, Ambrose, Athanasius, Jerome, Augustine, and others was a real interposition of our Lord! While the sincerity of those honored worthies is not for one moment questioned, their reliability is undermined and discredited. They were well meaning but deluded and therefore false witnesses! To me, a theory which must so discredit *them* is by that very fact *itself* discredited.

Next, the theory does not fit *the New Testament facts*. Its four peculiarities are as follows: (1) the miracle gifts were solely for the authentication of the Apostles—which we have found to be wrong; (2) only the Apostles could communicate them to others— which also we have seen to be incorrect; (3) only those on whom the Apostles laid their hands had the charismata—which we purpose now to disprove; and (4) those supernatural gifts ceased with the Apostles, or, to state the peculiarity exactly, with those who had *received* them from the Apostles. In other words, those on whom the Apostles laid hands *received* the charismata via the Apostles but could *not* transmit them in turn to others; so the charismata ceased with *them*.

Now items 3 and 4 just do not match the full New Testament data, as can be shown by quoting a further paragraph from Warfield.

The diffusion of these miraculous gifts [i.e., the charismata among those first Christian assemblies] is, perhaps, quite generally underestimated. One of the valuable features of the passage 1 Cor. 12-14, consists in the picture given in it of Christian worship in the Apostolic age (14:26ff.). "What is it, then, brethren?" the Apostle asks. "When ye come together, each one hath a psalm, hath a teaching, hath a revelation, hath a tongue, hath an interpretation. Let all things be done unto edifying. . . ." This . . . was the ordinary church worship at Corinth in the Apostles' day. . . . There is no reason to believe that the infant congregation at Corinth was singular in this. The Apostle does not write as if he were describing a marvellous state of affairs peculiar to that church. He even makes the transition to the next item of his advice in the significant words, "as in *all* churches of the saints". . . . The exception would be, not a church *with*, but a church *without*, such gifts.[10]

With that quotation we fully agree. But if those charismata were thus operating in *all* the churches as the then usual *modus operandi* of the Holy Spirit, what of those churches which had *not* been founded or even visited by any of the Apostles? If the charismata came only through the laying on of hands by the *Apostles*, how did they begin in those churches where the Apostles had *not* been?

It is generally agreed that neither Paul (Col. 1:7; 2:1) nor any other Apostle founded the church at Colossae. It is equally certain that the church at Rome was not founded by an Apostle. When Paul wrote his great Epistle to the Romans (c. A.D. 58 or 60), he himself had not yet visited Rome (1:10-16). Nor had Peter then been there. Peter was still in Jerusalem when the first Apostolic council was held there in A.D. 52 (Acts 15), and he stayed there for several more years before going up to Antioch (Gal. 2:11).

There are those who question whether Peter was ever in Rome at all—which we will not discuss here—but this is certain: he did not *found* the church there, nor had he been there before Paul wrote his Romans Epistle. Nor is there a fleck of tradition that any other Apostle founded that church. Yet already, when Paul dispatched his epistle to Rome, the assembly of believers there (or should we say the great Christian *crowd* there?) was so large and influential that the Apostle said of them, "Your faith is spoken of throughout the whole world" (1:8). Well, were there no supernatural spiritual "gifts" experienced at Colossae or Rome? Warfield says there *were*, and he is right: but how do you explain them if such "gifts" came *only* through laying on of hands by the Apostles?

Nor is that all. When one thinks how many, many thousands of Christian believers there were all over the civilized world before the

Apostles had all gone to heaven and how universally active the charismatic gifts then were (as Warfield says), how *could* the Apostles have laid hands on *all* who had those gifts?

Still further, as Paul makes emphatically clear in 1 Corinthians 12-14, the charismatic gifts were in general conferred *directly* by the Holy Spirit apart from human hands or intermediaries: "For to one is given by the Spirit [nine 'gifts' are enumerated] . . . But all these worketh that one and the selfsame Spirit, dividing to every man severally as He will" (12:8-11). All this, remember, was going on at Corinth, as elsewhere, in Paul's *absence*, without any Apostolic laying on of hands; and does not the wording clearly indicate that those "gifts" were imparted *directly* to each one whom the Holy Spirit sovereignly selected? So if they were thus communicated *independently* of the Apostles, where is there any authority to assert that they *ceased* with the Apostles? On all counts this theory, that the Holy Spirit's supernatural enduements ceased with the Apostles, breaks down.

The Second Theory

As mentioned, the second theory says that divine healings, along with other Christian miracles, dropped away permanently soon after the third century, coinciding approximately with Constantine's edict in 313, which proclaimed Christianity a leading and legitimate religion of the Roman Empire. Yet as with the first theory, so with this: in the New Testament there is neither preintimation nor even the faintest advance hint of any such intended cessation. Then *why* should the miracle gifts cease with the Constantine landmark? Well, the supposition is that miracles ceased then because their purpose as validating "evidences" of the new Christian religion had by that time been accomplished: they were no longer needed now that Christianity was sufficiently established throughout the world.

But just as the first theory was wrong in seeing the miracle gifts as being *only* for the authentication of the Apostles, so this second theory is wrong in seeing them *only* as Christian "evidences." Admittedly, those "signs and wonders" which were wrought at the Jewish capital, as recorded in the Acts, *were* meant to be evidential to old-time Jewry. But when we turn on to the New Testament Epistles, with their revelation of the hitherto "hidden" but now divulged "mystery" of the *Ecclesia*, we find there that the *first* purpose of the healings and other charismatic gifts in the Christian assemblies was *not* to furnish Christian "evidences" but for the *edification of the Church*

(1 Cor. 12:7,25,28-30; 14:5,12,26; Eph. 4:12). There is not the slightest suggestion that *those* charismata were meant to be only temporary. Nay, did not Paul give the distinct impression that he was instructing those Corinthians concerning activities of the Holy Spirit which were meant to *continue* in Christian assemblies right on ahead? There seems to be *no* anticipation of either withdrawal or suspension.

There are some who put this cessation theory in a rather different way. They tell us that the supernatural *pneumatikoi,* or "spirituals," were meant to continue only until the Church had the completed Scriptures of the New Testament, after which they would not be needed. We are asked to believe that Paul had this in mind when he wrote in 1 Corinthians 13:8-10: "Whether there be prophecies, they shall fail; whether there be tongues, they shall cease; whether there be knowledge, it shall vanish away. For we know in part, and we prophesy in part. But when that which is *perfect* is come, then that which is in part shall be *done away.*" The words "when that which is perfect is come" are supposed to refer to the completed New Testament Scriptures—which would bring us down to about 400 A.D., when the complete canon of the New Testament was ultimately certified at the Council of Carthage. Yet the words "when that which is perfect is come" in verse 10 simply cannot refer to the completion of the Scriptures for the obvious reason that the context flatly contradicts it. The "when" in verse 10 has its counterpart in the "then" of verse 12.

> *When* [v. 10] that which is perfect is come, . . . *then* [v. 12] we shall see face to face: . . . *then* shall I know even as also I am known.

That coming of the "perfect" did *not* happen with the completing of the Biblical canon, nor has it come even yet. What is more, if by the words "when that which is perfect is come" Paul had meant the completion of the inspired writings, the words would have been quite unintelligible to those Corinthians; for they had not the slightest suspicion that a body of divinely inspired oracles was being developed by a sovereign divine will for the permanent guidance of the Church through many subsequent centuries. Surely, then, the theory that the charismata intendedly disappeared when the New Testament Scriptures were eventually canonized is a vessel too leaky to hold water.

The Third Theory

Then there is the third theory, namely, that those heavenly manifestations of the first days gradually dwindled and then petered out as the spiritual condition of the church deteriorated slowly but surely into the torpidity of the Dark Ages. This theory, of course, does not either profess or require to base itself on Scripture. The New Testament Epistles do not anywhere state whether the charismatic gifts either would or would not continue through centuries yet to unroll; nor could the Scriptures very well foretell such continuance since at that time the second coming of our Lord was considered imminent. No, this theory of gradual cessation bases itself ostensibly on what *actually happened*, i.e., that the miracle gifts disappeared as the Church's downgrade reached low level.

In that, however, there are two fatal flaws. The first is that the diminution of the miraculous did *not* parallel the decadence of the Church. In actual fact, from about the middle of the fourth century, when deviations, perversions, and superstitions first appear to have become widespread, there is a numerical *upsurge* of healing and other miracles—or, rather, of *alleged* miracles. A second fault in the theory is its assumption (even if miracles *did* wane away) that their cessation meant their *final extinction*. May we not reasonably ask, If healing miracles ceased because of the Church's doctrinal defection and spiritual declivity, could they not reappear if the Church (or any group within it) should return to doctrinal fidelity and spiritual purity? Or again, if that supposed cessation of miracles long ago was indeed their *final* cancellation, what about all the *alleged* miracles in various Christian groups and at different times between then and now? Are they *all* indiscriminately make-believe? or ought they not at least be investigated? Clearly this third theory is disqualified in that it has neither Scriptural mooring nor provable grounding in actual fact.

The Fourth Theory

The fourth theory maintains that direct divine healings, along with other of the supernatural gifts, have *never* ceased among doctrinally sound and spiritually consecrated believers but have occurred from Apostolic days until now, though with intermissions for various reasons, mainly the condition of the professing Church. To me, this seems the most loyal to the total data, though for the moment I say so only tentatively.

Get these four theories clearly in mind. The first of them says that direct divine healings of the body *can't* happen today: they ended with the Apostles. The second theory says that they *won't* happen today: they served their purpose and were withdrawn. The third theory says they *don't* happen today: they faded out and are seen no more. The fourth theory says they *can* happen today where the required conditions are fulfilled. My own choice *has* to be the fourth because of the patent inconsistencies in the other three and because it *seems* to be the truest to available facts.

A follow-up factor which confirms me in rejecting the first three misconcepts is that their advocates sometimes, unwittingly perhaps, puncture their own theories by stray admissions. Let me give an instance. I referred earlier to Sir Robert Anderson's trenchant product, *The Silence of God*, and showed by quotation how decidedly he sponsored the view that miracles passed away once for all with the Apostles. What, then, about the following admission in note 1 of the appendix? He refers to cases of "*extraordinary* cures from serious illness" and concedes that "some at least of these appear to be supported by *evidence sufficient to establish their truth.*" Then he slips into this gratifying admission:

> But while the vast majority of seemingly miraculous cures may be explained on natural principles, there may perhaps be some which are *genuine miracles*. There are no limits to the possibilities of faith; and *God may thus declare Himself at times.*

Surely by that one admission he scuttles his own theory; for if "genuine miracles" of healing *do* happen today and God still *does* "thus declare Himself at times," then to say that healing miracles were *terminated* at the close of the Apostolic juncture is obviously a contradiction of fact.

That highly esteemed scholar the late Principal A. C. Headlam held the usual Anglican view, i.e., that Christian miracles ceased after the early A.D. centuries. Yet he, too, slips into a similar admission of *later* healing miracles. Addressing a church congress in Middlesborough, England, in 1912, he referred to the miracles reputed to have happened at the tomb of Thomas à Becket, early archbishop of Canterbury (c. 1118-1170). Headlam said:

> The stories of miraculous happenings . . . worked by his dead body . . . are exactly of the same character as those recorded at Lourdes, for example, at the present day. Many of them represent answers to prayers which were offered up in different parts of the world in the name of St. Thomas; many of them are trivial, and some are repellant. Some doubtless represent *real cures*.[11]

THE MIDDLE AGES

One thing which needs emphasizing as we now scan the Middle Ages (the more so because insufficiently recognized) is that in the early days it was not so much the miracles which confirmed Christianity as that Christianity confirmed the miracles. Whether with or without physical miracles, Christianity was *in itself* divine revelation and redeeming truth. The visible miracles certainly were *one* form of attestation to that; but if similar miracles occurred *apart* from the divine truth of Christianity, then, even though they were *real* miracles, they were not *divine* miracles. In other words, it was Christianity which carried the miracles, not the miracles which carried Christianity. To be strictly accurate, Christianity and the miracles were mutually corroborative. I am not just toying with words when I add that although genuine divine miracles are *proofs* of Christianity, they are not meant as *tests* of Christianity. No, for everything that is called "Christian" must be tested solely and wholly by *the written Word of God*, the Holy Scriptures; and miracles themselves must be tested by that same final touchstone.

Let me give just one more quotation from Sir Robert Anderson. Illustrating how the Bible and not miracle is the decisive test, he says:

> A stranger appears, say in London, claiming to be the bearer of a Divine revelation to mankind; and in order to accredit his message he proceeds to display miraculous power. Let us assume for the moment that after the strictest enquiry the reality of the miracles is established. If the argument is sound (that such miracles prove the *message* genuine) we are bound to accept whatever gospel this prophet proclaims. . . . The Christian, however, would be kept back by the words of the inspired Apostle: "But though we *or an angel from heaven* should preach unto you any gospel other than that which *we* preached unto you, let him be accursed." In a word, the Christian would at once . . . insist on bringing the new miracle-accredited gospel to the test of Holy Writ, and finding it inconsistent with the Gospel he had already received, he would reject it. That is to say, he would test the message, not by the miracles, but by a preceding revelation known to be Divine.

Quite so: for it is a principle truly Scriptural (see Deut. 13:1ff.) that even a proven miracle is to be discounted if it is wrought in propagation of error.

During the Middle Ages, many miraculous physical cures were recorded as happening, not to mention other alleged supernatural interventions. The first question, then, is, Were these cures genuinely miracles? Yet even if some of them *were* proven miracles, that does not necessarily make them *divine* miracles. Some may have been demonic or Satanic. It should be axiomatic in our thinking that unless miracles are wrought in alliance with the clear teaching of the divinely inspired Scriptures, they are not genuinely Christian miracles: they are not of God; they are either clever impostures or supernatural intrusions of lying spirits. It is with such distinctions clearly in mind that we should assess what we encounter in the Middle Ages. If we come across what appear to be actual miracles of healing and find ourselves asking, "But how could they be wrought through a Church of such corruption and superstition as that of medieval Christendom?" it will be well to reflect that not a few of those miracles may have been *Satanic* "devices" to further the influence of deadly error. That is what I meant in my earlier comment: Real miracles are always *proofs* but not really *tests* of Christianity. Real miracles *are* proofs. They are *always* proofs of something supernatural, but they are not always proofs of *God*.

What, then, do we find as to the number and nature of healing or other miracles, whether actual or alleged, during the Dark Ages and later medieval centuries? It would seem as though most Anglican theologians have leaned to the theory, already examined, that such miracles clung only to the first and purest centuries of Christianity, dying out as Christianity became firmly established or as the organized church became doctrinally and spiritually decadent. On the other hand, Roman Catholic chroniclers unhesitatingly claim miracles for their church in every subsequent century. Warfield *(ut supra)* says, "Before this assertion, . . . the Anglican theory is helpless . . . because the evidence for the later miracles [i.e., in the Middle Ages] . . . is very much greater *in volume and cogency* than that for the earlier miracles" (emphasis mine).[12] I find myself demurring at the two words "volume" and "cogency"; for miracles during the Middle Ages were *not* greater in average than the numerous, world-wide Christian miracles reported by the early Fathers. Nor had they greater "cogency" inasmuch as we have only the word of doctrinally unsound, prejudiced, and often superstitious Romish zealots for the miracles of the Middle Ages whereas for those of the first three or four centuries we have the stable, unbiased, complementive testimony of the accredited Christian Fathers.

There is one point, though, at which we gratefully "amen" Warfield. He asks, If the miracles of the first three centuries were real and useful *then*, may we not argue that they would be equally useful in the Church's missionary endeavors today? So why not miracles now? To that we echo, "Yes, *why* not?" That is one of the present-day questions to which these studies are making their way. Meanwhile, however, we ask, *Have* there been genuinely divine healings and other provenly divine miracles *since* those first centuries? Or, more restrictedly for the moment, Were there such during the Middle Ages?

Truth Versus Fiction

The available material spreading through the long stretch of the Middle Ages is so plentiful and wide-scattered that it would be a hopeless task for us to present illustrations one after another. All we can do here is to take a few representative records at different successive points. Regrettably, too, there is such profusion of the obviously superstitious and credulously inventive mixed in with whatever was real that often the first problem is to separate the wheat from the chaff, the pure gold from glittery tinsel, the real pearls from paste imitations, or, in the words of Jeremiah 15:19, "the precious from the vile."

Alas, even as early as Cyprian and Ambrose, in the third and fourth centuries, far-fetched "wonders" had begun to mushroom around the Eucharist. The following incidents are cited by Warfield.[13] When a Christian woman who had lapsed during persecution tried to receive the sacrament, fire shot out of it and stopped her. Another found that the element given him by the priest had become a cinder. Ambrose tells of a certain Satyrus who, being in a shipwreck, tied the eucharistic "mysteries" in a handkerchief round his neck and plunged into the sea, from where, without need of plank or help, he was first of the company to reach shore. Gregory the Great (540-604) tells of a young monk who slipped away without permit to visit his parents but died the day he returned; and even then he could not rest quiet in death until the eucharistic "host" had been placed on his grave. Gregory of Tours (c. 538-594) tells how on one occasion the consecrated bread flew away from the hand of an unworthy deacon and placed itself back on the altar. These are but some of the many, all indicating superstition-ridden gullibility.

The Mary Legends

All too early, also, the *Mary legends* came in and began to proliferate until, by the end of the Middle Ages, they were as widespread as they were numerous. From the at first innocently naive there devel-

oped the most fatuously absurd, sickening, and disgusting fictions
imaginable. By the middle of the fifth century, Mary was head, or
queen, of all the saints. Earle E. Cairns has made the following
comment:

> The false interpretation of Scripture and the mass of miracles
> associated with Mary in the apocryphal gospels created great rever-
> ence for her. The Nestorian and other Christological controversies of
> the fourth century [had already] resulted in the acceptance of her as
> the "Mother of God" and entitled her to special honors in the
> liturgy. . . . What at first was merely acknowledgment of her exalted
> position as Christ's mother soon became belief in her intercessory
> powers. . . . In the sixth century Justinian asked her intercession on
> behalf of his Empire.[14]

The more papal, sacerdotal, superstitious, and geographically
powerful the Roman church became, the more it fostered the Mary
emphasis until finally the dividing line between superstitious veneration and actual Mariolatry was practically blurred away.

As this all bears on the question whether or not there were genuine
miracles of divine healing during the earlier and later Middle Ages,
let me submit two or three more quotations. Eventually, as Yrjo
Hirn writes:

> Mary was looked upon, not as an individual human being, but as
> an incarnation of an eternal principle which had exercised its power
> long before it became embodied in the figure of a Jewish girl. The
> Madonna's motherly care had previously been directed to all the
> faithful, who had been fed by her "milk" in the same way as the Child
> of Bethlehem. In Mechthild's revelations it is even more expressly
> said that the Madonna suckled the prophets before Christ descended
> into the world. Later, she fed, during His childhood, "the Son of God
> and all of us," and when He was full-grown she offered her milk to the
> Christian Church. . . . There is no question of symbolism when, in the
> miracle-histories, it is related that the Madonna *cured pious individuals*
> with her healing milk. It is also told of some holy men that they were
> quite literally refreshed by Mary's breast. . . . Bernard of Clairvaux,
> who merited the Virgin's gratitude more than any other man, was
> rewarded for all his panegyrics and poems by Mary visiting him in his
> cell and letting his lips be moistened by the food of the heavenly
> Child.[15]

Heinrich Gunter adds:

> In the age of the Mary-legend, the Virgin also had to become a
> miraculous nourisher, and that—in accordance with the exaggerated
> imagination of the times—with her own milk. A monk gets sick;
> mouth and throat are so swollen that he can take no nourishment; the

brethren expect the end. Then Mary appears—visible only to the sick man—and gives him her breast and announces to him his early recovery. Among the mystical women of the convent of Töf the same thing happened to Sister Adeheit of Frauenberg.[16]

We discontinue the quotation there to omit even worse sentimental sickliness.

Those dark and dreary centuries during which the Roman church acquired and then wielded its mastery over Western Christendom were also the deplorable era of ever-multiplying veneration for relics, tombs, and dead saints, all floridly draped with wonder-tales and intendedly appealing to an inflamed craving for the religiously marvelous. Some of the saints were accorded semidivine honors. During the first three centuries the prayers in funeral celebrations were solely for the soul of the departed, but by the beginning of the seventh century the prayers *for* saints had become prayers *through* them. Legends of miracles grew up from revered coffins like brilliant weeds in a tropical jungle. Nor was it *all* misguided veneration; it developed into a money-making racket for many who trafficked in them with a "callous rapacity which traded on the ignorance and superstition of the purchasers." Indeed, the exploiting of relics—bodies, bones, teeth, hair, etc.—became such a scandalous business that in A.D. 381 it was officially but unsuccessfully banned.

It is difficult for us Bible-reading Evangelicals today to credit the absurdities which were devotedly swallowed in those days of Christendom's "gross darkness." Think of professing Christians preserving "feathers dropped from the wings of Gabriel when he came to announce to Mary the birth of Jesus," of pilgrim monks "boasting of having seen at Jerusalem the finger of the Holy Spirit"![17]

Nay, the wretched relics pestilence has gone on and on. Warfield has this additional comment on relic veneration.

Any ordinary sense of the ridiculous, however, should be sufficiently satisfied by the solemn exhibition in the church of Saints Cosmas and Damien at Rome of a "vial of the milk of the blessed Virgin Mary." But Ossa is piled on Pelion when we learn that this is far from the only specimen of Mary's milk which is to be seen in the churches. Several churches in Rome have specimens, and many in France—at Evron, and Soulac, and Mans, and Reims, and Poitiers, and St. Denis, and Bouillac, and the Sainte Chapelle at Paris; the Cathedral of Soissons has two samples of it; and the Cathedral at Chartres three. Then there is some more at Toledo and at the convent of St. Peter d'Arlanza in Spain, and of course in other countries as well. We are fairly astonished at the amount of it.[18]

Surely the perpetuation of such irreverent inanities and gross frauds should give the pope, cardinals, bishops, and priests of Rome crimson faces!

Of course, looking back over the Middle Ages one has to remember that there was extensive illiteracy, and even those who could read could not easily get at the Scriptures. Until Gutenberg of Mainz in 1450, there was no printing press. The Scriptures were all in handwritten copies. Each copy took a year or more to write; and when written it was either kept away from the vulgar gaze by clerical lock and key or was too costly for ordinary folk to buy, which again made it inaccessible to the poor. Nor were the Scriptures taught in the churches. What with crass ignorance, abounding superstition, flourishing heresies, and legendary exaggerations, to extract the real truth about divine healings of the body during those centuries is like trying to identify the victims of a train wreck in a long, dark tunnel.

The Monastic Orders

Yet even then (let us seize on it) like torches amid surrounding darkness, there were many wonderful instances of intelligent and victorious Christian godliness. Moreover, those such who have become well known to us may presumably represent thousands more whose names we have never heard. Whatever demerits and abuses we may see in the monastic orders of those centuries, in many cases they stood for the purest and best at that time. As two resplendent representatives we mention Bernard of Clairvaux (1090-1153), to whom we owe those precious hymns "Jesus, the Very Thought of Thee" and "O Sacred Head Once Wounded," and Francis of Assisi (1182-1226). Many monks and friars were just as intensely sincere in their consecration as they were misguided in their mendicancy, celibacy, and ascetic self-flagellations. What is more, the grey friars of St. Francis and the black friars of St. Dominic broke out from cloistered monasticism and went preaching in the vernacular among the throngs in the towns and cities. Nor must it be overlooked here that the Franciscan order produced Roger Bacon, Bonaventura, Duns Scotus, and William of Ockham while from the Dominican order (founded by Dominic: 1170-1221) came Albertus Magnus and his yet more famous pupil Thomas Aquinas, who developed the standard system of Roman Catholic theology.

It seems fairly allowable that there *were* genuine instances of direct divine healing during those times, though, as already complained, a shiny haze of the mystically imaginative overhangs everything, hampering accurate perception. We are inclined to accept that the saintly Bernard of Clairvaux was used in at least *some* direct healings. He himself never recorded any such, though he told of many miracles wrought by his friend St. Malachi. The following is related by H. Delehaye in his *Les Légendes Hagiographiques*.

> When St. Bernard was preaching the crusade in the diocese of Constance, an archer in the following of the Duke of Zähringen jeered at his preaching and at the preacher himself, saying, "He cannot work miracles any more than I can." When the saint proceeded to lay his hands on the sick, the mocker saw it, and suddenly fell over as if dead; he remained a considerable time without consciousness. Alexander of Cologne adds, "I was close to him when the thing happened. . . . and this poor man could not get up until Bernard came, made a prayer, and lifted him up."

By about one century later, no less than three authors, or compilers of miracles, were circulating the incident in blown up form (so characteristic of the medieval craze for marvels), affirming that the archer had *died* and that Bernard raised him to life again!

Somewhat the same, perhaps, may be said about Francis Xavier (1506-1552). Whether there were actually miracle healings, who can now decide for certain? He, also, is said to have raised the dead. Although in his own writings there is no reference to any such miracle, nor in any contemporary account, resurrection stories began to appear soon after his death. At first some persons at Cape Comorin averred that he had raised one person. Later the one became two. By the time of his canonization in 1622, the two had become three. By the time of the Dominic father Bonhours, the three had become *fourteen*, with the name and place of the resurrected person and the attendant circumstances detailed in each case! So where are we? In those days the more miraculous stories were, the likelier they were to be adopted. The ecclesiastical system helped in manufacturing and disseminating them. They fed the diseased appetite created by the misconception that religion is essentially magical. The miracle mania of the Roman church advertized itself practically everywhere. Error was propagated as truth, fictions as facts, and make-believe as reality. We are inclined to agree with others that amid such an ecclesiastical jungle, it is almost impossible to distinguish real miracles of divine healing from the luxurious entanglements of fantasy and exaggeration. If some of the healing "miracles" associated with saintly Bernard of Clairvaux really *were* divine miracles, then they were interventions of sheer compassion to the sufferer and came, *despite* the mistaken emphases of medieval monasticism, *not* in endorsement of them.

The Waldenses

However, like a sudden sun shaft in a cloudy sky, there breaks through to us, even from those medieval centuries, a surprise evidence that wherever there is a return to New Testament sanity and evangelical purity accompanied by intelligent yieldedness to Christ, the *true* miracles of the Holy Spirit begin to reappear, both spiritual and physical. I am referring particularly to the *Waldenses* who came into the picture during the last quarter of the twelfth century.

Besides the movements such as the Cistercians, Franciscans, and Dominicans, which sought to reform the Church from within, there were a few which were brave enough to take the "fateful risk" of coming right out and being separate. It certainly *was* a fateful risk, for at that time the Roman church was practically conterminous with Western Christendom, which it dominated with iron-handed authority. The seceders were courageous souls who could accept no middle course between conscientious separation for the Lord's sake and compromise with the corrupt, unscriptural institution which called itself the Church.

The Waldensians originated with Peter Waldo, a well-to-do merchant of Lyons, France. Through reading a translation of the New Testament, he was so challenged that he relinquished all his possessions except what were needful to feed his family. Organizing a group known as the "Poor in Spirit," he and his followers essayed to preach as laymen; but they were interdicted by the pope. Soon afterwards they were excommunicated for noncompliance. Let me quote again from Earle E. Cairns:

> The Waldensians believed that every man should have the Bible in his own tongue and that it should be the final authority for faith and life. Following the example of Christ, they went out by twos, dressed in simple clothes, to preach to the poor in the vernacular. They accepted the standard confessions, the Lord's Supper and Baptism, and lay ordination to preach and minister the sacraments. Their society had its own clergy, with bishops, priests and deacons. . . . The Waldensians anticipated in many respects the ideas of the Protestants of the Reformation.[19]

Now it is evident that the Waldensians, expressing as they did this revival of the "primitive faith and Apostolical simplicity," knew by experience the Holy Spirit's ministry of supernatural healing. Such divine healings, as A. J. Gordon said, "attend the cradle of every spiritual reformation, as they did the birth of the Church herself. Waldenses, Moravians, Huguenots, Covenanters, Friends, Baptists and Methodists all have their record of them."[20] Of more than ordinary interest, then, is the following frank and simple confession of the Waldenses, who kept the lamp of saving truth "trimmed and burning" amid the gross darkness which had overspread those medieval peoples of Europe under papal jurisdiction. Note the words I emphasize here, printed in italics.

> Therefore, concerning this anointing of the sick, we hold it as an article of faith, and profess sincerely from the heart, that *sick persons, when they ask it, may lawfully be anointed with the anointing* oil by one who joins with them in praying that it may be efficacious to the *healing of the body* according to the design and end and effect mentioned by the Apostles: and we profess that such an anointing performed according to the Apostolic design and practice will be healing and profitable.
>
> Albeit we confess that the anointing of the sick, performed according to the design, end, and purpose of the Apostles, and according to their practice and power, of which St. Mark and St. James make mention, is lawful; and if any priest *possessing the grace of healings* has so anointed the sick and they have recovered we would exhort all, that when they are really ill they omit not to receive that ordinance at their hands, and in no way despise it, because despisers of that or of other ordinances, so far as they are ordained by Christ, are to be punished and corrected, according to the rules of the evangelical law.[21]

Sad to tell, when lesser measures failed to quench the evangelical witness of the Waldensians, crueller measures were employed. Not only did the Synod of Toulouse in 1229 forbid laymen the use of vernacular translations of Scripture, thus preventing exposure of Romanist departure from Scriptural truth, but the fearful Inquisition was invented. Secret ecclesiastical courts used torture and withheld the names of accusers, and also turned their helpless victims over to the state for confiscation of property or even burning at the stake. Yet neither Inquisitors nor fiery martyrdoms could extinguish the Waldensian witness. Such brutal persecutions often clarify to basic human common sense just where the truth really *is*, which party stands for true Christianity and which for Satanic darkness. As men watch Christian martyrs singing their way with unshaken conviction through flames to their Savior in heaven, they often see with startling vividness that it is better to die for truth than live for error!

Cairns well comments: "The unwillingness of the Roman Catholic Church to meet the need for spiritual reform desired by the sects tended toward an ossification that made the Reformation inevitable."[22] And with that reference to the Protestant Reformation, of which the Waldenses and others were advance signals, we take leave of the medieval centuries. Their testimony to the continuance of direct divine *healings* is just about what one might expect from a period when, through an apostatized church wielding a psuedo-Christian ecclesiastical tyranny, gross darkness covered the peoples.

NOTES

[1]Earle E. Cairns, *Christianity Through the Centuries* (Grand Rapids: Zondervan Publishing House, 1954), p. 179.

[2]Sir Robert Anderson, *The Silence of God*, 9th ed., preface.

[3]Ibid., pp. 17,49.

[4]Ibid., p. 58.

[5]Ibid., p. 162.

[6]B. B. Warfield, *Counterfeit Miracles* (1918; reprint ed., Edinburgh: Banner of Truth Trust, 1976), pp. 5-6,236.

[7]Ibid., p. 21.

[8]*The New Christian Quarterly*, vol. 4, no. 2, p. 38: quoted in Warfield, *Miracles*, p. 245, n. 52.

[9]Ibid., pp. 37-38.

[10]Ibid., pp. 4-5.

[11]Within a few years of Thomas's martyrdom, five hundred miracles were reported at Canterbury.

[12]Warfield, *Miracles*, p. 35.

[13]Ibid., pp. 51-52.

[14]Cairns, *Christianity*, p. 174.

[15]*The Sacred Shrine*, 1912, p. 363: quoted in Warfield, *Miracles,* p. 95.

[16]Warfield, *Miracles*, pp. 95-96.

[17]Henri Etienne, *Apologie pour Herodote, ou Traite de la Conformite des Merveilles anciennes avec les modernes*, 1735, cited by Warfield, *Miracles*, p. 94.

[18]Paul Parfait, *La Foire aux Reliques*, cited by Warfield, *Miracles*, p. 94.

[19]Cairns, *Christianity*, pp. 248-49.

[20]A. J. Gordon, *The Ministry of Healing*.

[21]Johannis Lukawitz, *Waldensis Confessio*, 1431.

[22]Cairns, *Christianity*, p. 249.

The More Recent Period

But there have been nevertheless certain evident tokens of spuriousness attaching to Romish miracles which have indicated their true character to believers. There is a kind of Egyptian crudeness about them which suggests the art of the sorcerer rather than the touch of God's finger. Alleged healings by contact with the bones of dead saints; pains assuaged by making the sign of the Cross over the sufferer; recoveries effected by pilgrimages to the shrines of martyrs, and evil spirits exorcised by the crucifix or the image of the virgin! Who does not see the vast contrast in these methods from the dignified and simple methods of Christ and his Apostles?

—A. J. Gordon

Why look ye so earnestly on us, as though by our own power or holiness we had made this man to walk? The God of Abraham, and of Isaac, and of Jacob, the God of our fathers, hath glorified his Son, Jesus. . . . And his name through faith in his name hath made this man strong, whom ye see and know.

(Acts 3:12-16)

CHAPTER FOUR

The More Recent Period

In the post-Reformation period, our feet are on much firmer stepping stones so far as divine healing of the body is concerned. As a result of the mighty liberation wrought by the Reformation, we find a burst of new and vigorous movements, all Biblically based and in the main relating themselves with new intelligence to the ministry of the Holy Spirit among the Lord's people. An exhaustive survey of these is neither possible nor necessary for our purpose here. I think it will be sufficient if we pick out from several of those movements post-Reformation evidence as to the *reappearance* of the Holy Spirit's healing ministry in Christian fellowships. At the moment I do not say whether I myself agree or disagree with certain incidental remarks in the testimonies given. My one concern here is to document briefly yet clearly enough the *fact* that miracles of heaven-sent healing began to occur again in the wake of the Reformation and that they have continued ever since, forging new links in the long chain of divine healing through the centuries.

Martin Luther

Perhaps we should begin with the lion-hearted champion of the Reformation, Martin Luther himself. Some of Luther's remarks about miracles could easily make us think that he did not believe in supernatural physical healings; but we need to remember that he was reacting against the superstitious *pseudo*-miracles of the corrupt ecclesiastical system which he was challenging. In contrast with those he said, "How often has it happened and still does, that devils have been driven out in the name of Christ; also that by calling on his Name in prayer *the sick have been healed!*" (emphasis mine). Seckendorf, in his *History of Lutheranism*, tells how a girl possessed with a demon was brought to Luther. Laying his hand on her head and pleading the promise of John 14:12, he prayed God that for Jesus' sake the evil spirit should be expelled—and it was. There was complete recovery, as also there was in cases of physically sick ones over whom he prayed. Seckendorf also records the outstanding case of Philip Melanchthon. Let me quote:

> Luther arrived and found Philip about to give up the ghost. His eyes were set; his consciousness was almost gone; his speech had failed, and also his hearing; his face had fallen; he knew no one, and had ceased to take either solids or liquids. At this spectacle Luther is filled with the utmost consternation, and turning to his fellow-travellers says: "Blessed Lord, how has the devil spoiled me of this instrument!" Then, turning away towards the window, he called most devoutly on God.
> After this, taking the hand of Philip. . . . he said, "Be of good courage, Philip, thou shalt not die". . . . While he uttered these things Philip began, as it were, to revive and to breathe, and, gradually recovering his strength, was at last restored to health.

But can we be sure at this late date that it really *was* a miraculous healing? Can anyone prove that it was *not?*—for the outward evidences, as preserved for us, certainly *seem* to indicate miracle. Do Melanchthon and Luther comment on it later? They do, in letters to friends. Melanchthon said, "I should have been a dead man had I not been *recalled from death itself* by the coming of Luther" (emphasis mine). As for Luther, he said, "Philip is very well after such an illness—for it was greater than I had supposed. I found him dead, but by an *evident miracle of God* he lives" (emphasis mine).

Let me refer to just one more healing miracle connected with Luther. Professor C. Ernst Luthardt of Leipzig, in his *Moral Truths of Christianity*, recalls the following:

> Myconius, the venerated superintendent of Gotha, was in the last stage of consumption and already speechless. Luther wrote to him that he must not die: "May God not let me hear, so long as I live, that you are dead, but cause you to survive me. I pray this earnestly and will have it granted; and my will shall be granted herein, Amen". . . .

And from that time Myconius was kept, as it were, from the grave by the power of Luther's prayers, and did not die till after Luther's death.

Was *that* a real miracle of healing? Myconius himself should know best; and he later wrote of himself: "Raised up in the year 1541, by the mandates, prayers and letter of the reverend Father Luther, *from death*" (emphasis mine). We by-pass further such instances clinging round Luther and pass on to the Moravians.

The Moravians

Under God, the movement which became the Moravian church was founded by Count von Zinzendorf of Dresden (1700-1760). From the first it had such a world outlook that even in its earlier years it sent missionaries out to the West Indies, Greenland, and Africa. Nor should it ever be forgotten that it was Moravian missionaries through whom the great awakening began in John Wesley. Is it surprising that a body of believers so firmly founded on the Bible, so zealous after Scriptural holiness, and so widely devoted to soul winning should find the Holy Spirit revealing Himself among them in supernatural gifts? For our next quotations we are indebted to a *History of the United Brethren,* written by A. Bost. He gives the following excerpt from the saintly Count Zinzendorf himself (note specially our italicized words).

> To believe against hope is the root of the gift of miracles; and I owe this testimony to our beloved Church, that Apostolic powers are therein manifested. We have had undeniable proofs thereof in the unequivocal discovery of things, persons, and circumstances, which could not humanly have been discovered; in *the healing of maladies in themselves incurable, such as cancers, consumptions, when the patient was in the agonies of death, etc.,* all by means of prayer, or of a single word.

Later on, in his history of the United Brethren and speaking of the year 1730, our narrator adds (pp. 405-6):

> At this juncture various *supernatural gifts were manifested in the Church, and miraculous cures were wrought.* . . . The Count [Zinzendorf] rejoiced at it with all his heart, and silently praised the Saviour who thus willingly condescended to what is poor and little. . . . At the same time he did not wish the brethren and sisters to make too much noise about these matters and regard them as extraordinary, but when, for example, a brother *was cured of disease, even of the worst kind,* by a single word or by some prayer, he viewed this as a very simple matter, calling to mind ever the saying of Scripture, that signs were not for those who believe, but for those who believed not.

The implicitness with which those early Moravians trusted our Lord's promises in Holy Writ is a shining challenge to us all. We get a glimpse of healing miracles going on among them in an incident (one of many) concerning a brother named Jean de Watteville. A married woman at Hernnhut (the first Moravian center) had become critically ill. The doctor had now given up all hopes. Her husband was grief-stricken.

> Watteville visited the patient, found her joyfully expecting her removal, and took his leave after having encouraged her in this happy frame. It was at that time still the custom of unmarried brethren, on Sunday evenings, to go about singing hymns before the brethren's houses, with an instrumental accompaniment. Watteville made them sing some appropriate hymns under the window of the sick sister, at the same time praying in his heart to the Lord that He would be pleased, if He thought good, to restore her to health. He was given a hope of this so full of sweetness and faith that he sang with confidence these lines:
>
> > When I reach my dying hour,
> > Only let them speak Thy name;
> > By its all-prevailing power
> > Back my voice returns again.
>
> What was the astonishment of those who surrounded the bed of this dying sister when they saw her sit up and join with a tone of animation in singing the last line: "Back my voice returns again"! To his great amazement and delight he [Watteville] found her, on ascending to her chamber, *quite well.* She recovered perfectly, and not till thirty-five years after did he attend her earthly tabernacle to its final resting-place (emphasis mine).[1]

The Scottish Covenanters

In the land of the heather and the thistle the name "Covenanters" belongs to those early Protestants of Scotland who struggled for religious liberty from 1638, or more intensively from 1662, until the Reformation in Britain was decisively achieved after William of Orange landed there in 1688. Those Covenanters wrote a tragic but noble chapter with a pen dipped in their own blood and tears, an epic of which every Scot may be proud. The Scottish reformers had already drawn up and signed a Confession of Faith in 1557, followed by a repeat in 1581, in which, as the *British Encyclopedia* puts it, "all the errors of Popery were explicitly abjured"—to which King James VI and his council subscribed.[2] It was again subscribed in 1590,

1596, and 1638. Then came *The Solemn League and Covenant* of 1643, a solemn contract between the Church of Scotland and the English Parliament to effect uniformity of Protestant doctrine, worship, and discipline throughout Britain. Two decades later, in 1662, a turnabout English Parliament denounced the "Solemn League" as seditious and replaced it with a new "Act of Uniformity," restoring episcopacy, opening the door to a comeback of Romanism, and imposing heavy penalties for noncompliance. The supporters of the earlier covenants were thus betrayed and in loyalty to those covenants, especially that of 1643, withstood king and parliament and the new "bishops" appointed by them. I quote again from the excellent synopsis in the *British Encyclopedia*.

> The Presbyterian ministers who refused to acknowledge the bishops were ejected from their parishes and gathered round them crowds of their people on the hillsides, or any lonely spot, to attend their ministrations. These meetings, called "coventicles," were denounced as seditious, and to frequent them or to hold communication with those frequenting them was forbidden on pain of death. . . . [Later] An oath was required of all who would free themselves of suspicion of complicity with the Covenanters; and the dragoons who were sent out to hunt down the rebels were empowered to kill any one who refused to take the oath. During this "killing time," as it was called, the sufferings of the Covenanters were extreme.

I have before me an old volume published first in 1775 and now long out of print. It is a large work of some 650 pages with the title *The Scots Worthies*, and it was authored by John Howie. What a book! What a record of costly loyalty to evangelical truth under relentless oppression by Roman Catholic prelates encouraged by the nodding connivance of corrupt kings and councils! The book consists of seventy-one longer or shorter sketches, mainly of Scottish ministers belonging to that period of the Covenanters (1638-1688). It certainly was never written merely to please. In fact its style tends to be tedious. Yet never in my life was I more moved by any other book. As I read the record of those "worthies" who for Jesus' sake endured privation and prison, torture and martyrdom, with such singing fortitude and eager willingness, I began to feel unworthy by comparison to call myself a Christian. What men! What devotion! What vivid experience of Christ! What instruments of the Holy Spirit!

Think how sparse was the population of Scotland at that time, and then think what the following statistics tell. During only twenty-eight years 18,000 persons suffered death or else penalties of uttermost hardship. Of those who were not executed, 1,700 were shipped to plantations overseas. Another 750 were banished to desolate northern islands, and of those 750 about 200 were wilfully murdered. It is calculated that some 2,800 were imprisoned, and in not a few cases tortured, while another 800 were outlawed, with no means of sustenance, many of them with a price on their head and pre-sentenced to execution if and when apprehended. Those who were driven into voluntary banishment to other countries are estimated at 7,000. Nearly 500 were murdered in cold blood and some 360 executed by legal sentence. Among the overall figure of 18,000 there were the many who perished through winter cold, hunger, and other distresses, being driven out among the mountains, continually hunted by dragoons, and often murdered on the spot when dis-covered. And all that ugly baptism in blood and grief was perpe-trated in the name of religion, upon the godliest men of the realm, by Roman Catholic officials in alliance with a corrupt civil government.

Yet like other paradoxes of history, that half-century or more was one of the most glorious *spiritually* in the experience of the Lord's true people. The human extremity was the divine opportunity. The tyrannical pressure was not always at peak heat. In different places and at spaced intervals there was some degree of liberty allowed, but always the suspense was there; and eventually as the covenanting ministers and their congregations were de-churched, they were obliged to hold their meetings more or less secretly out-of-doors among the hills or in other lonely places. Oh, what prayer it begot! What mighty wrestlers with God those ministers and many of their people became! And what surrender to Christ for life or death! And what holiness of life!

Is it surprising that the *"gifts"* of the Spirit broke loose afresh through such men and among their people? There were no "Pen-tecostal" groups in those grim days, no "charismatic" movement, no "glossolalia" emphasis, no special seeking of the supernatural "gifts"; but in divine answer to the mighty prayerfulness of those Covenanters and the severities of the times, the "gifts" just *came*, in one way or another—including *healings*.

Those memoirs in *The Scots Worthies* are the more impressive because John Howie (1735-1793), the compiler, deliberately erred on the side of overcautiousness, conservatism, and punctilious ver-ification. He seemed afraid lest some occurrences might seem too remarkable to be easily digested. He would sooner understate or completely omit than have any detail doubtful. So we may read trustfully. What is recorded really happened.

As I perused the successive memoirs, perhaps the keenest surprise to me was the "gift" of foreseeing and foretelling which then reappeared, accompanied by a supernatural discerning of hearts and sometimes the pronouncing of immediate judgment upon wicked opposers—which judgments had fulfillments in such detail as to exclude all possibility of mere coincidence. In the ministries of John Knox, George Wishart, John Craig, John Davidson, James Wood, John Welch, Richard Cameron, John Semple, Donald Cargill, Alexander Peden, Thomas Hogg, and others, these discernings and predictings of future events occurred again and again like solemn attestations of the Holy Spirit that these godly men, although ejected, penalized, reviled, driven out, tortured, executed, were indeed the *true* servants of Christ. They were all men constantly in prayer, clean vessels, men under the monopoly of the Holy Spirit. Let me give just a couple of quotations from Howie. They are about John Semple in particular, but they are representative of various others.

Mr. Semple was a man who knew much of his Master's mind, as evidently appears by his discovering of several future events. When news came that Cromwell and those with him were engaged in the trial of Charles I., some persons asked him, what he thought would become of the king. He went into his closet a little, and coming back, he said to them, "The king is gone, he will neither do us good nor ill any more:" which of a truth came to pass. At another time, passing by the house at Kenmuir, as the masons were making some additions thereunto, he said, "Lads, ye are busy, enlarging and repairing the house, but it will be burnt like a crow's nest in a misty morning," which accordingly came to pass, for it was burnt in a dark misty morning by the English. Upon a certain time, when a neighbouring minister was distributing tokens before the Sacrament, and was reaching a token to a certain woman, Mr. Semple (standing by) said, "Hold your hand, she hath gotten too many tokens already; she is a witch;" which, though none suspected her then, she herself confessed to be true, and was deservedly put to death for the same.

At another time, a minister in the shire of Galloway sent one of his elders to Mr. Semple with a letter, earnestly desiring his help at the Sacrament, which was to be in three weeks after. He read the letter, went to his closet, and coming back, he said to the elder, "I am sorry you have come so far on a needless errand; go home, and tell your minister, he hath had all the communions that ever he will have, for he is guilty of fornication, and God will bring it to light ere that time." This likewise came to pass.

All these Scottish Worthies were men of scholarship as well as of evangelical conviction. One such was the Reverend Alexander Peden. More than once he had to flee from Scotland to Ireland, to escape his vengeful detractors. Even in Ireland he had to veil his identity and seek whatever employ he could. Howie says:

> In the same year he [Peden] went to Ireland again, and coming to the house of William Steel in Glenwhary, in the country of Antrim, he inquired at Mrs. Steel, if she wanted a servant for threshing of victual. She said they did, and asked what his wages were a-day and a-week. He said the common rate was a common rule; to which she assented. At night he was put to bed in the barn with the servant lad, and that night he spent in prayer and groaning. Next day, he threshed with the lad, and the next night he spent in the same way. The second day, the lad said to his mistress, "This man sleeps none, but groans and prays all night; I can get no sleep with him; he threshes very well, not sparing himself, though I think he hath not been used to it; and when I put the barn in order, he goes to such a place, and prays for the afflicted Church of Scotland, and names so many people in the furnace." He wrought the second day. His mistress watched and overheard him praying, as the lad had said. At night she desired her husband to inquire if he was a minister; which he did, and desired him to be free with him, and he should not only be no enemy to him, but a friend. Mr. Peden said he was not ashamed of his office, and gave an account of his circumstances; and he was no more set to work, or to lie with the lad. He stayed some considerable time in that place, and was a blessed instrument in the conversion of some, and the civilizing of others. There was a servant lass in that house whom he could not look upon but with frowns; and at last he said to William Steel and his wife, "Put her away, for she will be a stain to your family; she is with child and will murder it, and will be punished for the same." This accordingly came to pass; for which she was burned at Carrickfergus—the usual punishment of malefactors in that country.

The above anecdotes are picked almost at random. Some of the predictions by those men of God were national in scope, reaching years ahead. All came true, some with startling preciseness. To quote amply would run away with pages which we cannot spare here. I wonder whether the late B. B. Warfield ever read the evidence and whether others who aver with him that divine miracles ceased with the Apostles have pondered it. The predictings and discernings are too many, too authentic, and too genuinely fulfilled to be theorized away.

But of course we are primarily concerned in these present studies with the evidence for *divine healings of the body* which then reappeared. Among Howie's Worthies is the Reverend John Scrimgeour, who in the late fifteen hundreds was for a time minister in Kinghorn, Fifeshire, also for a time a chaplain to King James VI. He was "very learned, especially in Hebrew." He was also "an eminent wrestler in prayer." Let me quote a paragraph from Howie concerning the supernatural healing of his daughter.

> Mr. Scrimgeour had several friends and children taken away by death. The only daughter who at that time survived, and whom he dearly loved, was seized with the king's evil [scrofula: tuberculosis of the lymphatic glands], by which she was reduced to the very point of death, so that he was called up to see her die. Finding her in this condition, he went out to the fields, as he himself told, in the night-time, in great grief and anxiety, and began to expostulate with the Lord, with such expressions as for all the world he durst not again utter. In a fit of displeasure he said, "Thou, O Lord, knowest that I have been serving Thee in the uprightness of my heart, according to my power and measure; nor have I stood in awe to declare Thy mind even unto the greatest in the time, and Thou seest that I take pleasure in this child. O that I could obtain such a thing at Thy hand as to spare her!" And being in great agony of spirit, at last it was said to him from the Lord, "I have heard thee at this time, but use not the like boldness in time coming for such particulars." When he came home the child was recovered, and, sitting up in bed, took some meat; and when he looked at her arm it was perfectly whole.

Another among those mighty men of valor was the Reverend Thomas Hogg. So often did supernatural healings occur in connection with him that he became noted for them. Here are a few instances.

> (1) A good woman having come with this sore lamentation, that her daughter was distracted, Mr. Hogg charged one or two devout persons (for he frequently employed such on extraordinary occasions) to set apart a day and a night for fasting and prayer, and join with him in prayer for the maid next day. Accordingly, when this appointment was performed, she recovered her senses as well as before.
>
> (2) A daughter of the laird of Park, his brother-in-law, who lodged with him, was seized with a high fever which left little hope of life. Mr. Hogg loved the child dearly, and while he and his wife were jointly supplicating the Lord in prayer, acknowledging their own and the child's iniquity, the fever instantly left her. This passage was found in his own diary, which he concludes with admiration upon the goodness of God, to whom he ascribes the praise of all.
>
> (3) In like manner, a child of the Reverend Mr. Urquhart having been at the point of death, those present pressed Mr. Hogg to pray, for he was now become so esteemed that none other would in such case do it, while he was present; upon which he solemnly charged them to join with him, and after his having fervently wrestled in prayer for some time, the child was restored to health.
>
> (4) David Dunbar, who lived at a distance, being in a frenzy

[dementing paroxysm] came to Mr. Hogg's house in one of his fits. Mr. Hogg caused him to sit down, and advised with Mr. Fraser of Brea and some others present what could be done for the lad. Some were for letting blood, but Mr. Hogg said, "The prelates have deprived us of money wherewith to pay physicians, therefore let us employ Him who cures freely." . . . So, after commanding the distracted person to be still, he prayed fervently for the poor man, who was immediately restored to his right mind. This is faithfully attested by those who were eye and ear witnesses.

(5) Mr. Hogg having once gone to see a gracious woman in great extremity of distress, both of body and mind, he prayed with her and for her, using this remarkable expression among many others, 'O Lord, rebuke this temptation, and we in Thy name rebuke the same." Immediately the woman was restored both in body and mind. Yet, notwithstanding the Lord had honoured him in such a manner, it is doubtful if any in his day more carefully guarded against delusions than he did, it being his custom, whenever he bowed a knee, to request to be saved from delusions.[3]

Take now just one short paragraph about the Reverend Robert Bruce, famed for his scholarship, saintliness, and preaching gifts. Howie says of him:

Robert Bruce was also a man who had somewhat of the spirit of discerning future events, and did prophetically speak of several things that afterwards came to pass. Yea, and divers persons distracted (says Fleming in his *Fulfilling of the Scripture*) and those who were past all recovery with epileptic disease or with falling sickness were brought to him, and were, after prayer by him in their behalf, fully restored from that malady. This may seem strange, but it is true, for he was such a wrestler with God, and had more than ordinary familiarity with Him.

It would seem as though there were even resuscitations of deceased persons. I am always trebly skeptical about *any* report of an alleged resurgence from death. It is not that I doubt the Lord's power, but I question the likelihood and the rationale or suspect the validity of the "evidence." But what can one say about the following incident reported in connection with the Reverend John Welch? Before I quote from Howie's account, let me premise a comment or two about the said John Welch. I doubt whether in the history of the Church any man prayed more. He averaged some seven hours daily. In those times there were no cars, no railways, no radio or television, no automotive machinery, no big industrial plants, no population congestion, no public schools, no hospitals, no medical service. Life was simpler, slower, and in Scotland much severer. There were far less distractions for ministers, but there were far less comforts; and those regular seven hours daily in prayer were the more remarkable amid such unconducive circumstances. And, as never a man prayed more, so no man was more prophetic than John Welch since the days of the Apostles; for he had the supernatural gift of discerning hearts, of predicting impending happenings (with literal fulfilments), and pronouncing divine requitals on wicked-doers, which surely befell them with striking exactness. He was persecuted, driven from home, imprisoned first at lonely Blackness Castle, later in Edinburgh Castle; and eventually, on November 7, 1606, he was banished from his beloved Scotland, never to see it again. During his exile in France, he exercised a powerful ministry "in the Spirit." Now let me quote from Howie's pages.

There was in his house, among many others who boarded with him for good education, a young gentleman of great quality and suitable expectations, the heir of Lord Ochiltree, Governor of the Castle of Edinburgh. This young gentleman, after he had gained very much upon Mr. Welch's affections, fell ill of a grievous sickness, and after he had been long wasted by it, closed his eyes and expired, to the apprehension of all spectators; and was therefore taken out of his bed, and laid on a pallet on the floor, that his body might be more conveniently dressed. This was to Mr. Welch a very great grief, and therefore he stayed with the body fully three hours, lamenting over him with great tenderness. After twelve hours the friends brought in a coffin whereinto they desired the corpse to be put, as the custom was; but Mr. Welch desired that for the satisfaction of his affections they would forbear for a time; which they granted, and returned not till twenty-four hours after the death. Then they desired with great importunity that the corpse might be coffined and speedily buried, the weather being extremely hot. Yet he persisted in his request, earnestly begging them to excuse him once more. So they left the corpse upon the pallet for full thirty-six hours. Even after all that, though he was urged not only with great earnestness but with displeasure, they were constrained to forbear for twelve hours more. After forty-eight hours were past, Mr. Welch still held out against them; and then his friends perceiving that he believed the young man was not really dead, but under some apoplectic fit, proposed to him for his satisfaction that trial should be made upon the body by doctors and chirurgeons, if possibly any spark of life might be found in him; and with this he was content. So the physicians were set to work, who pinched him with pinchers in the fleshy parts of his body, and twisted a bow-string about his head with great force; but no sign of life appearing in him, the physicians pronounced him stark dead, and said that there was no more delay to be made. Yet Mr. Welch begged of them once more that they would but step into the next room for an hour or two, and leave him with the dead youth; and this they granted.

Then Mr. Welch fell down before the pallet and cried to the Lord with all his might, and sometimes looked upon the dead body, continuing to wrestle with the Lord, till at length the dead youth opened his eyes and cried out to Mr. Welch, whom he distinctly knew, "O sir, I am all whole, except my head and my legs" (the places they had sorely hurt with their pinching). When Mr. Welch perceived this he called upon his friends and showed them the dead young man restored to life again, to their great astonishment. And this young nobleman, though he lost the estate of Ochiltree, lived to acquire a great estate in Ireland, became Lord Castlestuart, and was a man of such excellent parts that he was courted by the Earl of Stafford to be a counsellor in Ireland. This he refused to be until the godly but silenced Scottish ministers, who suffered under the bishops in the north of Ireland, were restored to the exercise of their ministry. Then he accepted and continued so all his life, not only in honour and power, but in the profession and practice of godliness, to the great comfort of the country where he lived. This story *the nobleman himself* communicated to his friends in Ireland.

Well, what are we to say about that? I make no comment. It must speak for itself, as indeed must all the other supernatural effluences of the Holy Spirit through those Scottish Covenanters. A. J. Gordon finely says,

> When we reflect that these things are recorded by the pens of some of the holiest men the church of God has ever seen, and recorded too as the experiences of their own ministry of faith and prayer, the fact must at least furnish food for reflection to those who continue to assert with such confident assurance that the age of miracles is past. . . . It is Apostolic *men* who make an Apostolic *age*, not a certain date of Anno Domini. . . . When by the stress of violent persecution, or by the sore discipline of reproach and rejection by the world, the old faith is revived, then we catch glimpses once more of the Apostolic age. And such perhaps beyond all others in modern times was the age of the Covenanters.[4]

Richard Baxter

How some of us have reveled in the writings of Richard Baxter, the most prolific penman of the English Puritans! Like the Scottish Covenanters, he too lived during that turmoiled seventeenth century. As England swayed to and fro between Romanism and Protestantism, between Anglicanism and Presbyterianism, between Royalists and Cromwellian Roundheads, Richard Baxter acted according to Christian conscience as wisely as he knew how, inevitably clashing with those of strong views. Yet his transparent piety won him the respect of *all* parties. Eventually, in 1662, the same Act of Uniformity which provoked the Scottish Covenanters to recusancy had a like effect on Richard Baxter, from which time he threw in his lot entirely with the nonconformists. Later, this brought him imprisonment, which he bore joyfully for his Lord's sake.

Perhaps Baxter's most treasured work is *The Saints' Everlasting Rest*. In it he refers to direct divine healings of the body and does so in his characteristically frank, engaging way. Many experienced Christians, he said, can testify how God has made good "the promises of Scripture to his servants; some in desperate *diseases of the body*, some in other apparent dangers, *delivered so suddenly*, or so much against the common course of nature *when all the best remedies have failed*, that no second cause could have had any hand in their deliverance." Or take this further passage:

> I know men's atheism and infidelity will never lack somewhat to say against the most eminent providences, though they were *miracles*. . . . But when mercies [i.e., of healing] are granted in the very time of prayer, and when, to reason, there is no hope, and without the use or help of any other means. . . . is not this as plain as if God from heaven should say to us: I am fulfilling to thee the true word of my promise in Christ my Sonne? How many times have I known the prayer of faith to *save the sick when all physicians have given them up as dead!*

Besides those general references to miraculous healings, Richard Baxter details an experience of his own, a healing just as real to *him* as it is curious to *us*.

> Among the abundance of instances that I could give, my conscience commandeth me here to give you this one . . . I had a tumor rise on one of the tonsils or almonds of my throat, round like a pease, and at first no bigger; and at last no bigger than a small button, and hard like a bone. The fear lest it should prove a cancer troubled me more than the thing itself. I used first dissolving medicines, and after-lenient [emollient] for palliation, but all in vain for about a quarter of a year. At last my conscience smote me for silencing so many former deliverences. . . . Lest I should be derided as making ostentation of God's special mercies to myself, as if I were a special favorite of heaven, I had made no public mention of them. I was that morning to preach . . . and in obedience to my conscience I spoke these words which are now in this page: *"How many times have I known the prayer of faith to save the sick when all physicians had given them up as dead!"*. . . When I went to church I had my tumor as before (for I frequently saw it in the glasse, and felt it constantly). As soon as I had done preaching, I

felt it was gone; and, hasting to the glasse, I saw that there was not the vestigium or cicatrix or mark wherever it had been; nor did I at all discern what became of it. I am sure I neither swallowed it nor spit it out, and it was unlikely to dissolve by any natural cause, as it had been like a bone a quarter of a year, notwithstanding all dissolving gargarismes. I thought fit to mention this because it was done *just before I spoke the words* here written on this page.

I know how easily a certain type of mind can dismiss or explain away a simple testimony like that. I myself have been both harassed and blessed by an incurably skeptical mind toward alleged miracles, whether of physical healing or of any other nature. But if there is one man more than another whose combined sanity and sincerity I could trust, that man is Richard Baxter.

George Fox

I used to have Quaker friends in Ireland who never tired of talking about George Fox. That seventeenth century cynosure (1624-1691) certainly was shaped in an unusual mold, but were not his mystical and "inner light" and other peculiarities quite eclipsed by his transformed character and thoroughgoing exemplification of practical Christianity? If ever a man was heavenly minded yet down-to-earth, George Fox was. He has been rightly called one of the few religious geniuses of English history. His founding and guiding of the Society of Friends, or Quakers, proved him to be so. He himself was "a friend of God" as truly as Abraham was; and he "walked with God" as closely as Enoch did. I by-pass all other reference to the man and the movement, however, simply to mention the fact that miracles of healing reappeared once again in conjunction with *that* devout movement. I turn again to A. J. Gordon's *Ministry of Healing* for two brief incidents, both taken from George Fox's journal.

> Now there was in that town (Twy-Cross in Lincolnshire, England), a great man that had long lain sick and was given over by the physicians: and some friends in that town desired me to go and see him; and I went up to him in his chamber, and spoke the Word of Life to him, and was moved to pray for him; and the Lord was entreated, and *restored him to health* (emphasis mine). . . .
>
> John Rush of Bedfordshire went along with me to visit her [a woman in Hertfordshire, England], and when we came in there were many people in the house who were tender about her. They told me she was not a woman for this world [i.e., not long to live] but that if I had anything to comfort her concerning the world to come, I might speak to her. So I was moved of the Lord to speak to her; and the Lord *raised her up again* to the astonishment of the town and country.

Johann Albrecht Bengel

All students of historical theology know the name of Johann Albrecht Bengel (1687-1752). He was a scholar and principal of the theological seminary in Denkendorf, Wurttenberg. His *Gnomon,* or Index, of the New Testament was "the most remarkable commentary thus far produced," says Williston Walker in his *History of the Christian Church.* Later, the illustrious John Wesley made it the basis of his *Notes upon the New Testament.* Commenting on James 5:17, Bengel says, "It [the gift of healing] seems to have been given by God that it might *always remain with the Church* as a specimen of other gifts. . . . O happy simplicity! Interrupted or lost through unbelief!" (emphasis mine). This is endorsed by a particular instance of healing.

> At Leonberg, a town of Wirtembergh, A.D. 1644, thirteenth Sunday after Trinity, a girl of twenty-three years of age was so disabled in her limbs as hardly to be able to creep along by the help of crutches. But whilst the Dean, Raumier was his name, was from the pulpit dwelling on the miraculous power of Jesus' name *she suddenly was raised up, and restored to the use of her limbs.*[5]

It is good to see that Bengel's faculty of faith was not impaired by this faculty for exegesis. He was not the kind of reporter to confuse fact with fancy or to be taken in by mere appearances. None of us can be blamed for having a predilection in favor of believing him.

Others More Recent

There is no lack of material, but our pages here are becoming too many for what is meant only as a quick panorama. I pass by Edward Irving (1792-1834) and the Irvingites, or Catholic Apostolic Church, as also Baptist, Methodist, and Presbyterian groups during the seventeen and eighteen hundreds. A. J. Gordon gave instances of healing miracles among them; and others can be found in the written histories of various movements or bodies such as the English and Welsh Baptists or of Presbyterianism in Scotland. B. B. Warfield submits what I consider to be a rightful refutation of one much-publicized miracle healing associated with the Irvingites. That, however, only underlines his inability to undermine the many others, which he does not attempt to do. It is good to have a relentless scrutiny like his turned upon them all so long as we do not let prejudice blind us to real fact and honest testimony. I pass over these different groups only because I am now wanting to come to healings which link the nineteenth century to our own.

The Miracles at Lourdes

What of the healing "miracles" at Lourdes? For one thing, they must always be appraised in their Roman Catholic orientation. Saint worship, relic worship, shrine veneration, and miracle proneness have inhered in the Roman church right from the early days of its ascendancy. Supposedly supernatural wonders, which to us more calculating, Bible-based Protestants seem like sentimental impositions, are unquestioningly ingested by the dyed-in-the-wool Roman Catholic. That is not an unkindly biased statement.

Nor is it an overstatement that relics are central in the miracle-life of the Roman church. Yrjo Hirn has it that the whole Roman Catholic worship in reality now gathers round a relic chest; for with the lapse of time even the altar has become a kind of coffin, enclosing the bones of departed saints. It is a rule of long standing now that every Roman Catholic altar shall contain some relic.[6] Apparently saint-and-relic veneration has so ingrained itself even into the Mass that the very altar is finally turned into a saint's shrine.

That of necessity must be the background to our thinking on the "miracles" at Lourdes. Therefore we cannot but question at the outset: How many of them have been *real* healings directly from God?—for there is a vapory unclearness overhanging so much of what goes on there. I had rueful feelings as I read the depressing figures supplied by Warfield. Up to 1908, the fiftieth anniversary of Lourdes as a healing Mecca, about ten million people had visited there, though not all had gone there for healing. The full mixture of cures, whether reported as "complete" or only "partial," was at that time 3,962. The average works out at about one "cure" to every 2,500 pilgrims while the failures (which Lourdes never registers) are a minimum of 50,000. What heartbreak and disillusionment that represents! A French medical writer worked out the "cures" at about one-half of one percent.[7]

I have not sought out figures and percentages between then and now, for such further statistics are not in the least necessary to our present purpose, which is to show that direct divine healings of the body have continued, at intervals, from Apostolic days until the present. So many are the trustable instances of it that we neither need nor ask the equivocal assistance of Lourdes. We mention Lourdes only because if we did not do so, some would wonder why.

The truth is, in my judgment, that the whole showcase of the Lourdes "miracles" is not only suspect but disqualified as serious evidence; for in both its origin and nature there is a theatrical drapery and ungenuineness which belie it. There seems to have been a little epidemic of Mary apparitions in France during the latter half of the nineteenth century: (1) La Salette in 1846, where Mary was seen as a "beautiful lady" by two young shepherd children; (2) Lourdes in 1858, where Mary appeared as a "girl in white," no bigger than the country-bred girl who saw her; (3) Pellevoisin in 1876, where she appeared as "the Mother All-Merciful" to an ailing maidservant; (4) Le Pontinet in 1889, suppositionally seen as the "Queen of Heaven" by a girl aged eleven. The first of these was twice "pronounced fraudulent by the French courts."[8] The last of them was later disallowed by Roman Catholic officialdom.[9] As for the second (Lourdes), is it without significance that it occurred just after 1854, when the imagination of Roman Catholics everywhere was stirred into new and emotional adoration of Mary by that Roman-invented and now papally proclaimed dogma of "the Immaculate Conception of Mary"? In the aggregate, thousands of young, impressionable, and religiously sentimental Roman Catholic girls have had dreams and visions of Mary. With their type of religious upbringing, is that surprising? Fourteen-year-old Bernadette Soubirous of Lourdes was no exception. She seems to have been a nice wee girlie, though unfortunately, so I gather, she grew up to be a "somewhat colorless, not to say weak, and certainly very diseased, woman."[10]

What are we to say about all those alleged self-revealings of Mary? My answer is that they may well have been real enough *apparitions*, but they certainly were not real *appearings*. Can we be sure that they were not optically real? We can. Let this be put straight once for all in the thinking of both Protestants and Roman Catholics. Not one of all our departed Christian loved ones, not one of all the ecclesiastically canonized "saints" now gone beyond the grave, not one of them, nor Mary herself through whom our Lord's temporary flesh-and-blood body was given birth, can either hear or answer the prayers which we pray here on earth. Not one of them either can or does reveal himself (or herself) to us here on earth. A moment's thought will clarify and certify this. The only Being in existence who has the infinite attributes of omnipotence, omniscience, and omnipresence is *God*, for the simple but profound reason that only God is boundless in dimension and eternal in duration. Every created being, whether angel or demon or human, is *finite;* and every finite creature is *local,* i.e., can be in only one place at any given instant. No created being is omnipresent; therefore, no created being can be simultaneously present *everywhere.* Even Michael, the illustrious archangel, can be in only one place at any given moment. And likewise Satan, the powerful archfiend, can be in only one place at any given moment—and the same is true of all his demon accomplices.

So wherever that "heaven" is to which all departed Christians have gone, whether it be (to us) some invisible realm near this earth or near Venus or in the "empty space" of the sidereal heavens beyond the earth's North Pole (Job 26:7) or millions of light-years away from tiny planet earth—*wherever* they are in that vast space realm, they are there *locally.* They cannot be there and here at the same time; and since they are *not* hovering here, they are locally *there,* including dear Mary. Even if that heaven is nearer than Venus, they are all millions of miles too far away from us to hear prayers prayed to them here on earth even though we shout our prayers with voices of thunder. Nor does any one of them have the power to *answer* such prayers if he (or she) *could* hear them, for only *God* can move those cosmic forces which are involved in the answering of prayer. Moreover, even if departed Christian saints *tried* to reveal themselves to us optically or bodily, they could not do so, for they are now *bodiless.* In the words of 2 Corinthians 5:8, they are "absent from the body." That is equally true of the "highly favored" Mary.[11] Yes, and that is equally true whether we think of the departed as being in "heaven" or in "hades" or in "outer space" or in a suppositionary "Purgatory." They are localized; they are bodiless; they are sexless (Mary is no longer female); and they have neither the power nor the permit to come revealing themselves to us human beings still on earth. Let us be grateful that God has ordered it so.

Back in 1940, as the Nazi attack on Paris, France, got swiftly underway and France's defeat trembled in the balance, there was much panic praying. The Roman Catholic *Universe* of June 21 that year said, "The great Church of the Madeleine was packed all day—packed to the doors. And continually the cry went up: 'Our Lady of Lourdes, save France! Saint Genevieve, save France! Saint Joan of Arc, save France!'" But France was not saved. Those prayers were not answered. They were prayers to the wrong persons, and the Roman Catholic Church was to blame. Neither "our Lady of Lourdes" nor either of the other supposedly still-female "saints" who were so excitedly implored could hear those prayers or intervene to save France. Amid those misdirected intercessory wailings France fell, in thorough humiliation. Perhaps it is not irrelevant to add that some while *before* 1940, France had expunged the word "God" from all her government documents!

But let us try to imagine that for some mysterious reason God *had* given Mary some phantom body by which to reveal herself and then sent her through a million leagues to appear with occasional suddenness to people on this earth; what kind of appearances and communications would we have expected? Surely any such epiphanies would have been to reveal something of high moral and spiritual import or of momentous relevance for the times. Yet what do we find? Her appearings are apparently to the lesser intelligent: to two young shepherd children, to a rustic lassie of fourteen, to another girl aged eleven. Even the Roman Catholic author J. K. Huysmans, in his *La Cathédrale*, putting the most favorable construction on it, says, "First, she manifests herself only to the poor and humble. Secondly, she accommodates herself to their intelligence and shows herself under the poor images which these lowly people love."[12] As for the figure "seen" at Lourdes, even the Roman clergy themselves seem to admit that it was such as has often been seen, mainly by young Roman Catholic girls, under circumstances without any objective value whatever.[13]

As for the supposed *communication* at Lourdes, what? After characteristically keen but fair scrutiny, the scholarly B. B. Warfield gives this verdict: "The plain fact is that the communications attributed to the Virgin are silly with the silliness of a backward child, repeating, without in the least comprehending their meaning, phrases with which [at that time] the air was palpitant"[14]—i.e., just after the newly proclaimed dogma of Mary's immaculate conception had shaken Roman Catholics everywhere with "emotional tremors," some of which could scarcely fail to have registered in the imagination of young Bernadette in Lourdes.

I shrink from saying that those "apparitions" of Mary were anything *worse* than by-products of hyperemotional religious fervidity. Let me err on the side of charity rather than be wrongly drastic. Yet Roman Catholics everywhere, indeed all of us, may well be jolted by such Mary manifestations as are occurring in *our own* days. All around us there is a large-scale recrudescence of astrology, occultism, psychic practice, clairvoyance, spiritism, Satanic and demonic communication, and mediumistic traffic with the spirit realm. Rene Noorbergen's recently published book *The Soul Hustlers* is an eyeopener. At one point he reports an interview with George King, one of today's best-known "psychic masters." King has been for a long while a chief recipient of communications from intelligences in the spirit world. In January 1957 the˙spirit-informers foretold through him that in various places there would be visions of the woman commonly known as the mother of Jesus. "The fulfilment of this," says Noorbergen, "was printed in the London *Evening News* of 11 September 1957, when the *Associated Press* released the following news item. . . ."

> WARSCHAU—In Krakau, the appearance of the Virgin Mary has created great disturbance among civic and church authorities. For the last two weeks, every evening a large number of people gathered in front of the house where Miss Cseslawa Janusz, 49, has seen the vision of the Virgin Mary for two times. The crowd sings spiritual songs hoping that she will also appear to them. The Polish Catholic newspaper, Tygwonik Powzsechny, has warned against hysteria.[15]

How did those evil spirit beings foretell through George King those Mary apparitions? Did *Mary* tell them beforehand? Unthinkable! Did *God* foreapprise them? Heaven forbid! The only answer seems to be that they were able to *predict* them because it was they who were going to *effect* them, in which case Mary apparitions certainly *would* be contrivances of Satan himself to deepen and widen superstitious religious delusion.

But now, back to Lourdes. Not without reason has it been said that the immense success of Lourdes as a place of pilgrimage has been achieved in spite of the meanness of its origin, and it is to be attributed to the skill with which it has been exploited.

Ten thousand pities that such exploitation of saints, shrines, relics, apparitions, etc., have disgraced the Roman church through centuries. Even lowly Mary, of such sacred memory, has been equally worshiped and exploited. Back in the sixteenth century, that giant of erudite scholarship Desiderius Erasmus and his coadjutors were busy collecting and collating the Greek manuscripts of the New Testament which eventually became the Textus Receptus on which our English Authorized or King James Version of the New Testament is based. During the earliest phase of the Protestant Reformation, Erasmus sided with Luther but later disagreed with him because, unlike Luther, he preferred *not* to break away from the Roman Catholic Church but to attempt reform of it from within. Therefore Erasmus should have the ready ears of Roman Catholics. Let me quote his eminently sensible and outspoken words about superstition and pretending and lying which had crept into the Roman church under the guise of religion.

> Even Augustine, an honest old man and a lover of truth, can repeat a tale as authentic which Lucian had ridiculed under other names so many years before Augustine was born. What wonder, therefore, that fools can be found to listen to the legends of the saints, or to stories about hell such as frighten cowards or old women? There is not a martyr, there is not a virgin, whose biographies have not been disfigured by these monstrous absurdities.
>
> Smiths and carpenters were sent [by the Protestant Reformers at Basle] to remove the images from the churches. The roods [crosses, crucifixes] and the unfortunate saints were cruelly handled. Strange that none of them worked a miracle to avenge their dignity, when before they had worked so many [miracles] at the slightest provocation.
>
> No blood was shed, but there was a cruel assault on altars, images and pictures. We are told that St. Francis used to resent light remarks about his five wounds; and several other saints are said to have shown displeasure on similar occasions. It was strange that at Basle not a saint stirred a finger.
>
> What would Jerome say could he see the Virgin's milk exhibited for money, with as much honor paid to it as to the consecrated body of Christ; the miraculous oil, and portions of the true cross, enough if they were collected to freight a large ship [!]? Here we have the head of St. Francis, there our Lady's petticoat, or St. Anne's cowl, or St. Thomas of Canterbury's shoes; not presented as innocent aids to religion, but as the substance itself—and all through the avarice of priests and the hypocrisy of monks playing on the credulity of the people. Even bishops play their parts in these fantastic shows, and approve and dwell on them in their rescripts.[16]

In fine, then, what of those largely advertised miracles of healing at Lourdes? Well, first, the *non*-healings greatly outnumber the *alleged* healings. Second, even among the low percentage of alleged healings, many are not *real* healings. Third, among those which *seem* to be real, many are merely temporary remissions rather than permanent cures. Fourth, most of the comparatively small remainder which seem indeed to be thorough healings are in the area of the mental, nervous, emotional, i.e., *functional* disorders, forms of pathological and physiological dysfunction which could be corrected or largely ameliorated by modern medical skills or by powerful psychological influence. I am not convinced that there has ever been a really proven healing of any skeletal luxation, congenital lameness, or, for that matter, any fracture which might be repaired by modern surgery. Is that because however strong is the power of mind over body, it just cannot rejoin two separated parts of a broken bone?

Fifth, I believe that *some* of the alleged healings, even though only a small fraction, have indeed been direct divine acts. At that point I sharply diverge from Warfield's dictum, that *no* reported miracle, whether at Lourdes or anywhere else, can truly be a *divine* miracle. He is forced to take that view, of course, in line with the theory which he and others hold, viz., that divine miracles (both the evidential and the compassionate) *ceased* abruptly and finally with the close of the Apostolic period. Therefore, when he asserts that there have been absolutely *no* divinely wrought miracle cures at Lourdes, he is not so much uttering a conclusion drawn from impartial scrutiny of total evidence as he is defending an a priori necessity of his preformed theory. My own belief is that there have been *some* direct divine cures at Lourdes and that they have been wrought purely out of heavenly compassion for suffering, bewildered, sincerely godly souls. Those healings have *not* been evidential; that is, they have not been in confirmation of the unscriptural ecclesiastical system which has exploited Lourdes. They have not been *because* of Lourdes but rather *despite* it.

There are those who would remind us, perhaps, that some "miracles" which really *are* miracles may not be divine but *Satanic*. They would have us think that many of the healings at Lourdes were works of Satan, using a corrupt, pseudo-Christian church in that way so as to deceive human beings yet the more. Into that I will not delve here. Our particular concern is whether there have been *divine* healings there. I believe that there *have* and must leave it there. Lourdes has already taken more space than I intended. At best its testimony to divine healing through the centuries is cloudy; nor do we need its doubtful contribution inasmuch as we have far saner and safer evidence without it.

Torrey, Cullis, Simpson, Others

In finishing this section of our inquiries, I want to get right into our own twentieth century and up to the present day. Let me first call R. A. Torrey to our witness stand. In my judgment never was there a sounder or more squarely Bible-based evangelist than he. It was conservatively estimated (so I recall reading) that in his succession of city campaigns right round the English-speaking world, some sixty-four thousand instances of serious conversion to Christ were registered. At one time he was dean of the Moody Bible Institute in

Chicago. Later he became founder-president at the Bible Institute of Los Angeles. If it was ever true of any man, it was true of Torrey: "he knew his Bible" and knew how to teach it—as can still be seen in the practical forthrightness of the books he has left us. I have before me his pamphlet *Divine Healing*. Its primary purpose is not to argue *for* divine healing but rather to guard people against the way it was being preached at that time. He was just about the last man to be deceived by the merely seeming, but just the right man to tell us with reliable frankness about the real, if it was actually happening. He thought it best to give cases from his own experience; so here we reproduce a couple of them.

How often God has given to me *faith* as I have prayed for some sick one, and healing immediate, complete and wonderful has followed. When I was Superintendent of City Missions in Minneapolis, I found on my desk one day a request to go to a home three miles distant. The people were unknown to me. Upon reaching the home I learned that they were French, and had been Roman Catholics, but the husband and wife had been converted, though many of their relatives were still Roman Catholics. I learned that the woman had been sick for four years and had had *nine different physicians, none of whom could help her. She was helpless.* She could move her hands, but she had to be lifted upon a sheet when they made the bed. I sat down by the sick-bed and asked the woman what she wished me to do. She replied that she wished me to pray that she might be healed. . . .

I read to the sick woman this very passage that we are expounding, James 5:14,15. Then I asked her, "Do you believe God will heal you?" She replied that she believed that He could heal her. "But," I said, "do you believe that He *will* heal you?" And after my reading to her various promises from the Word she said she believed that He would. I then explained to her very fully the meaning of the anointing and that on her part it meant a full surrender to God of all her physical powers. Then I knelt by her bedside and, "having anointed her with oil in the name of the Lord," I prayed that God would come in with the healing power of His Holy Spirit and restore her to perfect health then and there. As I prayed God gave me faith that He heard my prayer. I prayed "the prayer of faith," and as I arose I said to the woman, "I expect you as soon as I am gone to get up and go about your work." I went from that home with the full assurance that God had answered my prayer. The night of the day following, before I began our evening meeting, I said to one of my missionaries, "Polly, you are going to hear something tonight." I was sure someone would come down from the neighbourhood and say that the sick woman was well. And, sure enough, when the meeting was opened for testimony a neighbour of this woman arose and said that God had completely healed the woman, and that immediately after my departure she did get up, dress, and go out for a call. And the following Sunday she was down at our services, three miles away. And she remained a strong, healthy woman as long as I remained in Minneapolis. Afterwards they went South and I lost track of her. But many years later, when I was holding meetings in Los Angeles in a tabernacle that was erected for me by the churches of that city, down on the corner of Seventh and Los Angeles Streets, I told this story one afternoon in speaking on the subject of "Prayer." A man sprang up in the audience and said, "Mr. Torrey, that was my wife. We are living in Los Angeles now, and my wife is a well woman." . . . She has been a well woman from that day, about thirty-five years ago, until this day.

Take another illustration. There was a Methodist minister in Dakota who had a child that was improperly formed. There was some defect in her backbone so that the little child was bent together and the abdomen protruded, causing constant pain, and the child could not sleep. The parents brought the child to Minneapolis to see what specialists could do, but the specialists told them that there was no hope for the child, that they might put her in a plaster-cast so that she might live, deformed, not longer than two or three years. Though the parents were Methodists they were so desirous for the health of their child that they tried "Christian Science," but found no help in that system of error. Then the minister said to his wife, "Let us take her to brother Torrey." They brought her over to my house, a little child of about two years of age, terribly misshapen and greatly suffering. I took the child in my arms and prayed for her. God gave the necessary faith and the child was healed. Relief came immediately. That night she slept normally for the first time, even the defective part of her body was made right. Something like eighteen years later I was holding meetings in Petoskey, Michigan. In one of the afternoon meetings a Methodist minister from one of the neighbouring towns came in. He got up in the meeting and told this story, saying he was the father of that daughter and that she was completely healed and a candidate for the foreign mission field. She herself came in a few days later, a beautiful, perfectly formed young woman. She was in our Auditorium in Los Angeles at our Sunday morning services a few weeks ago. . . . I know in my own personal experience that the promise of this verse [James 5:15] *holds for the present day* .[17]

I am tempted (and am yielding) just to add Torrey's testimony to a healing in his own body. Here it is:

Let me relate carefully one instance. When I was very young, so young that I have no recollection of it, I suffered a very severe attack of scarlet fever which left me with an infected ear. It was necessary to operate at the time, back of the ear. But for years I had a discharge from that ear. Even when I had attained to manhood it was necessary to carry absorbent cotton with me constantly and most of the time keep it in the ear. The drum was perforated, and I heard with such

difficulty with that ear (the left ear) that whenever I used the telephone it was necessary to bring the ear-piece way around to the other,
the sound ear. I went to a very well-known ear specialist in Cleveland,
Ohio, and found temporary relief from the discharges, but in a little
time they returned. My ear continued in this diseased condition for
several years longer. While working in Minneapolis I had a severe
attack of pain in the ear. I said to myself, You pray for the healing of
others, why do you not ask God to heal your own ear? I at once knelt
down alone in my own home and asked God to heal that ear. He
healed me instantly, and for many years I had no discharge from that
ear and no pain in it, the drum healed over and I can now hear well
with both ears. I have told this to two ear specialists and they both
asked me to let them look into my ear, which, of course, I did; and
both stated that the drum was evidently once perforated and is now
healed over.[18]

I will not give "case histories" from the next witness who is available
to us. I am referring to him particularly because he himself was a
doctor, a medical man of high repute among his fellow professionals.
He was Charles Cullis, a practicing physician in Boston, Mas-
sachusetts; and he had such a portfolio of authentic healing miracles
that we dare not start selecting. In lieu of my relating in detail, let me
furnish the following summary tribute to him by my recently deceased friend, Rowland V. Bingham, one of the greatest missionary
statesmen of our time.

While Christian Science was being conceived in the disordered
mind of Mrs. Eddy, in the same city of Boston God was raising up a
man who combined in himself the qualities of a true scientist and of a
humble, earnest and enlightened Christian.

Dr. Charles Cullis was a practising physician, of whom the profession might well be proud. He was really one of the advance guard to
wage war on that modern scourge of mankind, tuberculosis.

He was not only a physician, but a philanthropist, founding an
institution where he could minister to many sick and suffering ones
who would otherwise have been unable to afford the care which he
gave.

But, while he was a busy doctor, he was a diligent student of the
Word of God, and a man of prayer. In his medical work he often came
to the end of his own resources, and, like every honest physician, had
to acknowledge that human aid and medical help had reached their
limit. It was under these circumstances he was led to seek divine
assistance, and the answers to his prayers were many.

A careful study of the Scriptures convinced him that there were
promises which he could rightly plead on behalf of the sick. Especially
did he make use of the promise and instruction in the fifth chapter of
the Epistle of James.

It was his custom to render what medical aid he could. Then he would seek to administer spiritual comfort or admonition from the Word. Where he perceived that the patient had faith to be healed, he was always ready to pray the prayer of faith. Many were those who were past all help from human sources who were restored in answer to prayer.

But, with Dr. Cullis there was no attempt to resolve these experiences of healing into a system of theology, nor did he ever see any incongruity between the use of his medical knowledge and seeking divine intervention. He did not presume to dictate to God as to the plane on which He would operate, the natural or the supernatural.

And yet, far from showing divine displeasure that this man continued to act as the beloved physician in all cases where the natural healing was possible, God blessed his ministry in supernatural healing beyond almost any other instrument of our day, *until the record of the cases restored to health would require volumes.*

Then, of course, there is that now-venerated "mighty man of valor" in the Christian faith, the late A. B. Simpson (1843-1919), founder, under God, of the evangelical denomination known as the Christian and Missionary Alliance. His writings on direct divine healing and his testimony to its occurrence are so well known, so often quoted, and so easily available that to start giving examples here might seem a superfluity. Who among Evangelicals does not know the classic of Simpson's own healing from humanly incurable heart disease? We may not see eye-to-eye with the beloved leader in certain aspects of his *theory* as to divine healing, but as for the *reality* of the healings to which he bore witness, can there be any reasonable doubt? It has been truly conceded by one who was not too sympathetic with Simpson's viewpoint that having been a semi-invalid for years, he (Simpson), "instead of going to an early grave, was restored to a fulness of health which enabled him for more than a quarter of a century to do as much work as two ordinary men." No, in the case of A. B. Simpson, so well known after such long, critical scrutiny, we hardly need start supplying anecdotal corroborations. The monumental evidence cannot be demolished by the most determined skeptic.

In Retrospect, What?

What then are we to decide as we now look back over our gathered findings? I shall not hesitate to say that in my own opinion there is ample evidence through sufficiently trustworthy witnesses to establish the fact that direct divine healing of the body has been taught, experienced, observed, and faithfully reported among Christian believers, at intervals longer or shorter, right from post-Apostolic times until now. However cleverly some of the testimony may be devaluated (supposedly), more than enough remains which is unimpeachable.

The theory held by Warfield and others, that heaven-wrought healings along with other divine miracles were abruptly, completely, and finally terminated as the Apostolic generation folded up, simply must be rejected for the following reasons: (1) it has not even a wisp of Scripture to foretoken it; (2) while it endeavors to discount this or that witness, it leaves far more of the evidence altogether unmentioned and is therefore unfair to the full data; (3) all the way through, it fails to distinguish between miracles of *healing* and miracles of other kind and purpose.

I think it is correct to say that miracles fall into four main categories: (1) the *demonstrative*, exhibiting the presence and power of God; (2) the *evidential*, giving attestation to a message or doctrine; (3) the *symbolical*, illuminating some spiritual truth; (4) the *compassionate*, conveying succour or healing to the suffering. Now even if I were to allow that miracles of the first three categories ceased with the passing of the Apostles (which I am disinclined to do), I could *not* concede that miracles of divine *compassion* ceased along with them; for not only is the factual evidence against such cessation, but, in the very nature of the case, both *likelihood* and Christian *reasoning* run counter to it.

Even if we allow for the moment that demonstrative, evidential, and symbolical miracles have ceased, as being (argumentatively) no longer necessary, is there no longer any need for *healing* miracles? Does not Scripture itself afford strong presupposition that such miracles of healing *would* continue? Think again over the many miracles in Scripture which were *not* primarily demonstrative, evidential, or illustrative but were at least partly or often *solely* miracles of compassionate *healing*, whether in the Old Testament or in our Lord's ministry or in the Acts of the Apostles. With all those miracles of sympathetic grace in view, do we not see the obvious suggestion, nay, the strong *likelihood* that such healings would continue, if not indeed increase, in this present age, which is distinctively the dispensation of *grace?*

Both factually and logically, so it seems to me, the cessation theory breaks down. Surely if divine miracles simply do *not* happen today and have not happened since New Testament times, it leaves many answers to prayer sheerly inexplicable. Years ago, for instance, when

my dear wife and I were visiting mission fields in Africa, India, and
other places, I was making a movie film for later use in advocating
the missionary cause after our return home to Scotland. Along with
two Christian missionaries we trekked from an Indian border town
into Nepal. The terrain around there was of a sandy, silty, almost
powdery sort underfoot, so much so that attempted roads or paths
soon became indistinguishable as the wind continually covered them
over with that dry, gritty earth. It was *there* that I unknowingly
dropped a disconnectable lens belonging to my camera—a tiny
gadget no larger than a twenty-five-cent piece but absolutely necessary to my photography! Forgive me, but my naughty question was
"Why, why did the Lord *allow* me to lose that gadget—and to lose it
there, of all places?"

When we thought of retracing our steps (for between one and two
miles), we just could not find any footprints in that silvery powder;
nor was there any house or curb or other object nearby to guide us
back along the way we had come. My next woebegone question was
"Could even the Lord find that little lens for me in those monotonous
acres of fine silt?" Well, anyway, we prayed that God would guide us
to it, though I had a sly suspicion that our two missionary compan-
ions were hiding a kind of humorous unbelief in their hearts! Which
way should we tramp back? How I prayed! "This is the way, walk ye
in it" came to my mind from Isaiah 30:21, and somehow I knew
which direction to go. So the four of us slowly walked back that way,
a little apart from one another so as to inspect more area. Suddenly
the remainder of Isaiah 30:21 came into play—"When ye turn to the
right hand, and when ye turn to the left." Quite distinctly I
"heard"—not auricularly but inwardly—"Turn left several paces."
I did so; and there, almost covered in the soft, dry dust, was the lens!

How do we explain such occurrences? Was it luck or chance or
some sudden attack of extrasensory perception on a phlegmatic,
middle-aged Britisher? We Christians do not believe in luck or
chance; nor am I the extrasensory type. It was an answer to prayer
and of such a kind as to be a miracle, for it cannot be explained on
any lesser supposition. But if divine miracles absolutely *never* happen
in this dispensation, as the Warfield theory says, then either it was
some evil spirit which guided me back to that lost lens (nonetheless a
miracle) or else the lens was never lost and found at all! Deep in my
own heart, however, I knew it was a *divine* miracle; and I realized this
all the more when my film began to be shown in different cities: for
not only did it raise money for the overseas missionary cause, but we

seldom if ever showed it without there being one or more of the younger men and women offering themselves for service in the overseas mission fields.

One night an intoxicated sot blundered through the door of the Water Street Mission in New York City. Bloated, bedraggled, be-fuddled, ragged, and filthy, he was dithering out of another terrifying bout of delirium tremens. Shoved inside the mission by an invisible hand of pity, he slumped down on one of the rear seats. There he sat for some time with sagging head and bleary eyes in a state of mental stupefaction. Gradually, however, under the genial warmth of the mission he began to be dozy and dreamy. After awhile his brain somehow cleared sufficiently for him to grasp where he was and what the preacher was saying to the little crowd of broken men like himself. For the first time he learned and grasped that almighty God, out of love for such human wrecks, had come into this world in the person of His beloved Son, the Lord Jesus; had endured crucifixion to purchase redemption for even the worst of sinners; had risen from the grave; and had come knocking for admission into human hearts. That night the forlorn Sam Hadley (for he it was) let the risen Savior into his life. It was an earthquake conversion. Not only was Sam Hadley born again, but he was instantaneously changed to the depth of his being, both mentally and physically. According to his own testimony, in that electrifying, transforming moment the very desire for whiskey, which since his first "glass" in youth had been like a legion of fiends in his mind and body, was *utterly* plucked out of his system, once for all, so that ever afterward he detested the very odor of that for which previously there had been an intolerable craving.

Now of course the new birth is a miracle—a miracle greater than any other healing—but the new birth in itself is exclusively a *spiritual* miracle. The accompanying deliverance which suddenly and forever eradicated that enslaving whiskey-lust from Sam Hadley's very constitution was a *physical* miracle. It was not a necessary part of his new birth, for many other drunkards have been saved and truly born again; yet the drink-thirst has remained, and they have had to battle with it in the imparted strength of the Lord. I have known wild and despairing drug addicts to experience a deliverance similar to that of Sam Hadley's. An invisible heavenly hand has somehow effected an instantaneous, inward surgery or drastic therapy which has changed them *bodily*.

Again I ask, What are we to say about the many such cases? I think we have to say, "Thank God, the theory which says that miracles cannot happen today is *wrong."* Quite apart from direct divine healings of functional and organic maladies, such psycho-physiological deliverances as those just mentioned are miracles in the truest sense of the word. Such is my admiration for Warfield that I find no pleasure in thus colliding with him. Even less do I relish dismantling a theory so brilliantly championed by him. Therefore I have not replied here to merely incidental aspects of it. This, too, will be realized: that if the theory is wrong which allows no divine miracle since the Apostles, so also are those other two theories which tell us, respectively, (1) that such miracles ceased when Christianity had become firmly established in the world, and (2) that they gradually but finally disappeared as the organized church became corrupt.

I submit that although the evidence is neither as full nor as detailed as we might have given, enough has been furnished to settle it, for anyone not wedded to a divergent theory, that from the first days of the Christian Church right on through the centuries until today, there have been divine miracles of direct bodily healing. That brings us to the second area of these studies, namely, Is divine healing as taught today Scriptural?

NOTES

[1]A. Bost, *History of the United Brethren.*

[2]*British Encyclopedia,* 1933 ed., s.v. "Covenanters."

[3]John Howie, *The Scots Worthies.*

[4]A. J. Gordon, *The Ministry of Healing.*

[5]Williston Walker, *History of the Christian Church.*

[6]*The Sacred Shrine,* 1912: quoted in B. B. Warfield, *Counterfeit Miracles,* (1918; reprint ed., Edinburgh: Banner of Truth Trust, 1976), p. 101.

[7]Warfield, *Miracles,* p. 107; see also Rouby, *La Verite sur Lourdes,* 1910.

[8]Warfield, *Miracles,* p 103; see also p. 278, n. 107, where Warfield cites A. D. White, *A History of the Warfare of Science with Theology,* 1896, 2:21-22.

[9]Leon Marillier, *Proceedings of the Society of Psychical Research* 7:100-110: quoted in Warfield, *Miracles,* p 103.

[10]Warfield, *Miracles,* p. 104.

[11]The egregious late-date invention, that Mary did not die but ascended bodily to heaven—or more precisely, that she was "assumed," both body and soul, into heaven—is utterly without scriptural warrant and destitute of any foundation in history. This so-called Assumption of Mary is pure fabrication, as should be evident from the fact that even the Roman Catholic Church did not accept it until it was recently proclaimed (in 1950) by Pope Pius XII. It was *denied* by an earlier pope (Benedict XIV in 1740). It is nothing *but* an assumption! Furthermore, it is physiological contradiction: *no* flesh-and-blood body could dwell in that purely *spirit* realm which is "heaven." Our Lord Jesus is at present the only Being in the

universe with a corporeal human body which disease cannot touch and death cannot destroy; and even *His* resurrection body is not one of flesh and blood (Luke 24:39).

[12]*La Cathedrale,* cited in Warfield, *Miracles,* p. 278, n. 109.

[13]*Proceedings of the Society of Psychical Research* 9:177.

[14]Warfield, *Miracles,* p. 106.

[15]Rene Noorbergen, *The Soul Hustlers* (Grand Rapids: Zondervan Publishing House, 1976), pp. 146-47.

[16]J. A. Froude, *Life and Letters of Erasmus,* 1894, pp. 301,359-60,121.

[17]R. A. Torrey, *Divine Healing* (Grand Rapids: Baker Book House, reprint 1974), pp. 27-32.

[18]Ibid., pp. 47-48.

PART TWO

Divine Healing
As Taught Today

Is the Teaching Scriptural?

When our Lord came down to earth He drew heaven with him. The signs which accompanied His ministry were but the trailing clouds of glory which He brought from heaven, which is His home. The number of miracles which He wrought may easily be underrated. It has been said that in effect He banished disease and death from Palestine for the three years of His ministry. If this is exaggeration it is pardonable exaggeration. Wherever He went, He brought a blessing.

> One hem but of the garment that He wore
> Could medicine whole countries of their pain;
> One touch of that pale hand could life restore.[1]

—B. B. Warfield

CHAPTER FIVE

What Say the Gospels and Acts?

Having reflected in some degree on the testimony of past centuries to miraculous divine healings in and through the Christian Church, we now inquire into divine healing as it is being taught today. It certainly *is* being taught again today with new vigor, but is the teaching truly Scriptural? That is the critical question.

In such an inquiry there is need for strict impartiality, which I shall endeavor to exercise. Perhaps I shall exercise it so carefully that it may seem to impede our journey to an eventually clear conclusion. I will not apologize on that score inasmuch as, for all evangelical Christians, the Bible is the final court of appeal; therefore our bounden duty is to investigate without prejudice what Scripture really teaches on this subject. So far as I have ascertained, those who maintain that we should still preach and experience direct divine healing of the body claim their warrant mainly on the following grounds:

1. Our Lord Jesus healed the sick when He was on earth. Should we not expect Him to do so still, seeing that He is "the same yesterday and to-day and for ever" (Heb. 13:8)?
2. The Apostles similarly performed numerous miracle healings after Pentecost. Are we not still in the same Pentecostal dispensation as the Apostles?
3. Healing for the body is included in the Atonement. Matthew

8:16-17 says, "He . . . healed all that were sick, that it might be fulfilled which was spoken by Isaiah, the prophet, saying, Himself took our infirmities, and bore our sicknesses."

4. The Scriptures prophesy that in "the last days" God will "pour out" the Holy Spirit as never before, with healing miracles and other supernatural manifestations. Are we not now living in those predicted last days?

5. All sickness is of Satan and is due to sin. It is therefore wrong and displeases God. His will is always to heal in the case of Christian believers; so healing should be claimed by faith.

6. The New Testament didactically ensures such healings by the Holy Spirit among Christian believers, particularly in 1 Corinthians 12 – 14 and James 5:14-16.

There may be other slants and aspects, but I think that the six which we have listed are the main bases. We shall briefly consider each of them in turn.

OUR LORD'S HEALINGS

The argument is that inasmuch as our Lord Jesus is the same today—both in His sympathy and in His power to heal—as when He was visibly on earth, should we not take it for granted that His *disposition* to heal sick ones remains the same now as then?

In such a plea there is that which at once has a tender appeal to all Christian hearts. We all like to think of Jesus in that way, especially when we recall words like those of Matthew 14:14: "Jesus . . . was moved with compassion . . . and he healed their sick" or Luke 4:40: "All they that had any sick with divers diseases brought them unto him; and he laid his hands on *every one of them*, and healed them." He sighed with them, wept with them, felt for them, and never said no to a single one of them. Is He not the same Jesus today, unchanged after His crucifixion and resurrection and ascension? Does He not *feel* the same today toward all the suffering ones who come to Him, even though we cannot now see Him?

There would seem to be some *statistical* support for such argument in the large proportion of space which Matthew, Mark, Luke, and John give to our Lord's healing miracles. Here are some approximate percentages. In Matthew there are 28 chapters and 1071 verses. Of those, 91 verses are given to our Lord's healing miracles and 66 to His other miracles such as quelling the storm on Galilee and feeding the five thousand. That means about one-eleventh part is used in reporting His healings and as much as a seventh to his miracles as a whole.

In Mark there are 16 chapters and 678 verses. Healings take 131 verses and other miracles 74, which means nearly one-fifth of Mark's space is given to the healings and almost one-third when the other miracles are included.

In Luke there are 24 chapters and 1151 verses. The healing runs away with 132 verses and the other supernatural works 124, which means no less than one-eighth of the narrative is given to healings and as much as a quarter of Luke's story is given to the miracles as a whole.

In John there are 21 chapters and 879 verses. The healings occupy 114 verses and the other miracles 64, making about one-eighth of John's Gospel assigned to healings and almost one-fifth to the "sign miracles" in total.

We may well be reminded, also, that besides all the separately recorded healings of *individuals*, there are in Matthew no less than eight places where *plural* healings are reported, indicating that in the aggregate hundreds (or even thousands eventually) were healed (4:23-25; 8:16-17; 9:35; 10:1,8; 11:5; 14:34-36; 15:29-31; 21:14). In Mark there are four such plural healings reported, in Luke five, and John concludes with a final, comprehensive retrospect: "And *many other* signs truly did Jesus in the presence of his disciples, which are not written in this book" (John 20:30).

Naturally, to us who love and adore Him, this compassionate ministry of our Lord as the sympathetic, all-powerful miraculous healer is everlastingly precious. Yet does it, in itself, give us any solid warrant to expect such supernatural healings to continue today? I think not, for the following reasons.

First, those miracles belonged peculiarly and *only* to the days when they were performed. They were not meant to indicate an activity which was to continue if our Lord's offer of Himself as Israel's Messiah-King was rejected. Although they truly did express the sympathy of His meek and lowly heart, their principal purpose, their *stated* purpose, was to furnish supernatural *credentials* that our Lord Jesus was genuinely the Messiah. They were sign-proofs intended for *then*, but they were not guarantees of healing for *now*.

That those healing wonders were intended as *Messianic* identification marks is clear from our Lord's reply when John the Baptist sent messengers asking, "Art thou he that should come, or do we look for another?" The reply was, "Go and show John again those things which ye do hear and see: the blind receive their sight, and the lame walk, the lepers are cleansed, and the deaf hear, the dead are raised up" (Matt. 11:2-5). Also, right at the end of the four Gospels John says that those miracles which *he* selected out of the many were "that ye might believe that Jesus is the *Messiah,* the Son of God" (see John 20:31).

Are there statements or indications anywhere that those healing miracles would continue? Well, in Matthew 10:1 we read, "And when he had called unto him his twelve disciples, he gave *them* power against unclean spirits, to cast them out, and to heal all manner of sickness and all manner of disease." Verse 8 adds that Jesus then commissioned them: "Heal the sick, cleanse the lepers, raise the dead, cast out demons." Yet that could *not* have indicated an intended continuance of such miracles *beyond* our Lord's offering Himself as Messiah nor a continuance of them in our present time because our Lord imposed the following restrictions: "Go *not* into the way of the Gentiles, and into any city of the Samaritans enter ye *not*" (v. 5). "And whosoever shall not receive you, nor hear your words, when ye depart out of that house or city, shake off the dust of your feet" (v. 14). Can you imagine any missionary of the Gospel going out on *that* basis today? That certainly was not the present dispensation of "grace"!

Present-day preachers of divine healing for the body often quote that commission of our Lord to the Apostles as belonging to us today: but understandably they hesitate to quote it in full, for our Lord not only said "Heal the sick" and "cleanse the lepers" but *"raise the dead"* as well! Quite apart from exegetical and dispensational considerations, such raisings of the dead are de facto non-occurrent today. If real raisings from the dead were actually happening, they would be headline news around the world. Nothing could suppress the publicizing of them. Claims have recently been made, as I readily acknowledge, by eager enthusiasts here and there that some dead person has been brought back to life; but certified evidence there has *not* been. There has been *seeming* death for some moments or for some short spell during which the pulse was apparently without a quiver and breathing was undetectable; but in no case has there been indubitable (even though tentative "clinical") certification of demise plus a long enough gap between the assumed death and the alleged "raising."

I am not doubting the possibility of such resuscitations, nor am I rejecting evidence of rare instances during the Christian centuries; but I *am* denying their present-day actuality until *irrefutable* proofs are forthcoming. Also, let me append: I cannot see anywhere in the Scriptural provisions for the Church any promised "gift" or power for the raising of dead ones in this present age.

Incidentally, in his tract *Divine Healing and Divine Healers*, the late M. R. De Haan has a pointed annotation on that commission of our Lord to the twelve Apostles in Matthew 10. First he refers to verses 9 and 10: "Provide neither gold, nor silver, nor brass in your purses, nor scrip for your journey, neither two coats, neither shoes, nor yet staves: for the workman is worthy of his meat." Then he comments:

> They were not to accept money for their services; they were not to take any provision, but to live on the kindness and charity and generosity of the people to whom they ministered. . . . No lolling around in luxury for those Apostles; no expensive hotel suites; but theirs was to be a life of rigor and self-denial; a life of poverty as became the followers of him who "had no place where to lay his head," who was born in a stable, depended on the charity of his friends, rode on a borrowed colt, and died on a sinner's cross. If, then, this commission in verse 8, "Heal the sick," is to be taken for us today, it also should involve all of these other instructions which the Lord gave in this connection. This verse (8) is constantly quoted as a reason for the same miracles today, but surely consistency alone demands that the rest of the passage be made to apply as well.[2]

In line with that, consider a recent healing mission concerning which Rowland V. Bingham says,

> Of the 7000 cases prayed for and anointed in Toronto, as far as we could ascertain by enquiry, there was not a single outstanding case of healing, although he [the missioner] received *thousands of dollars* for the two or three days' ministry here; and in less than a week's ministry in Washington, with results similarly disappointing, he took in just about *ten thousand dollars* in offerings from the multitudes of sick people for whom he did not procure healing![3]

Yet that dollar-hungry "healer" based himself on our Lord's commission to the moneyless Apostles in Matthew 10! Perhaps a further reminder may be pertinent, that in Matthew 10 the Apostles were sent out to proclaim exclusively to Jewry that "the *kingdom of heaven* is at hand" (v. 7). Let there be no misunderstanding: that message of the "kingdom" was *not* the Gospel of the grace of God which we are *now* to preach; for our Lord had not then gone to the Cross to make atonement for "the sin of the world" nor risen from the dead and come back to us at Pentecost as the indwelling Savior.

To take that pre-Calvary Apostolic commission and pin it as an instruction label on the Christian *Church* which was not then in historical existence is a dispensational anachronism. Please do not misapprehend that remark; I am no hyper-dispensationalist. If you will forgive the grammatical atrocity, I am an *anti-hyper*. Nonetheless, I submit that all of us, if we have open minds, *must* be "dispensational" to some degree. The old covenant through Moses was *not* the new covenant through our Lord Jesus. The dispensation of "law" is *not* the dispensation of "grace." The "kingdom," offered to Israel only, is *not* the Gospel of individual salvation now offered to the whole world. That kingdom, since Israel's rejection of Jesus as Messiah-King, is no longer being offered to Israel today; but the Gospel of God's grace to Jew and Gentile alike *is* being offered. Therefore, to claim warrant for bodily healings today on the ground that our Lord commissioned the twelve Apostles to heal the sick exclusively in Jewry two thousand years ago is gratuitous presumption, or so it seems to me. I know one or two preachers today who claim their authority on the basis of that long ago commission to the Twelve—and sincere servants of our Lord they certainly are—but I consider it rather reasonable to whisper in their ears, "Dear brother, if your name is not among that list of Twelve, the commission was never given to *you*."

Mark 16:17-18

But what about Mark 16:17-18? There our Lord says, "And these signs shall follow them that believe; In my name shall they cast out demons; they shall speak with new tongues; they shall take up serpents; and if they drink any deadly thing, it shall not hurt them; they shall *lay hands on the sick, and they shall recover*."

First, I accept that disputed passage (vv. 9-20) as authentic, including the two verses just quoted. Moreover, as I well realize, our Lord spoke the words after His resurrection, which means that they *do* look beyond His own days of visibility on earth. But do they look beyond the days of the Apostles and right down to our own times? To me that seems doubtful; for in foretelling that there would be those miracles wrought in His name, our Lord said they would be "signs." I am not just hair-splitting but am carefully differentiating when I say that there is a real difference between "signs" and the Holy Spirit's *"gifts."* Signs, intendedly, are more or less temporary whereas gifts are permanent (more on this later). In the Acts of the Apostles the "miracles" (including bodily healings) are called signs, if we translate the Greek word exactly. Therefore we have no clear permit to say that healings which were intended only as temporary signs (primarily to Israel) for a transitional period guarantee a continuance of such healings today.

Most of us have been brought up to believe that the Christian Church was inaugurated on that historic day of Pentecost which is graphically recorded in Acts 2. Yet that is an assumption without Scriptural support. When Peter heard his puzzled compatriots asking on that extraordinary day, "What meaneth this?" did he reply, "Ye men of Israel, this is a wonderful new movement of God in history; a new movement called the Church of Christ"? No. He said, "This is that which was spoken by the prophet Joel" (Acts 2:16). Turn back then then to the Joel passage partly quoted by Peter (Joel 2:28-32 and context). Has it anything to do with the Christian Church? Nothing whatever! It refers specifically to the covenant *nation,* to the regathering of scattered Israel, and to the Lord's "great and terrible day" of judgment on the Gentile nations. It predepicts a group of climactic events which are even yet future and will not break into occurrence until the end of this present age. If there is anything the Joel passage has *not* to do with, it is the Christian Church and this present, intervening age of grace.

What then? Why this: whatever else the Acts of the Apostles may or may not be, it is before all else the *second* offer of "the kingdom of heaven" and of Jesus as Messiah-Savior to the nation *Israel*—the speaking in tongues, bodily healings, and other miracles being God-given signs to certify the bona fide reality of the new offer.[4] As the transition period covered by the Acts elapsed and Israel's further, official rejection of Jesus became deep-fixed, the Holy Spirit began to reveal that the many scattered groups of "believers" who *did* accept Jesus were, by anticipative divine overruling, the first units of the Christian Church, the mystic body of God's dear Son. In that sense, of course, Pentecost was by divine overruling the *origin* of the Christian Church, but not its *inauguration* (which is no mere toying with words but a distinction vital to a true grasp of the Acts). Let this be clearly realized: the *primary* meaning of Pentecost was the new offer of the kingdom to Israel which it signaled. Therefore it did *not* set the norm for the *Church* throughout the present dispensation as is generally assumed.

I will not further press this here. For the moment the one point which I make is that in Mark 16 our Lord's foretelling those Pentecostal signs cannot be conclusively construed into meaning that such signs were to continue throughout the Church age; for as the very word *signs* indicates, they were not permanent gifts to the Church (which at that time was not even in historical existence). I will not insist inexorably that those signs simply *cannot* have been meant to continue through the Church age, but I do say that apart from corroboration elsewhere our warrant to assume so is slender.

However, there may be those who still think I am not being fair to the full force of our Savior's words here. They will tell me I am forgetting to couple them with the great commission to which our Lord coupled them:

> Go ye into all the world, and preach the *gospel* to every creature. He that believeth and is baptized shall be *saved*. . . . And these *signs* shall follow them that believe; In my name shall they cast out demons. . . . (etc.) (Mark 16:15-18).

I remember reading a challenge put out years ago by a well-known preacher of divine healing. He rightly claimed that there is not a verse in Scripture which says that those miraculous signs have ever been withdrawn and that therefore as long as the true Gospel is preached, those signs will accompany it to the end of time. Well, I think he has something there; yet it is reasonable also to reflect that although there is no Scripture which says that those signs would ever be withdrawn, neither is there any Scripture which actually says that they would *continue* "to the end of time."

Frankly, I would like to extract from Mark 16:17-18 as much as possible in favor of our preaching a present-day continuance of those promised signs, but there is need for precision as well as eagerness as we examine our Savior's promise. I am not just being pedantic when I point out the distinction between what our Lord *commanded* and what He *predicted*.

This is what He commanded: "Go ye into all the world and *preach the Gospel* to every creature."

This is what He predicted: "And these signs shall follow them that believe."

So the signs are not a part of the message but a prospective *accompaniment* of it. In other words, we are not commissioned to *preach* the supernatural healings and other signs. The message to be preached is "the gospel," which alone saves the *soul*. That is the one thing *we* are to do. The signs are what the *Lord* does.

Next observe that this is not a promise that *all* who "believe" will be healed. Therefore, even if those promised signs *do* reach down to today, we are not warranted even to *expect* that all will be healed.

Next, note that the promised signs are not to appear through *preachers* only but through the rank and file; for our Lord's words are: "These signs shall follow *those who believe*." So apparently they occur through "believers" in general, whomsoever among them our Lord may choose. (That indeed is what happened often in the early days of Christianity.)

Next, as to the *continuation* of those miracle signs, our Lord leaves that indefinite; but as already remarked, the very word *signs* suggests their being temporary rather than perpetual. Albeit, for the sake of being carefully exact in exegesis, I concede that our Lord's prediction does not necessarily *limit* those temporary signs to the Apostolic period. I do not know of any Scripture which so confines them. So I shall accept it that our Lord's words *may* reach on beyond then. He could well have meant that such signs would break out temporarily again and again as credentials of the Gospel to meet successive emergencies or challenges. Nevertheless, when we have said the most in that direction, it still remains that our Lord's words do *not* give us any authority to preach supernatural healings as a part of the Gospel message to men.

John 14:12

Then, of course, there is John 14:12: "Verily, verily I say unto you, He that believeth on me, the works that I do shall he do also; and greater works than these shall he do; because I go unto my Father."

As all will agree, this promise clearly does look beyond our Lord's days on earth. In so doing it neither sets any time limit nor is it restricted to the Apostles. It is a wide-open statement that they who "believe" on Jesus should do those same "works" and even "greater" after our Lord had returned to the Father.

We know that the Apostles and others in the period covered by the Acts *did* do healing miracles like those of Jesus; but what were those even "greater works" which were to be done? Our Lord could not have meant greater works in the *physical* realm; for although the Apostles and others performed healing miracles on a wide scale, they never did anything to equal such marvels as the feeding of the five thousand by a couple of sardines and five barley cookies or the quelling of the clamorous elements on storm-tossed Galilee or the miraculous haul of fishes or the causing of a fish to carry a coin in its mouth and then swim to Peter's waiting hook; for such miracles as those indicate an omniscience and an omnipotent command far surpassing the healing of human bodies.

The greater works which our Lord predicted must have been the *spiritual* triumphs of the Apostles and their coadjutors which, through the power of the Holy Spirit, brought millions into eternal salvation and even in the Apostles' lifetime were said to have "turned the world upside down" (Acts 17:6).

So, then, our Lord's promise, "the works that I do shall he do also," was amply fulfilled in the Apostles' days; but does it cover all the centuries *after* then, right down to the present? As we have noted, it is not limited to any specified period. So may we not say, at least tentatively, that it *could* apply still today? Hardly, for its indefiniteness as to time is the very feature which makes it inconclusive, especially when we remember what transpired after our Lord returned to the Father, i.e., His being further rejected by Jewry, then the withdrawing of the further "kingdom" offer to Israel, and the corresponding discontinuance of miracles as "signs" to that nation. Therefore, did not our Savior's forecast, "the works that I do shall he do also," have special reference to those miracle-filled Apostolic days? It did. Are we right, then, in stretching the promise to two thousand years *after* the Apostles and treating it as a promise to the *Church.* I scarcely think so.

Observe carefully the *wording:* "He that believeth on me, the works that I do [not just the healings but the other miracles too] shall he do also." By "works" our Lord meant *all* His miracles (as in John 5:36 et al., where the same Greek word occurs). Therefore, if we take His words, "the works that I do shall he do also," and insist on applying them *today*, we ought to be turning water into wine, walking on the sea, causing fish swarms, feeding multitudes with miraculously multiplying victuals, and fishing up coins to pay dues. We are inconsistent if we claim only the *healing* miracles while admitting that the others obviously do *not* apply today.

Therefore, with nothing but cordiality toward those who differ, I maintain that Matthew 10:1-15 and Mark 16:16-18 and John 14:12 do *not* make our Lord's healing miracles necessarily applicable today. This leaves us back where we began, namely, that our Lord's healing miracles away back *then* do not give us any clear certification that He purposes to continue such healings *now*. To argue that they *do* seems risky to me. I gratefully agree that our dear Lord is "the same yesterday, and to-day," but the unchangingness of His *nature* does not necessarily imply no change in His *modus operandi*. Nay, Scripture makes clear that God has had different ways of working in different dispensations. The one safe conclusion is that apart from clear statement in Scripture, we have *no valid warrant* to insist that because our Lord performed those many healings long ago we may preach them as part of the gospel message for today.

BODILY HEALINGS IN THE ACTS

A second argument why supernatural healings should be happening today is that such healings were numerous after that miracle-crowned Pentecost of two thousand years ago, which ushered in our Christian era. Are we not still in the same dispensation as the Apostles? Was not Pentecost, with its supernatural healings, the intended standard for the Church? Should we not, therefore, expect such healings to happen *now* just as they did then?

That reasoning, so it seems to me, is far more plausible than justifiable. We certainly find such healings prominent in the Acts, and it is useful to see them in proportion. Out of 1007 verses in the Acts, 63 are devoted to miraculous bodily healings and 118 to other miracles, which means about one-sixteenth apply only to healings and about one-fifth to miracles as a whole. However, some of the references indicate healings in great numbers (5:15-16; 8:6-7; 19:11-12); so in the aggregate, healings loom large. They are an outstanding phenomenon of that Pentecostal epoch. Yet there are powerful reasons why their prevalence then does *not* argue their continuance today.

Despite the oft-repeated assertion that we are still in the same dispensation as the Apostles, are we in it in the same *way?* Surely not! As already noted, the period covered by the Acts was a *suspense* interval during which everything hung (viewed from the human aspect) on whether Israel would say yes or no to Jesus, who was now being offered as Messiah-King to the nation for the *second* time, in the wake of His resurrection. Because of Israel's further and deeper refusal, that second offer of the kingdom was eventually withdrawn and the suspense period thereby became the *transition* period from the "kingdom" message of the Gospels to the "church" doctrine of the Epistles. It was for this reason, principally, that period was an *abnormal* interval; and its abnormalities, so it seems to me, were of such a nature that they could not possibly have been intended for continuance in the ministry of the *Church*, which was as yet a "mystery" to be revealed later.

Glance at some of those abnormalities. In chapter 5 we see Ananias and Sapphira struck dead on the spot for what in these days would be considered a comparatively mild duplicity. Who struck them dead? *God!* Was that the age of "grace"? Since then many have done far worse things in the Church than did Ananias and Sapphira. If God were dealing in that way today, there would be thousands of corpses in our churches around the world next Sunday!

In chapter 12 King Herod, who imprisoned Peter, is suddenly smitten by an angel, "immediately" eaten of worms, and then dies. In chapter 13 Elymas is instantaneously struck blind for resisting missionary Paul's message. Ask our overseas missionaries whether such drastic divine intervenings are recurrent among them today.

In chapter 5 the Apostles are arrested and put in the "common prison," but amid the darkness of the night an "angel of the Lord" opens the prison doors and leads them out.

In chapter 12 Peter is put in jail and guarded by four squads of four soldiers each; but some nights later, while he is sleeping in chains between two soldiers, an angel awakens him, snaps his chains, lights up the prison with a light which only Peter sees, guides him past the first and second guard posts to the great iron gate, which opens of its own accord to let Peter out! Do miracles of that order punctuate our Lord's method today?

In Acts 5:15-16 we are told that even Peter's shadow communicated healings wherever it fell, from which, apparently, a "multitude" were healed—"every one." Similarly, in chapter 19:11-12 "handkerchiefs," after contact with Paul's body, carried all kinds of healings and expelled demons far and wide. In recent days many have experimented with the handkerchief procedure, and I have tried to believe that possibly our Lord might even today honor the sincerity and faith exercised thereby; but inquiries have shown me that instead of healings there have been dashed hopes, nor are there "shadow" healings nowadays.

Acts 8:39 tells us that when Philip and the Ethiopian came up out of the wayside baptismal pool, "the Spirit of the Lord caught away Philip" so that Philip instantaneously disappeared from there and was immediately found miles away at Azotus. Does *that* peculiar kind of miracle happen today? Or again, in chapter 9, as Saul is making for Damascus, the risen Lord personally intercepts him (not a mere vision, but an actual appearing), strikes him down by a blinding light, and calls to him by an overpowering voice. Later, "scales" visibly fall from Saul's eyes as his sight is miraculously restored. There are "striking conversions" today, thank God, but never with such abnormal accompaniments as are recounted in Acts 9.

Nor is there anything today like the frequent intervention of angels as in those Apostolic days. They were not just *visions* of angels but actual *appearances* (5:19; 8:26; 10:30 with 11:13; 12:7-11,23; 27:23). Such visible interventions by angels were characteristic then, but they *never* occur today.

Nor, despite what some eager brethren report, are there clear and definite world-girdling predictions being made in Christian assemblies today such as those of Agabus (11:28-29; 21:10-12).

Nor in these days is it God's way to shake the premises where Christians meet for prayer (4:31) or to rock city jails with specially timed earthquakes which unfetter prisoners and fling open jail doors (16:26).

But that is by no means all. There are abnormalities of another category clinging around that Apostolic era, abnormalities which must be an insoluble puzzle to those who regard Pentecost as the inauguration of the *Church*. In Acts 6:7 we read, "And the word of God increased; and the number of the disciples multiplied in Jerusalem greatly; and *a great company of the priests were obedient to the faith*" (emphasis mine). Then why did those priests still go on offering animal sacrifices in the Jewish temple? Was not the old order of the priests and the sacrifices done away forever by the one perfect sacrifice and priesthood of our Lord Jesus? Yet those priests who were now obedient to the Jesus message and the Christian faith saw no inconsistency in their still continuing to offer up the usual temple sacrifices and to go on performing their usual priestly functions!

Even more jolting is Acts 15:5. "But there rose up [in the assembly of Christian believers] certain of the sect of the *Pharisees* which believed, saying, That it was needful . . . to keep the law of Moses" (italics mine). How on earth could a Jewish Pharisee be a true "believer" on the Lord Jesus as Savior and yet remain a Pharisee with his chains of legalism and self-righteousness clanking around him? Yet that is what happened in those early post-Pentecost years!

Again, in Acts 21:17-20 we find the leaders of the Christian assembly in Jerusalem saying to Paul, "Thou seest, brother, how many thousands of Jews there are which believe; and they are all *zealous of the law*" (italics mine). But how could they still be "zealous of the law" of Moses in that Jewish sense if they were really "believers" on the Lord Jesus for salvation "by grace" and "through faith" and "apart from the law" (Rom. 3:21) and "not of works" (Eph.

2:9)? Is not the whole point of the New Testament Epistles that "grace" and "law" are sheer opposites? Is not the Gospel message most plainly this, that all who would be saved by divine grace through faith must renounce all trust in self-merit or "law" works?

What about Paul's taking Jewish vows on himself (Acts 18:18,21)? What about chapter 8 where the Samaritans "believed" and were "baptized" into the Christian faith (v. 12); yet the Holy Spirit had come on "none of them" (vv. 15-16)? Do we not preach today (and rightly so) that when a person truly "believes" on our Lord Jesus Christ, accepting Him into the heart as Savior, such a person thereby becomes "born anew" of the Holy Spirit? That is not only what we preach, it is what is *experienced* by all who thus believe and receive. What, then, about those Samaritans of the Acts period who truly "believed" yet were still *unregenerate?* I say "unregenerate" because we are plainly told that one of them (Simon) had "believed" and had been "baptized" yet was *not* regenerated (vv. 21-23).

Do we need add more? Is it not pronouncedly evident, from all these combining peculiarities which we have mentioned, that the post-Pentecost epoch was an *abnormal* interstice? It was no more intended as a "norm" for the ensuing centuries of the Christian Church (which was as yet unrevealed and humanly unknown) than the Apostles were meant to live on earth forever. Whatever else the Acts of the Apostles is or is not, it is *primarily* the second offer of the "kingdom" to Israel. Not only are the "kingdom" and the Christian "Church" *not* the same as each other, they are *contrastively* different from each other. Oh, the bungled exegesis and mixed-up preaching which have resulted from confusing them! As Israel's further rejection of Jesus became crystalized and the Apostles died, the miracle "signs" and "wonders" to Israel dropped away. The kingdom offer was withdrawn, and its eventual realization was suspended until the second advent of Jesus. The Church as God's anticipative, long-hidden secret became revealed, and the Church age came in, which meanwhile continues.

So, then, in one final word, let it be emphasized again that the miraculous bodily healings belonging to the transition period covered by the Acts do *not* set the "norm" for the Church. They may to some degree be *patterns* to us of the ways in which the Holy Spirit chooses to work, but they were *not* meant to be a guarantee that such healings would continue throughout the history of the Church. I

uch healings *are* meant to feature in the Church's ministry, we must
ind clear statement elsewhere.

INTERIM CONCLUSION

*Neither from our Lord's miracle healings nor from those of the Apostles can
ie safely deduce that such are meant to continue today, nor should we presume so.
f such healings* were *divinely intended to continue in the same way today, then
ll who come for healing today would be healed without exception, as was the
ise in the days of our Lord and the Apostles. But thousands who come for
ealing today are* not *healed. Therefore, by that simple, practical test we* know
iat healings today are not on the same basis as in those days of long ago.*

NOTES

[1]B. B. Warfield, *Counterfeit Miracles* (1918; reprint ed., Edinburgh: Banner of
ruth Trust, 1976), p. 3.
[2]M. R. DeHaan, *Divine Healing and Divine Healers* (out of print).
[3]Rowland V. Bingham, *The Bible and the Body.*
[4]For more on this, see my book *The Strategic Grasp of the Bible* (Grand Rapids:
ondervan Publishing House, 1968), particularly the three chapters on "A Re-
urvey of the Acts."

Is Healing in the Atonement?

Perhaps as we move into this further chapter, we should pause for a moment to remind ourselves of two important considerations.

(1) A sound and basic principle in the interpretation of Scripture is that passages which seem obscure or doubtful should always be interpreted in the light of those which are unmistakably clear.

(2) It is a basic fact of our salvation that we are already delivered from the curse of the *Law* (Gal. 3:13); but we are *not* yet delivered from the hereditary curse of the *Fall* (Rom. 8:22-23).

—J.S.B.

8.30-01-7H That's a very useful principle to apply & teach.

CHAPTER SIX

Is Healing in the Atonement?

From a theological standpoint, the basic proposition of most who preach divine healing today is that such healing is *included in the Atonement* and may therefore be appropriated by faith, even as we receive the forgiveness of sins by faith through the Atonement.

As A. B. Simpson in his tract *Divine Healing in the Atonement* says, "If our healing is provided for by Jesus Christ, then it is a redemption right which we may humbly and boldly claim by walking obediently with the Lord."[1]

As mentioned in our introductory remarks, this contention is based mainly on the statement in Matthew 8:16-17: "When the even was come, they brought unto him many that were possessed with demons; and he cast out the spirits with his word, and healed all that were sick; that it might be fulfilled which was spoken by Isaiah the prophet, saying, Himself *took our infirmities, and bare our sicknesses*" (emphasis mine). This passage, indeed, has been called the Magna Charta of the divine-healing heralds. Even the late A. J. Gordon in his careful work *The Ministry of Healing* grants, though with a hesitancy unlike his usual definiteness, that the passage at least "seems" to give some footing for the theory.

In the atonement of Christ there *seems* to be a foundation laid for faith in bodily healing. *Seems*, we say, for the passage . . . is so profound and unsearchable in its meaning that one would be very careful not to speak dogmatically in regard to it ... The passage *seems* to teach that Christ endured vicariously our diseases as well as our iniquities (italics mine).[2]

There are those, however, who reply an adamant no! In fact the pros and cons have been discussed again and again by able expositors. Nevertheless it seems to me that even yet there are considerations which have been overlooked.

To my surprise, R. A. Torrey, who wrote *against* the usual kind of "divine-healing" preachers and practitioners, accepted Matthew 8:16-17 as teaching that healing is included in the Atonement. These are his words:

It is often said that this verse teaches that the atoning death of Jesus Christ avails for our sicknesses as well as for our sins; or, in other words, that "physical healing is in the atonement." I think that is a fair inference from these verses when looked at in their context.[3]

Strangely enough, no sooner has Torrey conceded this than he postpones its applicability until the return of Christ and the beginning of the Millennium (which seems the more peculiar to my own mind because then, in our immortal resurrection bodies, how can we ever *need* healing?). Even more strangely, after postponing its operativeness until then, he swings right back to admitting: "We do get in many, many, many cases physical healing through the atoning death of Jesus Christ even in the life that now is."[4] So in reality Torrey is saying, though in a rather hedging way, that on the basis of Matthew 8:17 bodily healing *is* included in the Atonement.

On the opposite bench is that prince among recent missionary statesmen Rowland V. Bingham. Let me quote him on Matthew 8:17.

They say that this teaches that divine healing is in the Atonement, and that on the ground of this every obedient child of God has the right to claim deliverance from all infirmity and disease. They quote the words, "Himself took our infirmities and bore our sicknesses" as though it settled the whole matter; and, linking it with I Peter 2:24, they claim that He bore our sicknesses just the same as He bore our sins—that *we* might not bear them. This seems quite plausible until we raise three serious questions.[5]

Bingham's three questions are as follows: (1) *When and where* did Christ bear our sicknesses? (2) *How* did Christ bear our sicknesses? (3) Where did Christ teach that sickness needs atonement?

As to "when and where" the bearing of our sicknesses occurred,

Bingham reminds us that Matthew 8:16-17 makes it some three years *prior* to our Lord's atoning death and at *Capernaum*, not at Calvary. So both time and place forbid our reading into it any substitutionary or propitiatory significance such as belongs solely to our Lord's sin-bearing on the Cross.

As to "how" our Lord bore those sicknesses, Bingham observes that in translating Isaiah 53:4, Matthew deliberately drops Isaiah's word for *substitutionary* "bearing" and uses a different word "which is never associated with propitiation or atonement."[6] That different word, says Bingham, is employed in the New Testament always "to express *sympathetic* bearing, as, for example, in Galatians 6:2, 'Bear ye one another's burdens'; or as in Romans 15:1, 'We then that are strong ought to bear the infirmities of the weak.'"[7] Also, as Bingham points out, that alternative word used by Matthew is *not* the word used by Peter: "His own self bare our sins" (1 Peter 2:24). "The only conclusion which can be drawn from this," adds Bingham, "is that Matthew is guided to use the spiritual figure of Isaiah 53:4 *illustratively*," i.e., as merely *illustrating* our Lord's ministry of physical healing (emphasis mine).[8]

As to whether our Lord ever *taught* that sickness needs atonement, Bingham replies: "Nowhere does He speak of dying for our sicknesses."[9] "Sin is the only thing that demands expiation by blood. For if sickness needed atonement, then sickness implies a clouded conscience and broken fellowship with God. Such a cruel doctrine is denied by the most saintly men in the Church, many of whom in the direst sickness have had sweetest fellowship with God."[10]

So then according to Bingham, Matthew's use of Isaiah 53:4 means that our Lord's "bearing" of human sicknesses was sympathetic but not vicarious. Other like-minded writers substantially agree with this. For instance, Charles W. Mayes, in his thoughtful pamphlet *Is Healing in the Atonement?* gives the following five reasons why the healing of our bodies is "not on the same basis as the forgiveness of sins."[11]

(1) God has promised to forgive "to the uttermost" (Heb. 7:15; Eph. 1:7; etc.). Nowhere has He promised to *heal* to the uttermost. If He had, we might keep on being healed even to the permanent postponing of death. (2) "If healing were on the same basis as the forgiveness of sins, such healing would of necessity produce a perfect, incorruptible body" even here and now. (3) The forgiveness of sins is for *every kind* of sin; not so with present bodily healing; for if it were, it would "assure us new teeth, new hair, or replaced hands." "Are teeth not included in the Atonement? Whoever had a finger replaced which

had been removed by accident? Are fingers not in the Atonement?"
(4) The forgiveness of sins is always *immediate* whereas, according to
the divine-healing advocates themselves, bodily healings are often
gradual, sometimes long processes. (5) The forgiveness of sins is *never*
withheld from the sincere and believing, whereas healing for the body
is often *refused* to sincere believers who earnestly pray and "believe"
for it—instances of this being reported even in the New Testament
(2 Cor. 12:8-9; 2 Tim. 4:20).[12]

Following those five reasons, Mayes links up with Bingham as he
adds,

> The verbs "took" and "bore" in this passage (Matt. 8:16-17)
> quoted from Isaiah 53:4 do not refer to the act of substitutionary
> suffering or death which Christ accomplished on the Cross. If we were
> to hold that Christ *took* and *bore* our sicknesses on the cross of Calvary,
> we would find ourselves coming to a very absurd conclusion . . . i.e.,
> that Christ suffered disease in our stead.[13]

Mayes quotes the late Alva J. McClain: "Sickness is not sin; it is the
result of sin. We punish men for sinning, but not for getting sick. A
man may become diseased by breaking the law: he is punished for
breaking the law, but sent to the hospital for the disease."[14] The
point is that God has "made him to be *sin* for us" (2 Cor. 5:21), but
He was never made *disease* for us.

I quote now from the pamphlet *Prayer and Healing* by James H.
McConkey, always a judicious interpreter of the Word. He sides
with Torrey in the view that although divine healing for the body
does somehow come *through* the Atonement, its applicability is not so
much for today as for the new age which will begin on earth at the
return of our Lord.

> It must be remembered that the atonement of Christ covers the
> millennial age to *come* as well as this age in which we now live. It does
> not follow that because the children of God are to be delivered from all
> disease and sickness, their deliverance is for *now* instead of hereafter
> when "the inhabitants of Jerusalem. . . . shall no longer say, I am
> sick." For it is clear that there are many blessings in the Atone-
> ment. . . . the enjoyment of which has not yet arrived. Thus deliver-
> ance from death is covered by the atonement of Christ, yet it is not
> ours in *this* age, but in an age yet to come. . . . So too it is argued that
> Christ was made a curse for us, and that we are therefore made free
> from all the curse of the Law, and that under this is included sickness.
> But that we are *not* made free *now* from all the curse [brought by sin] is
> obvious in that the curse upon the *earth* is clearly not removed until
> our Lord comes (Rom. 8:19-23). Thus we see plainly that we cannot
> claim *in this age* all that is included under the atonement of Christ; and

therefore we cannot claim universal exemption from sickness on the ground that it is in the atonement of our Lord (emphases mine).[15]

From the foregoing excerpts it will be seen that there is sharp disagreement as to both the interpretation and the present applicability of Matthew 8:16-17 and also that there is definite objection to its being used as a basis for the assertion that healing is in the Atonement. Which of these positions is right?

In favor of those who claim that healing *is* in the Atonement and against Bingham's plea that our Lord's miraculous healings only *paralleled* with Isaiah 53:4 rather than strictly fulfilled it is Matthew's word: "That it might be *fulfilled* which was spoken by Isaiah the prophet, saying : Himself took our infirmities, and bare our sicknesses" (Matt 8:17, emphasis mine). The word "fulfilled" surely settles it that our Lord's healing ministry was no mere illustration of Isaiah 53:4 but somehow the historical *fulfillment* of it. It is the Holy Spirit who says so through Matthew, and the statement is too clear for any of us to dodge it.

As for the two verbs "took" and "bare" in Matthew 8:17, both Bingham and Mayes insist that the two Greek words so translated do *not* have any substitutionary or vicarious connotation in them. Bingham asks his readers to note that "Matthew deliberately drops the word for 'bore' which Isaiah used [in Isaiah 53:4] and uses another word for 'bore' which is never associated with propitiation or atonement."[16] Bingham then adds:

> Who authorized Matthew to make such a change unless he was guided by the Holy Spirit? The word used by Matthew *(ebastasen)*, although quite common in the New Testament, is never linked with atonement, but is employed to express *sympathetic* bearing, as, for example, when it occurs in Galatians 6:2, 'Bear ye one another's burdens,' or as in Romans 15:1, 'We that are strong ought to bear the infirmities of the weak' (emphases mine).[17]

It seems to me that Bingham is on dangerous ground when he says that the Holy Spirit "authorized" Matthew "deliberately" to "change" Isaiah's word for substitutionary bearing and to put instead of it a word which means only "*sympathetic*" bearing. It makes the Holy Spirit say that Isaiah 53:4 was "fulfilled" by something which in reality did *not* fulfill it.

It seems even stranger to me that Bingham then adds that the "different" word which Matthew used (aorist of *bastazo*) is employed only "to express *sympathetic bearing*"; for in both the texts which he cites to show *how* it is used for "sympathetic" bearing (Gal. 6:2;

Rom. 15:1) it is used for *substitutionary* bearing! When Galatians 6:2
exhorts us, "Bear ye one another's burdens," it patently means the
bearing of someone *else's* burden.

It is wrong for Bingham to say that Matthew used a Greek word
which did not reproduce the sense of Isaiah 53:4. Admittedly,
Matthew's word is not that which 1 Peter 2:24 uses when it says that
our Lord bore "our sins in his own body on the tree," but there is
little or no significance in that; for Peter could have used Matthew's
word without detracting in the least from the substitutionary meaning of 1 Peter 2:24. When John 19:17 says that our Lord went to
Golgotha "*bearing* his cross" (italics mine), the Greek word for
bearing is again *bastazo*, which is used in Matthew 8:17. For whom
did Jesus bear that cross?—for Himself alone? or for others? His
bearing of that cross was both sympathetic *and* substitutionary.

All this leaves us with the real meaning of Matthew 8:16-17 still
unsolved. In telling us that our Lord's healing ministry "fulfilled"
Isaiah 53:4, *does* it or does it *not* teach us that healing is in the
Atonement? Surely the true answer is that it does *not*—for the
following reasons.

First, as already noted, Matthew 8:16-17 states something which
was occurring between two and three years *prior* to our Lord's
atoning death on Calvary. Whatever it may or may not connote, it
was a "taking" and "bearing" *distinct* from His substitutionary
sin-bearing for us later on the Cross. Both time and place separate it
from Calvary.

Second, our Lord's healing ministry was something which He was
doing *continuously* whereas His death on the Cross, as Romans 5:18
emphasizes, was "*one act* of righteousness" (ERV) and, according to
Romans 6:10; Hebrews 7:27; 10:10, was solitarily "once for all"
(Greek, *ephapax*).

Third, our Lord simply could *not* have borne our infirmities and
sicknesses in the way He bore our race's sin. Sickness is indeed a
transmitted *result* of original sin, of hereditary and racial sin-
infection; but sickness itself is not sin. It has much suffering attached
to it but no guilt and, therefore, no legal *penalty*. It calls for pity and
cure but not for punishment. Nay, it is in itself an inherited penalty
and punishment which we all helplessly incur as members of fallen
Adam's blighted posterity. Therefore, since sickness is itself a penalty, our Lord certainly never died to bear the penalty of a penalty!
Hereditary sickness does not incur judicial sentence; for while in sin
there is *motive*, in sickness there is *not*. Humanity's sickness calls forth

the divine sympathy, not punitive judgment. Sickness therefore is in a different category from sin. Let us do away once for all with any such idea as that human sickness *requires* atonement. It is sin and sin alone which necessitates it. So in that basic sense healing is *not* in the Atonement.

Fourth, because our Lord Jesus made a full and final propitiation for all the sins of all men, a full and free forgiveness is given to *all* sincere penitents for *all* their sins without any delay and without any exception. If then our Lord bore all the *sicknesses* of all men in the same way on Calvary, then there ought similarly to be a full and free *healing* given to all sincere applicants for *all* their ailments without any delay and without exception. But how vastly otherwise is the actual fact! The healings of sicknesses are *not* given in the way that forgiveness of sins is given. Healings are *not* given without exception. Therefore healing for human sicknesses simply *cannot* be in the Atonement in the same way that the forgiveness of sins is.

It is still true, however, that divine healing for sickness comes to us *through* the Atonement, just as all the other blessings of salvation do. Yet, as we have already been reminded, not all the blessings which the Atonement secured for us are appropriable here and now. Immortal bodies were thereby "bought with a price" for us, but they are not to be ours until the "last trumpet" unlocks the "mystery" of our age-end translation. The "white robes" and the victory palms, the millennial kingdom, the heavenly "mansions," the jasper walls, the golden streets, the fadeless glories of the New Jerusalem—all are ours *through* the Atonement, but not yet. A sinless, tearless, disease-less ecstasy of never-waning youth is yet to be ours through what happened on Calvary; but it is for then and there, not for here and now. In keeping with this I think it is presumptuous to assert solely on the basis of Matthew 8:16-17 that healing is in the Atonement in the sense of guaranteeing healing for us *now*. It certainly is *not* in the Atonement in the sense that expiation for our *sins* is. In the absence of clear Scriptural statement elsewhere to support it, we are wrong if we assert on the basis of Matthew 8:16-17 alone that healing is in the Atonement. Our risk of painful delusion is even acuter if, on a dubious exegesis of that text, we claim that divine healing for the body is guaranteed to us here and *now*.

Still, in all fairness it should be added that perhaps there is more in Matthew 8:17 than some brethren care to allow, whether they are among those who *claim* that healing is in the Atonement or among those who *deny* it. Glance again at the two parallel clauses:

Himself took our infirmities,
and bore our sicknesses.

Those who preach from this text that healing is in the Atonement
seldom if ever expatiate (so I glean) on the first half of its dual
statement. They major on that second member, "bore our sicknesses," but they soft-pedal or quite by-pass the preceding clause:
"took our *infirmities.*" Few such preachers, if any, would have the
temerity to urge that we may claim healing for all our "infirmities"
as well as all our "sicknesses." Yet if healing for sicknesses is in the
Atonement, equally so is healing for infirmities: and for any of us to
be exploiting the one yet excluding the other is conspicuous inconsistency.

I am thinking of infirmities such as common eye complaints which
require the wearing of spectacles, dental deficiencies which need
orthodontic correction, and defective hearing such as often accom-
panies elderliness and calls for technical aid. These and other such
infirmities, in some of their forms, are even worse to endure than
sicknesses. So we may well ask, Is supernatural healing for all such
infirmities in the Atonement and available to present-day appropriation? If we say it *is,* we are at once up against the stubborn facts of
contrary evidence. If we say that healing for infirmities is *not* in the
Atonement, then how can we say that healing for sicknesses *is?* The
two clauses in Matthew 8:17 are a poetic parallel, an inseparable
pair. What is true of one is equally true of the other. If healing for all
our infirmities is *not* in the Atonement, then neither is healing for all
our sicknesses.

I recall a prominent apostle of divine healing for the body (a
minister well worthy of high esteem) who forced himself not to wear
glasses in his public healing ministry but simply *had* to use them in
private study. Beyond all question, he had earlier been healed of a
serious organic disease; and he now thought that his audiences
would consider it a strange contradiction if they saw him wearing
glasses. Yet he need not have had any such qualms, for our heavenly
Healer never does the superfluous. He who could feed the hungry
thousands with five barley cookies and two little fishes was the
watchful economist who said, "Gather up the fragments which
remain, that nothing be lost." I think we may take it generally for
granted that where medical science and art can successfully cope
with infirmities, there will not be supernatural intervention. I do not
state that as a rule which has absolutely no exception, but I do aver
that exceptions to it are so rare as to *prove* the general rule. Or I may

put it alternatively, that only where the natural infirmity is a definite hindrance to Christian witness or other special service, and where there is no hope in medical skill, will a miracle healing occur.

On the other hand, those who *decry* the idea that healing is in the Atonement are so busy arguing that the verb in "*bore* our sicknesses" does not really mean a vicarious bearing, they seem scarcely to pay attention to the preceding verb in "*took* our infirmities." Yet in truth *that* verb may be the very key which unlocks the disputed meaning of Matthew's quotation. It is the usual Greek word for the act of taking something; so in some real way our Savior "took" our infirmities to Himself. But how? Therein lies a mystery bigger than the world, bigger than all worlds, bigger than the universe, big as infinity.

Our Lord Jesus is the "mystery" of God made manifest. He is *Immanuel,* "God with us." It is difficult for our finite minds to grasp that God is simultaneously and continuously everywhere, not just in vague diffusion, but personally and intensively. There is not a square inch in all the inconceivably vast universe where God is not. As the psalmist said, "If I ascend up into heaven, thou art there: if I make my bed in Sheol, behold, thou art there. If I take the wings of the morning, and dwell in the uttermost parts of the sea; even there shall thy hand lead me, and thy right hand shall hold me" (Ps. 139:8-10). Jesus, the all-knowing Wisdom from on high, has told us that the heavenly Father is so everywhere present that not a falling sparrow escapes His notice and "the very hairs of your head are all numbered" (Matt. 10:30). It is impossible for us to visualize realistically such boundless yet microscopic omnipresence; yet it is true, and (remember) *Jesus* is that God made visible in incarnation. He is omnipotence and omniscience and omnipresence looking at us through human eyes, talking to us through human lips, and feeling for us through human emotions. The whole universe coheres in Him, centers in Him, *registers* in Him. He knows and *feels* what is going on everywhere and what is being experienced everywhere. Mystery? I should say so! Yet none the less profoundest reality! And it was *HE* who "took" our infirmities.

Are there not many of us who at times, perhaps through our own suffering and that of others, have been so weighed down by contemplating the pain which ceaslessly racks mankind everywhere that we have feared it would sink us into incurable melancholy? Yet we are just little creature minds, utterly incapable of registering in ourselves any more than an infinitesimal pang of creation's gigantic travail. How must it all have registered in *HIM,* our Lord Jesus, the infinite Son of God incarnate! It is my considered persuasion that the whole groaning agony of sick and suffering mankind entered through the door of His human sympathy into His infinite capacity to suffer. He became so one with us that He suffered not only *for* us but *with* us. When He accosted the raging persecutor Saul on the Damascus road, He did not say, "Saul, Saul, why persecutest thou my followers?" It was "Why persecutest thou *ME?*" (Acts 9:4, emphasis mine). Every lash of the whip, every blow and flogging, every slash of the sword, and every other painful penalty borne by His disciples *HE* felt! Even as it is written in Isaiah 63:9, "In all their affliction *He* was afflicted" (emphasis mine).

Every time "virtue" or strength went out from Jesus to heal the sick, the "iron entered His own soul." Just as at His Jordon baptism He was immersed, not because He had any sin of His own to occasion repentance, but in token of His identification with the sin and need of those whom He had come to redeem, so He "took" to His infinite heart all the infirmities and sicknesses and sufferings of Adam's penalized posterity. As He hung on Calvary He was not only suffering *for* us as sinners but *with* us as sufferers. He was not only bearing the penalty of our *sin* as our Savior but also the pain of our total *sicknesses* in the exquisite sympathy and race consciousness of His sinless manhood and boundless godhead; for somehow, as He hung there, the Father saw in Him not only the black guilt of the whole race's sinning and the loathsome leprosy of the race's moral disease but all the aggregate misery of racial sickness and death.

Yes, I believe that all this was involved in the depthless mystery of Golgotha, that in a profoundly real way He "took our infirmities, and bare our sicknesses." Yet even that does *not* warrant us to assert that healing is in the Atonement. It was as our sinless *Substitute* that He bore our *sin*. It was as our sympathetic *Kinsman* that He bore our sicknesses. His bearing our sins *judicially* wrought our redemption. His bearing our sicknesses *representatively* as the One in whom all human suffering concentratedly registers itself demonstrated His uttermost *identification* with us in all our present suffering as human beings. It is all fathomlessly wonderful. I hold that we should believe nothing less than *that* about His taking our "infirmities" and bearing our "sicknesses"; but I also maintain that we should not outrun what Scripture allows and believe *more* than that.

Therefore, that healing is in the Atonement should *not* be preached on the basis of Matthew 8:16-17 unless it is endorsed by Scripture statement elsewhere. But it is *not* taught elsewhere, and it certainly cannot be safely adduced solely from Matthew 8:16-17. No, healing for our mortal bodies is *not* in the Atonement. This conclusion is supported at once by the fact that forgiveness of sins and cleansing from guilt are offered through the Cross freely and certainly and at the present moment to all who sincerely "believe" whereas healing for all our infirmities and sicknesses is *not* offered freely and certainly at present to all who believe. Not one of those who have believed for forgiveness and cleansing has ever been denied, but thousands and thousands who have believed for physical healing *have* been denied. That cannot be gainsaid—for a very pertinent reason. Permitted *sin* in the present is *never* a part of God's plan or purpose for us, but permitted sickness often *is*, as we learn both from Scripture and from Christian testimony (more on this later). Both Scripture and experience, then, say no; bodily healing is *not* in the Atonement.

NOTES

[1] A. B. Simpson, *Divine Healing in the Atonement.*
[2] A. J. Gordon, *The Ministry of Healing.*
[3] R. A. Torrey, *Divine Healing* (Grand Rapids: Baker Book House, reprint 1974), p. 53.
[4] Ibid., pp. 56-57.
[5] Rowland V. Bingham, *The Bible and the Body*, pp. 54-60.
[6] Ibid.
[7] Ibid.
[8] Ibid.
[9] Ibid.
[10] Ibid.
[11] Charles W. Mayes, *Is Healing in the Atonement?*
[12] Ibid.
[13] Ibid.
[14] Ibid.
[15] James H. McConkey, *Prayer and Healing.*
[16] Bingham, *The Bible and the Body.*
[17] Ibid.

The Last Days? The Divine Will?

The tenacity with which erroneous views continue to be held is often greater than the persistence shown in holding to the truth. Some misconceptions, though often corrected, keep reappearing with surprising vitality. . . . Hence the preeminent importance of getting and holding that true meaning of any particular passage which is consistent with the teaching of Scripture as a whole. We may well distrust any interpretation of a text which is not in harmony with the general tenor of the inspired Word.

—Arthur T. Pierson

One of the commonest causes of error in interpreting Holy Scripture is our being so fascinated with a theory that when we meet texts which contradict it, instead of relinquishing the theory we start bending, straining, or manipulating somewhat the awkward texts to fit our theory. . . . Another equally common cause of misleading deviation is the building of a doctrine or theory upon one text of Scripture or another in *isolation*, neglecting to interpret it in its relatedness to the *consensus* of Biblical teaching on that subject.

—J. S. B.

CHAPTER SEVEN

The Last Days?
The Divine Will?

A further argument why we should expect miraculous divine healings today is that we are now living in the predicted "last days," concerning which the Scriptures foretell us that there will then be a widespread outpouring of the Holy Spirit accompanied by healing miracles and other supernatural manifestations in a way never before known.

How often I have heard preachers of divine healing in effect say, "These are the 'last days'; so in the light of Scripture prophecy, are we not right in expecting the Holy Spirit to be working healing miracles in copious measure today?" Only a few days ago I was reading a book in which the gifted author writes: "It is encouraging to recall that our lives are set in the era prophesied by the Old Testament prophet Joel:

> And it shall come to pass *in the last days*, saith God, I will pour out my Spirit upon all flesh . . . and your young men shall see visions and your old men shall dream dreams."

That appropriation of Joel 2:18-32 is not only representative of those who preach direct divine healing today, it is a main plank in their platform. Yet their argument stems from a curious misuse of the phrase "the last days," as may easily be shown.

I agree with many others that the long-awaited Second Coming of our Lord Jesus to this earth is now probably very near and that therefore we have now reached what may be called the last days of this present age. But when Scripture prophecy refers to "the last days," it does not mean the last days of this present age: it means the yet future Millennium which follows on *after* our Lord's return and which will indeed be the *last* of those "ages" or dispensations which compose the time-scheme of Adamic human history, ending with the final, general judgment of the race at the great white throne. *Those* days have not yet come; so the "pouring out" of the Spirit "upon all flesh" promised for *then*, in that "age to come," obviously cannot be happening *now*. The applying of the phrase "the last days" to the present time, so I believe, is dispensationally wrong.

It may be well to look up a couple of those passages which speak about "the last days." Take Isaiah 2:1-5. Note carefully the words which we italicize.

> The word that Isaiah the son of Amoz saw
> Concerning *Judah* and *Jerusalem*.
> And it shall come to pass in *the last days*,
> That the mountain of the LORD's house
> Shall be established in the top of the mountains,
> And shall be exalted above the hills;
> And all nations shall flow unto it.
> And many peoples shall go and say,
> Come ye, and let us go up to the mountain of the LORD,
> To the house of the God of *Jacob;*
> And he will teach us of his ways,
> And we will walk in his paths:
> For out of *Zion* shall go forth the law,
> And the word of the LORD from *Jerusalem*.
> And he shall judge among the nations,
> And shall rebuke many people:
> And they shall beat their swords into plowshares,
> And their spears into pruninghooks;
> Nation shall not lift up sword against nation,
> Neither shall they learn war any more.

Observe (1) that the prediction refers exclusively to the covenant nation, i.e., to "Judah," to "Jerusalem," to the "house of Jacob"— *not* to the *Church;* (2) that the prediction is not to be fulfilled until "the last days"; and (3) that what it forepictures of Israel's headship among the nations, Jerusalem's juridical centricity, and the absolute abolition of war have *not yet* happened—which means that we have not yet reached those predicted "last days." Therefore the present time (the 1970s) *cannot* be the "last days" in that prophetic sense.

Take the following selected verses from Micah 3:12 to 4:8 concerning those same "last days." In part they are a repeat of the Isaiah forecast which we have just consulted (incidentally, a useful piece of evidence as to the early date of Isaiah). The italics are mine.

> Therefore shall Zion for your sake
> Be plowed as a field,
> And Jerusalem shall become heaps,
> And the mountain of the house
> As the high places of the forest.
>
> But in *the last days* it shall come to pass,
> That the mountain of the house of the LORD
> Shall be established in the top of the mountains,
> And it shall be exalted above the hills. . . .
> But they shall sit every man
> Under his vine and under his fig tree;
> And none shall make them afraid. . . .
> In that day, saith the LORD, will I assemble her that halteth
> And I will gather her that is driven out,
> And her that I have afflicted;
> And I will make her that halted a remnant,
> And her that was cast far off a *strong nation:*
> And the LORD shall reign over *them* in mount Zion
> From henceforth, even for ever. . . .
> Unto *thee* shall it come, even the first dominion;
> The *kingdom* shall come to the daughter of *Jerusalem.*

Let it be noted again that the reference is specifically to Jerusalem and the covenant nation, not to the Church. Also, that which is forepictured to happen in "the last days" certainly has *not* happened yet, which proves that we are *not* at present in those "last days."

Only one other passage need detain us. It is Joel 2:28-32, and I refer to it because it is the prophecy which Peter quoted hundreds of years later, on the day of Pentecost (Acts 2:14-21). Indeed, it may be preferable to quote it as reproduced by Peter on that epochal day so as to see how he used it.

> Ye men of Judaea, and all ye that dwell at Jerusalem, be this known unto you, and hearken to my words. . . . This is that which was spoken by the prophet Joel: And it shall come to pass *in the last days,* saith God, I will pour out of my Spirit upon all flesh; and your sons and your daughters shall prophesy, and your young men shall see visions, and your old men shall dream dreams; and on my servants and on my handmaidens I will pour out in those days of my Spirit; and they shall prophesy: and I will show wonders in heaven above, and signs in the earth beneath; blood, and fire, and vapour of smoke:

the sun shall be turned into darkness, and the moon into blood, before
that great and notable day of the Lord come.

(Acts 2:14-20)

Joel added some further features which Peter did not include but
which belong to those same "last days."

> For, behold, *in those days,* and in that time, when I shall bring again
> the captivity of *Judah* and *Jerusalem,* I will also gather all nations, and
> will bring them down into the valley of Jehoshaphat, and will plead
> with them there for my people and for my heritage *Israel,* whom they
> have scattered among the nations. . . . for the *day of the LORD* is
> near. . . . The *sun* and the *moon* shall be *darkened,* and the *stars* shall
> *withdraw* their shining.

(Joel 3:1-2,14-15)

Surely no one will try to make out that those fearful portents in the
heavens appeared in Peter's days—"blood, and fire, and vapour of
smoke," the "sun and the moon . . . darkened," the "great and
notable day of the Lord," with judgment upon the Gentile nations
for their treatment of Israel and the regathering of Israel's "scattered" millions. All those are yet future. The "last days" to which
they belong are *not* our own days, as is now being wrongly preached.

But *why,* then, did Peter connect Joel's prophecy with that Pentecost of two thousand years ago if those were not the "last days"? It
was because the outpouring of the Holy Spirit upon that first band of
believers on Jesus was the wonderful evidence that the promised
"last days" of renewal and restoration were being genuinely *offered*
to the Jewish people, if they would respond repentantly. All the Old
Testament promises concerning those "last days" which were to
bring Israel's national regathering and regeneration and the outpouring of the divine Spirit were *Messianic;* that is, they all pertained
to the predicted reign of the coming *Messiah.* Jesus had now offered
Himself as Israel's Messiah but had been rejected and even crucified. Yet the nation was being given a further chance to receive Him,
in the new light of that supreme credential, His bodily resurrection
from the dead.

The promised "last days" might have come then if only Israel had
believingly responded. Peter said so quite plainly in Acts 3:19-21.

> Repent ye therefore, and turn again, that your sins may be blotted
> out, that so there may come *the times of refreshing* [another name for the
> "last days"] from the presence of the Lord; and *that he may send* the
> Christ who hath been proclaimed unto you, even Jesus: whom heaven
> must [now] receive until the *times of restoration* [another name for the

"last days"] of all things, whereof God spake by the mouth of his holy prophets from of old (ASV).

Could anything be more explicit? Had the nation Israel reciprocated penitently, our Lord Jesus would have returned *then* in His Messianic role as Davidic Savior-King; and the "last days" of spiritual refreshing and national restoration and kingdom glories would have begun. But did not God know in advance of Israel's refusal? How then could the offer to Israel have been truly meant for *then?* The reply is that although *God* foreknew Israel's refusal, no one else did; and inasmuch as God never violates human free will, history was (as always) allowed to move on in its natural sequences. God similarly foreknew Israel's supreme infidelity in crucifying our Lord, but He did not predetermine that infidelity—for God is never the author of evil. He foreknew it, anticipated it, and overruled it. So was it with Israel's further and deeper rejection of Jesus in the days of the Apostles: the renewed offer of Jesus as Messiah-Savior-King to Israel was thoroughly real, but its repudiation by Israel was divinely foreknown, anticipated, and overruled to the bringing in of this present age of grace and of the Church. Meanwhile the "last days," which are distinctively the age of the reigning Messiah, are suspended until the archangel's trumpet signals our Lord's yet future descent in flaming splendor.

Other passages might be cited in further confirmation that our own times are not the "last days" envisioned in Messianic prophecy, but I think that the foregoing should suffice. I am well aware that the New Testament Epistles refer in several places to the last days of this present age (e.g., 2 Tim. 3:1; 2 Peter 3:3) and actually call them "the last days"; but unfortunately for those preachers who say that these closing days of the present age are those of the Spirit's being outpoured on all flesh, the Epistles say the reverse. The italics are mine.

> This know also, that *in the last days* perilous times shall come. For men shall be lovers of their own selves, covetous, boasters, proud, blasphemers, disobedient to parents, unthankful, unholy . . . traitors, heady, highminded, lovers of pleasures more than lovers of God (2 Tim. 3:1-4).
>
> There shall come *in the last days* scoffers, walking after their own lusts, and saying, Where is the promise of his coming? for since the fathers fell asleep, all things continue as they were from the beginning of the creation (2 Peter 3:3).
>
> Now the Spirit speaketh expressly, that *in the latter times* some shall depart from the faith, giving heed to seducing spirits, and doctrines of [demons] (1 Tim. 4:1-3).

These and other warnings which we find in the Epistles make it only too clear that the last days of this present age are very different from those predicted "last days" when Messiah Jesus is to reign on David's throne and the Holy Spirit is to be outpoured everywhere as never hitherto in human history. Therefore, the divine healings and other accompaniments of that still future era *cannot* consistently be claimed as being in fulfillment today.

Having emphasized that, however, I readily concede that today there are startling developments everywhere around us which may well suggest the likelihood of increased miracle healings.

These age end decades are undoubtedly abnormal times. During the past century Satan's grand strategy has been to destroy belief in the divine inspiration of the Bible. To accomplish that is to cut away the very foundations of Christianity. How largely the evil schemer has succeeded is only too evident. Beginning early in the nineteenth century, with the innocuous-seeming queries of a few theological scholars concerning the authorship of the Pentateuch, Satan fathered the German schools of the rationalistic Higher Criticism which later became known as the New theology and eventually Modernism or Liberalism. Under the guise of modern learning and scientific method, the movement challenged the most sacred fundamentals of the evangelical faith and gradually undermined faith in the supernatural inspiration of the Bible throughout Christendom—bringing the biggest crisis in Protestant Christianity since the Reformation. It has been Satan's big-scale retaliation. Flanked by the evolution theory in the realm of science and by the "new psychology" in the domain of morals, it has wrought havoc immeasurable. The resultant breakdown of faith in the Bible, inevitably accompanied by collapse of respect for Christian ethics and social standards, has left a fearful gap into which the archenemy of Christ has masterminded a tremendous invasion by anti-God philosophies, sensual vulgarity, sexual license, television propagation of violence, and the biggest recrudescence of occultism, witchcraft, spiritism, demon traffic, and demon possession in A.D. history.

I can well believe, therefore, that in these last laps of this present age we may witness supernormal manifestations of the Holy Spirit. The enemy has surged in like an evil flood. May we not expect, therefore, that Isaiah 59:19 may have a spectacular fulfillment today: "When the enemy shall come in like a flood, the Spirit of the Lord shall lift up a standard against him"?

Yes, there seems reason to expect extraordinary operations by the

Holy Spirit today in answer to unprecedented challenge. Yet it is wrong to confuse any such with what is yet to happen in those Messianic "last days" after our Lord's return. *Those* "last days" are not *these* days; so they do not furnish a basis on which to preach the certainty of divine healings in the present. Any such arguing is Biblically baseless. Our only safe warrant at any time is clear Scripture statement.

The Divine Will?

Still another position held by sponsors of divine healing is that all sickness is of Satan and thus against the will of God. They assure us that the will of God is *always* to heal sickness in the case of Christian believers and should therefore be unhesitatingly claimed by faith. I have before me at this moment a leaflet to that effect issued by a minister of the Gospel who is well known for his healing itinerations. I have met him and heard him and formed a high opinion of him as a gifted, sincere servant of our Lord, but what are we to say about such tenets as the following in his manifesto?

> Recognize where your sickness comes from. It must come from somewhere. Find your Bible and read the following verses: Job 2:7, Luke 13:11, Acts 10:38, Matt. 12:22, Luke 11:14. Can you see the origin of disease? It comes through *sin* and Satan. When you are living a perfectly normal life you are *well and healthy.* When you are diseased and sick you are being robbed of your health by the devil.
>
> Sin and sickness come from the same source. They came into the world by Adam's transgression. *Make sure your sins are forgiven, that Christ is your Saviour and living in your heart.* Recognize that your disease is the devil's oppression. *God hates sickness as much as sin.* He wants you to be whole and well. He wants to save and heal you. Healing is your right and inheritance once you are a committed Christian.
>
> Recognizing this foundation truth, begin to take up the challenge *yourself.* You have no right to suffer. Read Matthew 8:17. See what God did with your diseases 2000 years ago. Disease has no right to bind your body. *Right now, recognizing this great truth, command your sickness to leave you, in the name of Jesus.* . . . God will acknowledge your prayer of faith in the name of his Son, Jesus. Sickness must leave you *now,* as you pray. *Disease cannot resist you any longer.* The Christ in you is bigger than the disease. *It must go now* . . .
>
> Now rise up. Yes, rise up in the name of Jesus. Dare to move your limbs. Leave your sick bed. Vacate your wheelchair. Eat normally. Breathe freely. Act your healing, whatever was wrong with you. . . . As you act in faith, *God heals* . . . Throw yourself upon God and his Word . . . Continue in this act until every trace of your disease has left you . . . (etc.).

It requires much courage as well as sincerity to march under such a bold escutcheon as that. To preach such a doctrine, then "lay hands on the sick" and "command" each sickness to depart "in the name of the Lord," expecting it to occur each time in the presence of a keenly watching public, is notable bravery, to say the least; and I admire it. Albeit, if I may say so with courtesy, I believe the bravery of it is equalled by the error of it. Despite the forthrightness of the preacher's manifesto, I can hardly find Scripture for a single component in it.

We all recognize, along with him, that sickness in our human race originated with Adam's sin. In that sense, yes, sickness "comes through sin and Satan." Yet to argue on the strength of that— "When you are living a perfectly normal life you are well and healthy"—is dreamily unrealistic. What *is* a "perfectly normal life"? In the present providential management of our human race, a normal life is neither sinless nor diseaseless. Although sin and sickness were not part of the original design for mankind, they were mysteriously permitted; and now, alas, they are all too patently "normal" to mankind in its present, fallen condition. We are all sinners, even by heredity; and sickness comes to the "perfectly normal" as well as to all others.

It is even further off kilter to add: "When you are diseased and sick you are being robbed of your health by the devil." Nay, in most cases that is not true, except indirectly. Our Lord Jesus settled that conclusively in His reply to the disciples' question about the blind man in John 9:1-3: "Master, who did sin, this man, or his parents, that he was born blind?" Our Lord replied, "Neither hath this man sinned, nor his parents: but [he was born blind] that the works of God should be made manifest in him." So it was *not* "by the devil"! It was an overruling "of *God*"!

I need not linger here over the deep mystery of divine prevenience wrapped up in that ill-clad, sightless beggar sitting by the wayside, though one cannot but marvel that such an apparent nonentity was particularly in the precognitive purpose of God before ever time began! The one point at issue here (which many faith healers need to recognize) is that in the divinely permitted present scheme of things there is as truly a use for sickness as for healing. I can attest to that from my own experience. After knowing both illness and direct divine healing, my testimony is that there has been equally a ministry in suffering as in supernatural cure.

Do we need to elaborate our remark as to the present providential use of sickness? Does not the Bible make emphatic that mankind today is neither as God originally created nor as He ultimately intends? During these intervening sixty centuries we are living in what is rightly called the *permissive* providence of God. Eventually, in a promised consummation, planet Earth will be lifted back again, in Christ, to the higher level of God's *direct* will. But meanwhile much that now happens is in God's *permissive* will, in which He *overrules* all He allows. That congenitally blind Palestinian beggar of two thousand years ago is both startling and comforting. If *he* was in the purposive precognition of God, then so were all the others whom Jesus healed—and so were all the others whom Jesus did *not* heal—and so are all those *today* whom He heals—and so are all the others who are *not* healed by Him. It cannot be otherwise. However mysterious, however astounding, this pretemporal divine cognizance of us as human individuals—infinitesimals though we may seem—it is true. Indeed, when one reflects, how terrifying if it were *not* so!—if we were all unforeseen accidents in a haphazard creation!

Yes, in this midway condition of mankind, by the permissive wisdom of God, sickness is allowed to scourge our fallen race, though in controlled subservience to an ultimate "restitution of all things" (Acts 3:21). All that lies within the present permissive will of God is foreknown, anticipated, and so overruled that in the words of Romans 8:28: "All things work together for good to them that love God, to them who are the called according to his purpose." God may sometimes *send* sickness for some incidental purpose, as in the case of Lazarus (John 11:4; cf. Isa. 38:1; Acts 12:23). With specific purpose He may even use Satan or other evil spirits to inflict calamity or sickness (1 Sam. 16:14; Job 1:12, 2:6; 2 Cor. 12:7), but all such concession to evil agencies is bounded by sovereign restriction (Job 1:12; 2:6; 1 Cor. 10:13). The truth in general is that God *permits* sickness rather than directly inflicts it, by allowing the ordinary laws of cause and effect to take their normal course.

I repeat, for emphasis: In the present status quo there can be a designed ministry in permitted sickness; and I therefore label as delusively wrong the teaching that all sickness is directly effected by the devil. Let me quote from James McConkey's sympathetic tract *Prayer and Healing*.

> After all, is it not a fact of every-day observation that God does use physical affliction for the chastening and purification of His children, and that He suffers it to remain until He has accomplished His purpose of love and child-training with them? Surely this is the case in

the lives of myriads of His godliest saints. Who is there of us who has not seen a strong, perhaps rebellious life, go into the crucible of affliction of all kinds, bodily included, and come forth strengthened and purified as no other dealing of God seemed hitherto able to accomplish? We recall the case of one of the most devoted and successful workers in the Lord's vineyard. For sixteen years she lay a helpless invalid, suffering keenly much of the time. At the end of all these long and weary years she awoke one midnight to the consciousness that she had never been wholly submitted to the will of God in her illness—that deep in her heart there had always been a root of bitterness, a spirit of rebellion that God should permit her thus to suffer. Then and there, with the vision of her rebellious will vividly before her, she yielded that will wholly and unconditionally to her Father in heaven, to bear patiently all that He might permit to come into her life in the way of bodily affliction. She was, as she expressed it, *just as willing to lie there a thousand years, if it were God's will, or to be raised up to health if that were His will* (emphases mine).[1]

Later that Christian woman was miraculously healed, but not until the sickness had done its intended work in her life. Let me quote further.

And do we not see Him permitting others of His own thus to be afflicted not only for years, but for a whole lifetime, *without* the ensuing healing which came in that case? And as we mark the Christlike patience, gentleness, and long-suffering which are wrought out in those lives, in the chamber of affliction, must we not confess that for some reason God is allowing it to be thus? And dare we assert that the only reason such godly souls are not healed of their diseases is that they do not have faith in God? Such an inference is incredible to those who know the saintliness of many such lives. . . . Some He heals marvelously, miraculously. Others, for causes best known to himself, He permits to stay in the place of infirmity and affliction. It seems clear that it is not because these lack faith to be healed, if God will, but that it is *not* his will to heal (emphases mine).[2]

Catherine Marshall, in her recent, eloquent *Something More,* pays tribute to the disciplinary and educative influence of physical illness. So do not a few others who are contemporary. We think, also, of glorious saints like Frances Ridley Havergal and Annie Johnson Flint, in the one case continuously weakened and in the other excruciatingly pained by prolonged and crippling arthritis, yet both of them chastened, sanctified, enriched by it to the blessing of countless thousands by their hymns and poems. Was their continued tuition in the school of suffering a penalty for lack of faith?

To teach that "God hates *sickness* as much as *sin*" and that it is *always* His will to heal in the case of true Christians ("healing is your right and inheritance") seems to me a dangerous presuming on Biblical *silence*. If bodily healing were always God's will, would there not be some clear pronouncement to that effect somewhere in the New Testament? So sensitively painful a concern is it that I cannot conceive a complete no-promise of it anywhere, if it were true. The fact is that there is no unqualified statement anywhere in Scripture that it is *always* the will of God to heal bodily ailments.

Those who say that healing is promised in the Word turn us to Matthew 21:22, Mark 11:23-24, and John 14:13-14. Through the centuries such promises have been both a shining challenge and (at times) a sore problem to Christian hearts amid their trials, endeavors, and sufferings. Into that I need not go here. I simply call attention to the circumstance that not one of those promises specifically mentions physical healing much less do they even hint that it is always God's will to heal sick believers. Then, of course, we shall be asked, What about James 5:15? Well, we note at once that even it is limited to Christians and is carefully guarded against being taken as a guarantee of healing without exception (but more on that later).

If it is always God's will to heal our sicknesses as Christians, then we cannot help asking (as many others have): Why do we find Paul saying in 2 Timothy 4:20, "Trophimus have I left at Miletum *sick*"? The fall-out of a valuable comrade when Paul needed him! Yet Paul, who had healed thousands through the name and power of Jesus, left him there ill! Why was Paul himself not healed of his own persisting malady? I do not press, as some do, that Paul's "thorn in the flesh" was ophthalmia (2 Cor. 12:7). The word "thorn" itself may be a questionable translation. Yet is it not inferable from Galatians 4:13-15 and 6:11 ("large letters" or scrawl) and 2 Corinthians 10:1,7,10 that there *was* some eye trouble with disfiguring facial effects? Paul has told us why the "thorn" was not removed. But why was the other hampering defect not healed? And why were Timothy's "frequent sicknesses" *(astheneias)* and stomach weakness (1 Tim. 5:23) not remedied by the Lord once for all? These are awkward questions for those who maintain that it is *always* God's will to heal sickness in Christian believers.

It may well come as a surprise to some that in 2 Corinthians 12:7 Paul actually says that his affliction of the body was a *gift* from God ("There was *given* to me a thorn in the flesh")! And what are we to say about his exultation in it: "Most gladly therefore will I rather *glory* in my infirmities *(astheneias)*, that the power of Christ may rest upon me" (v. 9)? In that instance the power was *not* healing power

but the imparted power to endure victoriously an *un*healed malady
Think of it: Paul, the Lord's vehicle of healing to thousands, ye
himself *not* healed but exulting in his illness!—"I take pleasure ir
infirmities" (*astheneias* again! v. 10). How can it all be explainec
except on the premise that there is often a divine ministry in permitted ailment? Still more: What about 1 Corinthians 11:30, wher
sickness and infirmities and even death are stated to be divinel\
permitted as correctives for blameworthy behavior?

With nothing but sincere esteem for the courageous ministe:
whose manifesto I quoted in earlier paragraphs, let me add that]
attended one of his meetings. He is a gifted, consecrated servant o
our Lord. With mingling grace and urgency he gave a fine message
followed by an invitation for all those who were seeking healing tc
gather at the platform. If ever anyone watched and listened witl
sympathetic openness of mind, *I* did, praying all the while both fo\
him and for the needy ones who had gone to him. In each case there
was the "laying on of hands" and the strong command "in the nam
of Jesus" that the malady should at once quit the body. Somehow]
sensed that not all, if any, in that particular meeting were healed—
though I may have been mistaken.

I had to leave before the final dispersal, but I had the chance tc
speak to at least one of those who had gone forward for healing. H
had been sitting next to me; so after the laying on of hands for hi:
healing, he came back and resumed his place beside me. He hac
been "healed" presumably of eye trouble; but when I asked hin
whether it had really happened, he gave me a strange reply: "Well
no, not really; not yet. You can't expect this kind of trouble to b
healed immediately."

So there was a fault somewhere. Was it in the preacher?—or in the
patient?—or in the theory? I have good reason to believe that a\
times there have been remarkable healings in that dear preacher'\
meetings; but I wonder how many *un*healed others have been dashec
down into deeper suffering through the theory that it is *always* God'\
will to heal Christians of their physical ills, if only their faith is simpl
enough or strong enough.

NOTES

[1]James McConkey, *Prayer and Healing.*
[2]Ibid.

Is There True Scriptural Basis?

That the life also of Jesus might be made manifest in our mortal
flesh.

—2 Corinthians 4:11

There is a reverence for the one true God
  Which needs no cloister or cathedral high;
A path of worship godly hearts have trod
  Which needs no symbol for the outward eye:
A deep, maturer adoration, freed
  From sacerdotal forms and liturgies,
A fellowship with God beyond the need
  Of kindergarten pomp and pageantries.

There is a faith in God which has outgrown
  Such trappings of religious infancy;
Which fastens on God's written Word alone,
  And finds that Word its all-sufficiency:
What need of candles, ikons, rosaries,
  To make "religion" seem more tangible?
True faith disdains such sensory vagaries,
  Trusts God direct, and "*sees* the Invisible."

There is a deep-down, glowing daily tryst
  With heaven, by the consecrated soul,
Which so absorbs the healing life of Christ
  That somehow mind and spirit are made whole:
The nervous system too is calmed and healed,
  Both mind and body are renewed and blest,
The Lord of life and health is thus revealed
  And through the mortal flesh made manifest.

—J.S.B.

CHAPTER EIGHT

Is There True
Scriptural Basis?

We now come to the heart of our subject. What is the verifiable
teaching of the New Testament on miracle healing? Up to this point
may have seemed to harbor reservations against believing in such
curative divine intervention: but no, my mind is open. Any hesitancy
is simply because it is wisdom to question what is questionable and
doubt what is doubtful. This whole matter of healing from heaven
needs freeing from assumptions which are seemingly Scriptural yet
not *really* so. Maybe if we can cleave through to the uncluttered
dictates of Scripture we can iron out some of the puzzles and
safeguard the healing message from dud miracles, no-cures, and
psychosomatic caricatures.

Let us sum up our findings thus far. First, the right to preach
divine healing of human bodies today cannot be safely claimed on
the ground that our Lord healed the sick when He was visibly on
earth. Second, we cannot firmly infer that such healings should
continue today because they were prominent during the period
covered by the Acts of the Apostles. Third, a true exegesis of
Matthew 8:17 gives no warrant to preach salvation from sickness as
a twin doctrine to salvation from sin. Fourth, we cannot validly
assume that miracle cures are for today on the plea that we are living
in "the last days," for in the Biblical foreview these are *not* "the last

155

156   *Divine Healing As Taught Today*

days." Fifth, it is unscriptural to preach that all sickness is directly
from Satan or that it is *always* God's will to heal.

So can we now pick out what *is* Scriptural teaching? Our first
question is, Where does the New Testament teach healing for bodily
sickness in suchwise as makes it clearly applicable today? The
following seem to be the only passages where it is definitely stated or
promised, along with several others from which perhaps we may
reasonably infer its availability to Christians in general. I will quote
them each in turn.

1. Now there are diversities of gifts, but the same Spirit. . . . For to
   one is given by the Spirit the word of wisdom; to another the word
   of knowledge by the same Spirit; to another faith by the same
   Spirit; to another the *gifts of healings* by the same Spirit; to another
   the working of miracles; to another prophecy; to another discerning of spirits; to another divers kinds of tongues. . . . But all these
   worketh that one and the selfsame Spirit, dividing to every man
   severally as he will.   (1 Corinthians 12:4, 8-11)

2. Now ye are the body of Christ, and members in particular. And
   God hath set some in the church: first apostles, secondarily prophets, thirdly teachers, after that miracles, then *gifts of healings*, helps,
   governments, diversities of tongues. Are all apostles? are all
   prophets? are all teachers? are all workers of miracles? Have all *the
   gifts of healings?* do all speak with tongues? do all interpret?
                                            (1 Corinthians 12:27-30)

3. Is any among you afflicted? let him pray. Is any merry? let him sing
   psalms. Is any *sick* among you? let him call for the elders of the
   church; and let them pray over him, anointing him with oil in the
   name of the Lord. And *the prayer of faith shall save the sick, and the Lord
   shall raise him up;* and if he have committed sins, they shall be
   forgiven him. Confess your faults one to another, and pray for one
   another, *that ye may be healed.* The effectual fervent prayer of a
   righteous man availeth much [i.e., in this praying for healing].
                                            (James 5:13-16)

4. We are troubled on every side, yet not distressed; we are per-
   plexed, but not in despair; persecuted, but not forsaken; cast
   down, but not destroyed; always bearing about in the body the
   dying of the Lord Jesus, *that the life also of Jesus might be made manifest
   in our body.* For we which live are alway delivered unto death for
   Jesus' sake, that the life also of Jesus might be made *manifest in our
   mortal flesh.*   (2 Corinthians 4:8-10)

5. But if the Spirit of him that raised up Jesus from the dead dwell in
   you, he that raised up Christ from the dead shall also *quicken your
   mortal bodies* by his Spirit that dwelleth in you.
                                            (Romans 8:11)

Those seem to be all there is in the Epistles by way of clear promise or statement concerning divine healing or renewal of the human body in this present age. What is the first thought which leaps to mind? Is it not the *very small space* given to physical healing? In a way, it seems disappointingly small. Let it tell us the comparatively small importance which *God* puts upon it. Let it indicate its comparatively minor place over against the major emphases of the New Testament letters to Christian believers.

Note that I describe it as of *comparatively* diminutive concern. In itself it is important enough, like various other weighty matters which are given only scant reference in Scripture; but *relatively*, that is, over against the great spiritual and eternal issues which are the heart of the Christian message, it is among the incidentals of lesser concern.

This sparse mention of the subject in the Epistles strikes a sharp contrast with the frequency of miracle healings in the four Gospels and the Acts of the Apostles. And let us be reminded, it is the New Testament *Epistles*, not the Gospels or the Acts, which are specifically addressed to the Church as a whole, to local churches, and to individual Christians as such. It is the Epistles which are exclusively the property of the Church and which furnish all those teachings which are specifically "church" doctrines and which reveal all the Lord's special provisions for His Church and which set the norm for the Church's life, fellowship, witness, and experience throughout the present age. So, seeing this matter of divine healing in true perspective, let us now examine those five texts in which we have found reference to it.

1 Corinthians 12:4, 8-11

We halt again at 1 Corinthians 12:4, 8-9. "Now there are diversities of gifts, but the same Spirit. . . . For to one is given by the Spirit the word of wisdom; to another the word of knowledge by the same Spirit; to another faith by the same Spirit; to another the *gifts of healings* by the same Spirit."

Are those "gifts of healings" plainly included among the Spirit's supernatural *gifts?* Yes. Are they plainly stated to be part of the Holy Spirit's activity in the Church? Yes. In teaching that local Corinthian church, did Paul do so in such a way as plainly applies to the Church as a whole? Yes. Is that teaching plainly meant to indicate a norm, or intendedly continuing *experience* in the Church? Yes, for those "gifts" were not merely temporary "signs." They were specifically to the Church, with no indication of any time limit. Therefore, are those "gifts of healings" meant to be still operating in the true Church today? Who can say no unless it is someone who is a slave to Bullingerian hyper-dispensationalism?[1]

Let us indulge no misgivings about it: those "gifts of healings" are meant for today. I do *not* say they are meant as part of the Church's message to the public at large. In preaching the "whosoever" Gospel to the unconverted, we have no warrant to offer healing for the body as well as the forgiveness of sins. The Gospel message to men in general concerns the salvation of the *soul*, not the cure of physical ailments. Therefore, so it seems to me, public healing campaigns, which understandably attract big crowds of cure-seekers and wonder-watchers, are basically unscriptural when they preach bodily healing for everybody as a concomitant of trusting in Jesus for the salvation of the soul. I am not denying that miracle healings often take place in such campaigns (and shall offer careful comment on that later); but I cannot find anywhere in Scripture that supernatural healing for the body is an intended component of our Gospel message to the promiscuous public. That, however, in no wise detracts from the fact that a ministry of healing for born-again Christians *is* meant to be experienced today *inside* the fellowship of our Lord's own people.

Notice how that Corinthian passage describes the healing ministry: "To another . . . *gifts* of healings." So the healings then occurring were not effected *directly* by the Holy Spirit but through human intermediaries sovereignly selected by God Himself for that purpose.

Let us recognize that as it was then, so it is meant to be now. In any local evangelical church which is closely adhering to the New Testament pattern, those heaven-imparted "gifts" may rightly be expected to reappear.

The Holy Spirit imparts only through *some* the "gifts of healings." He may or may not single out the pastor or any of the elders for that particular use. As often as not He may select the seemingly unlikely, thereby emphasizing His own sovereignty of operation. The distribution of healing "gifts" is not on the basis of office or seniority or even of spiritual maturity. The transmitter may be older or younger, office-bearer or ordinary member, someone more deeply seasoned spiritually or someone less evidently mature. As the Word says, the Holy Spirit distributes gifts "to every man . . . *as he will*" (1 Cor. 12:11).

If, therefore, the all-controlling Spirit chooses to impart healing gifts through any member of the fellowship, let that one be humbled by such responsibility; and let none of the others be foolishly envious. Nor let the one through whom healings are transmitted envy those who have greater gifts than that of merely physical healing.

The singling out of someone through whom to communicate healings is not necessarily a sign of spiritual merit, nor does it mean that our Lord loves the selected vessel more than others. It is solely a matter of the utmost benefit to the assembly as a whole, every member of which is *equally* dear to our royal Savior because He paid the same costly redemption price for each one.

1 Corinthians 12:27-30

"Now ye are the body of Christ, and members in particular. And God hath set some in the church, first apostles, secondarily prophets, thirdly teachers, after that miracles [works of power], then *gifts of healings*, helps, governments, diversities of tongues. Are all apostles? are all prophets? are all teachers? are all workers of miracles? Have all the gifts of healings? do all speak with tongues? do all interpret?"

Who can read this Corinthian passage without seeing that it is not merely of local or temporary relevance? When Paul said, "God hath set some in the Church," he obviously meant the Church in all places, not just the assembly at Corinth. When he said, "First apostles," he did so because they, with their inspired writings and decisive authority, belong to the *whole* Church, in which all the local churches are contributive units.

In our earlier quotation from 1 Corinthians 12, it was the "gifts" which were particularized. Here, in verses 27 to 30, it is the human *agents* who are classified; and the nine classes are divided (according to order of importance) into a primary three and a subsidiary six. First come "apostles," "prophets," "teachers" and "*after* that" the other six. Supernatural healings belong only to the latter, along with the other *sensory* gifts—"miracles," "tongues," "interpretation of tongues" (cf. v. 10).

Yes, that is where bodily healings belong. They are of far less importance to the Church than the spiritual gifts of prophetic preaching and Spirit-anointed teaching. Yet that must not blind us to the fact that the gifts of healings are *there* as a part of the Holy Spirit's movement in the Church, intended for the benefit of believers everywhere. Has that healing ministry of the Holy Spirit through chosen human vessels ever been formally withdrawn? If so, who will give us Scripture for it? Is there any valid reason why it should not be operating today among assemblies of believers who are soundly evangelical and consecrated to Christ?

James 5:13-16

The Epistle of James acquires added interest from its probably being the first-written document in the New Testament. It gives us a specimen of the earliest teachings to Christian groups, which in the first days, be it remembered, were mainly Jewish.

In the structure of the New Testament, which I for one believe to be by the Holy Spirit's designing, the Epistle of James comes second in the ninefold group often called the "Christian Hebrew Epistles." By reason of its early date, its Jewish slant, its nonmention of the Church *(ecclesia)*, and its supposed evangelical elementariness, certain hyper-dispensationalists will again interrupt us with their objection that this epistle does not apply to Christian believers today as do those epistles which were written *after* the Pauline disclosure of the Church as the "body of Christ"—the "mystery" which had been hidden during preceding ages.

We reply to those hyper-dispensationalists by reminding them that *all* the New Testament Epistles are *Christian*. They are all distinctly directed to Christians. It is true that James addressed his epistle "to the twelve tribes which are in the dispersion" (literal Greek). He did so as "a servant of God and of the *Lord Jesus Christ*" (1:1, emphasis mine). And he exhorted them to "have not the faith of our Lord Jesus Christ, the Lord of Glory [i.e., as taking the place of the Shekinah] with respect of persons"—for in the light of "Christ the Glory" earthly distinctions vanish (2:1). True, James spoke to them as adherents of their synagogues ("assembly" v. 2), for the complete cleavage of Judaism from the new Christian faith had not yet occurred; but in James 5:14 he exhorted sick ones who need physical healing to "call for the elders of the *ecclesia*" (i.e., the local Christian church).

We reject the hyper-dispensational notion that there is some interior division of the Epistles based on date: a division which *suspends* large parts of them from any applicability to the present-day church. We repudiate the theory that the so-named Christian Hebrew Epistles (Hebrews to Revelation) are Jewish in a way which denudes them of reference to Gentile Christians today. I am all in favor of "rightly dividing the word of truth" (2 Tim. 2:15), but the hyper-dispensational splitting of the Epistles into one part for Gentile believers and another for Jewish is *wrongly* dividing the Word; and it is banefully misleading. If I understand them rightly, they would rob us Gentiles of nearly all the New Testament except the later Epistles of Paul!

The New Testament Epistles are arranged according to a pattern superimposed by the Holy Spirit: first the Church Epistles (Romans to 2 Thessalonians), then the Pastoral Epistles (1 Timothy to Philemon), then the Christian Hebrew Epistles (Hebrews to Revelation). They each occupy an intended place, and all conform to a developing progress. In the nine Pauline Epistles to the churches, the first four outstandingly emphasize the *Cross;* the middle three the *Church;* the final two the yet future *Coming.* In the nine Christian Hebrew Epistles, Hebrews comes first, emphasizing *faith;* but it is followed by the Epistle of James with its balancing emphasis on *works.* Next comes 1 Peter with its glad emphasis on Christian *hope* looking to the future; but immediately following is 2 Peter with its balancing insistence on *growth* here and now. Then come the three Epistles of John with their emphasis on *love,* followed by the Jude fragment with its keynote of godly *contending* "for the faith," reminding us that Christian love is not a wishy-washy tolerating of error, yet indicating also that we are never safely ready for "contending" *until* we have that constraining and *re*straining love in our hearts which is expounded in the preceding Johannine Epistles. Finally comes the Apocalypse (which in reality is an epistle of our Lord Jesus Himself through the apostle John) with its crowning emphasis on *overcoming* and *inheriting.* Isn't that an obviously designed progress?

Reflect again: the three main writers of the New Testament Epistles were Paul, Peter, and John; and their writings occur in that order. In Paul the distinctive emphasis is *faith,* in Peter it is *hope,* in John it is *love.* Is not that also an intended overall pattern? And is that not the usual order of Christian experience? And does it not all bear against the hyper-dispensational idea that this or that or the other epistle has little or no applicability to the Church today? If I may reverently say so, the divine Designer of Biblical structure seems to have *ignored* the mere date on which each composition was written so as to shape all of them into a logically progressive design.

Admittedly, in the nine Christian Hebrew Epistles there is nothing about the *Ecclesia,* the Church, as the "mystery." There is nothing about the Church either mystical or organizational, either historical or spiritual, either collective or local; but does that lessen the relevance of these epistles to us Gentile believers who largely comprise the Church today? Not one whit! Think what we *have* in those Christian Hebrew writings. In the first of them there is (along with other splendors) the only place in the New Testament where we have a full-scale treatment of our risen Lord's intercessory ministry as our Great High Priest in the heavenly Holy of Holies. In James, the second of them, is the only passage where the stickling relationship between "faith" and "works" is squarely faced. Faith without works and works without faith are equally dead. Justification before God through Christ is by faith *apart* from works; but the *proof* of that faith before both God and men is its expression in good works. In 1 and 2 Peter, Christian hope and growth are treated as nowhere else; while finally, in John's three epistles a sublime goal is reached in the "perfect *love*" which "casts out fear."

Ponder it well: if we are willing to be guided by the structural progress of the New Testament Epistles, then however gripping to heart and mind the "Evangel," the "Mystery," the "Church," the "Wisdom," and the "Parousia" explicated to us in the nine Church Epistles (Romans to 2 Thessalonians), all is lost on us unless it issues in the practical, individual godliness and spirituality reiterated in the Christian Hebrew Epistles (Hebrews to Revelation). It is no accident that the profound doctrines of those nine Pauline masterpieces lead to the individual faith, works, hope, growth, love, contending, and overcoming of that final ninefold group. We cannot do without any one of them or any *part* of any one. All of them, without exception, were meant to inform *all* Christian believers through *all* the Church's history, including today.

With that firmly in mind, let us thank God anew for the Epistle of James, particularly for that flashing jewel of a promise in 5:13-16. This is the boldest, most explicit pronouncement anywhere in the New Testament on the subject of supernatural bodily healing for Christians.

> Is any among you afflicted? let him pray. Is any merry? let him sing psalms. Is any *sick* among you? let him call for the elders of the church; and let them pray over him, anointing him with oil in the name of the LORD: and *the prayer of faith shall save the sick, and the LORD shall raise him up;* and if he have committed sins, they shall be forgiven him. Confess your faults one to another, and pray one for another, *that ye may be healed.* The effectual fervent prayer of a righteous man availeth much (i.e., in this prayer for healing).

Mark the salient features. First, the promise is *definite*—three times over: (1) "the prayer of faith shall save the sick"; (2) "the Lord shall raise him up"; (3) "if he have committed sins, they shall be forgiven him." Three positives and no negatives! There is nothing doubtful such as "the prayer of faith *may* save the sick" or "the LORD *may* raise him up." There is no subjunctive hedging such as "though perhaps not in every instance" or "perhaps not immediately." If ever a statement was definite, James 5:15 is.

Second, the promise is *specific*. It describes the invalid as "anyone *sick*." Does the Greek word here *(asthenei)* really mean physical sickness? Yes, it is the word used again and again for bodily ailments. Its literal meaning is "without strength"; and in James 5:14 it points to such strengthlessness or weakness in wearying degree, for in the ensuing clause, "shall save the sick one," James uses an alternative word *(kamnonta)*, which means "the exhausted one." The implication is that the sick one is so ill as to be unable to get up or get out—hence the calling of the elders to his dwelling.

As incidental to that, perhaps some brethren need to realize that this promise of healing is not meant as a petty cure—for every time they have a headache or a sore toe or some other minor pain—lest they turn the praying elders themselves into sagging invalids through overmuch traipsing around! The text specifies serious illness, apparently that which is beyond cure through natural means or medical skills.

Again, the promise is *inclusive*. It excludes none who are truly Christian believers and members of a Christian group: "Is *anyone* among you sick?" So it is not a provision only for the elderly but not the younger; for leaders and office-bearers but not ordinary members; for the saintly and mature but not the undeveloped new disciple; for masters but not servants; for those in some full-time Christian vocation but not those in secular employ. No, this promise of healing is the property of *every* born-again Christian.

Notice now, however, that it promises healing only *in private*. It does not say that if anyone is sick, he is supposed to go to some big healing campaign, or if too incapacitated to go by himself, he is to get a group of his friends to take him. Nor does it say that he is to be taken to some well-known faith healer or to a charismatic clinic where there are reported healings. No, the promised healing is to be in the quiet of one's own home.

I shall be asked, "What then about those big public gatherings where divine healing for the body is preached and often apparently occurs? Do you not believe in them?" My interim reply, until I return to the matter later, is, In some cases no, in others yes—but with certain uncompromising reservations. They would not be needed were it not that the average local church today is spiritually decadent or far removed in other ways from the New Testament original. In the usual run of churches, where can you find a half-dozen office-bearers who even *believe* in divine healing for the sick in answer to the "anointing" and the "prayer of faith"? Where are those who are living near enough to the Lord and sufficiently experiencing the Spirit's power to *qualify* for such miracle ministry in the sickroom?

We must leave that for the moment. Beyond any peradventure James 5:15 expresses our Lord's own *preference* in His healing of our sicknesses. It is the opposite of anything ostentatiously loud. There is nothing of the fleshly excitement, crowd psychology, artificial galvanizing of "faith for healing," and sometimes (we suspect) hypnotism or personal magnetism such as characterize too many healing crusades. Let James 5:14-15 stamp upon our minds our *Lord's* preferred way: a little group of reverent, praying, believing men gathered around the sick brother's bed, in the calm and quiet of his home; conferring, sympathizing, expecting, praying with utter, reverent blending of hearts. *That* is the way our heavenly Physician has here prescribed.

Next, the text is *directive*. It directs the sick one as to what *he* is to do: he is to "call for the elders." Then the text tells the elders what *they* are to do: they are to "pray over him, having anointed him with oil in the name of the Lord." There is no suggestion of elders going *unbidden*. Even less does it authorize *others* who vainly presume themselves the Lord's mouthpieces to call without invitation on sick persons, pressing the matter of healing upon them in such a way as to make any use of medical aid appear sinful—often engendering in them a guilt complex for (supposedly) not having enough faith to be healed. Pertaining to this, R. A. Torrey's book *Divine Healing* gives us some pretty sharp jabs.

> Note also for Whom he is to send, "the elders of the church." He is not to send for some self-appointed busy-body who goes about with a little bottle of oil to be used in his loudly-advertised "ministry of healing" to which he has been called, or fancies he has been called. He is not to send for some woman who is peculiarly gifted in prayer, or who thinks she is, and who has a peculiarly psychological or magnetic or hypnotic personality. He is not to send for any man or woman or group of such. No, he is to "call for *the elders*," the word is always masculine. He is not to "attend meetings for three days" (or three hours, or three

minutes) to get under the spell of psychological influences that are akin to Coueistic auto-suggestively therapeutic influences. He is not to be brought into the mesmeric atmosphere of a meeting where there is skillfully-planned, highly-emotional music and swaying of the body, and passings of the hand and shouts of hallelujahs, that excite the imagination and thrill the body.[2]

And now notice further that the text is *instructive*, particularly as to procedure. The visiting elders are to do three things: (1) anoint him in the name of the Lord, (2) pray over him, (3) exercise "faith" for his restoration to health—"the prayer of *faith* shall save the sick."

The anointing is to precede the praying, for in the Greek the clauses read, "Let them pray over him, *having* anointed him." What, then, are we to deduce from this instruction to "anoint"? To me it is surprising to find anyone arguing that it was meant as a medication; yet many seem to insist so. They tell us that such anointing with oils was a common resort because it was almost the only remedial agent known in those times. They are wrong, however, on two counts. (1) There was a much more extensive and developed medical skill at that time than has hitero been generally allowed. (2) If the anointing was for *medical* amelioration, why follow it with prayer for nonmedical, *supernatural* healing?

It is from Scripture itself that we must learn the significance of the anointing. So far as I can ascertain, it was *never* intended curatively. In ancient Israel there were anointings into the priesthood, into kingship, and into the prophetic office, but there were none for healing. In Genesis 28 we are told how God spoke to the fugitive Jacob in a nocturnal vision-and-voice dream as he slept on the moors with a "pillow" of stones for his hard headrest. Next morning Jacob turned the "pillow" into a memorial "pillar" and then *anointed* it with oil (Gen. 28:18; 31:13). That anointing certainly was not therapeutic! In various places we find oil anointing used for cosmetic purposes (Ruth 3:3; Amos 6:6; Matt. 6:17). Not surprisingly, therefore, it is also used figuratively of joy (Pss. 23:5; 45:7). As a matter of fact, such anointing is always associated with health and gladness, never with sickness and sadness.

If we would know the *religious* significance of such oil-anointing, we must turn to Leviticus, which in reality was a manual for the Aaronic priests. See Leviticus 8:10-12. Note the occurrences of the word "sanctify."

> And Moses took the anointing oil, and anointed the tabernacle and all that was therein, and *sanctified* them. And he sprinkled thereof

upon the altar seven times, and anointed the altar and all its vessels, both the laver and its foot, to *sanctify* them. Also he poured of the anointing oil upon Aaron's head, and anointed him, to *sanctify* him (emphases mine).

In this passage we clearly see that the primary intent of oil-anointing was a *ritual* one, solemnly signifying a "sanctification" or setting apart of the anointed person or article for sacred use. That is still the understood religious meaning in New Testament times (Luke 4:18; Acts 4:27; 10:38). The prescribed anointing in James 5:14 is symbolic. It is meant to symbolize outwardly something which happens inwardly, namely, a voluntary, complete consecration; it symbolizes a setting apart of the sick body to God by the elders and a complete self-yielding of the sick person to Him in hope of a direct healing.

But now take one further look at the promise in James 5:14-16. As remarked, it is definite, specific, inclusive, directive, and instructive; yet in one feature it is *conditional*. That in itself need not surprise us, for is there *any* promise of Scripture or any transaction between a human soul and God without *some* condition which must be fulfilled on the human side? Accordingly, in our text, even after the calling of faithful elders and the anointing with oil in the name of the Lord, there is *not* a guarantee that *every* prayer for healing will bring the longed-for cure. It has to be "the prayer of *faith*."

That may come as a disturbing jolt for some and pose an ironic problem for others. It still perplexes some of us who have lingered with long ponderings over it. All else goes well in the promise; then, suddenly at this point, the electric current of divine energy flowing through it "blows a fuse": there seems to be an area with the power shut off! It carries the suggestion that there is a short-circuiting somewhere so that in some instances instead of healing power coming through there is refusal. Only the "prayer of *faith*" shall save the "sick one."

Disappointing though this conditional element may seem, however, it puts us wise as to why many prayers for healing are not granted. It is that they were *not* prayers of "faith" in the way meant by James 5:15. It raises the question: What *is* the "prayer of faith"? And, first, this "faith" is not the faith of the new convert, the faith which we exercise toward Christ when we believe the Gospel and accept Him as our Savior. No, that is not the "faith" denoted in James 5:15; and we need to nail that firmly into our thinking.

In 1 Corinthians 12:8-9, when Paul said, "For to one is given by the Spirit the word of wisdom; to another the word of knowledge by the same Spirit; to another *faith* by the same Spirit; to another the gifts of healings," he was evidently speaking, not of faith in Christ for salvation, but of a special kind of faith which is one of the *pneumatika,* or special "gifts" of the Spirit, for use among the members of the assembly. It is an in-wrought capacity to lay hold on some answer to prayer, some required blessing, some healing miracle, or some other work of divine power to match a necessitous situation. Similarly, in James 5:15 the "prayer of faith" is *that* kind of faith, a faith directly infused into those "elders" for their vicarious appropriating of healing.

That may appear to cast a pall of frustrating uncertainty over the at-first seemingly radiant promise. Is it not ironically like "arguing in a circle"? We are told that we *must* have a special kind of faith in God in order to receive the healing; yet we just cannot have that special faith unless God Himself *gives* it to us. We may pray and plead and cry and weep for healing, but all is in vain unless we have that special faith; yet though we long, yearn, burn to *have* it, it never comes unless God gives it to us!

Yes, there is this seeming breakdown in the availability of James 5:14-16. Yet it need not cast us into dejection. The cloud of apparent uncertainty has a rainbow glistening through it, for the very fact that such a promise is given indicates a predisposition in God to answer the sincere. If special faith must be the agent which grasps and brings the healing, then God will inspire such faith. The only instances (whether few or more) in which such faith is *not* imparted are those in which God designs some important spiritual ministry through the permitted sickness. It may sound strangely paradoxical, but I myself have known sick Christians to be healed, not *of* their sickness, but *by* it! Through their physical malady has come a healing of the soul, for it has brought them into a communion with our Lord such as they had never known before.

This seeming irony, that we *must* pray with a special "faith" and yet cannot have it unless God gives it, becomes more intelligible the more one ponders it. Forgive for a moment the absurd supposition: but if you or I were God (!), could *we,* under the present state of things on earth, commit ourselves to a carte blanche promise to heal every sick Christian in answer to prayer? I think not. We would see (as of course God does) that in some cases it could not be for the highest interests or eternal good of those concerned. Yet would we on that account withhold *any* such promise of healing which could benefit many, many others? No, we would give the promise so as to indicate our purpose in general yet guard it by some proviso in the wording. That is exactly what God has done and for a twofold reason: (1) to prevent presumption, (2) to emphasize His own sovereignty in dispensing supernatural healing. Whatever promises God makes, to whomever about whatever, He never does so in any way which could blur His own absolute sovereignty. That should be remembered in our consideration of any promise given to us in Holy Writ.

Perhaps we can discern somewhat how that sovereignty operates through James 5:14-16. Let me illustrate by several parallels. Consider a foreign missionary who has given himself to work among an ugly, dirty, repellent people. On settling among them, he shudders at their repulsiveness and cries, "Oh, God, I simply cannot love these people, not with my own imperfect capacity. Yet somehow I *must* love them if I am to win them. You tell me to love them; yet I *cannot* of myself. You Yourself must give the love I need." You catch the parallel: our Lord says we are to have that love; yet we cannot have it unless He Himself *gives* it (which He does, cf. Rom. 5:5; 2 Cor. 5:14).

Here is another parallel. Our Lord gave the following injunction: "When men shall revile you, and persecute you, and shall say all manner of evil against you falsely, for my sake, *rejoice*, and be exceeding glad" (Matt. 5:11-12). Echoes of that run through Romans 5:3, James 1:2, and elsewhere. We are to "joy" in testings and "glory" in tribulations! Yet of ourselves alone we just cannot do it. That extraordinary joy can be ours only by its being divinely imparted. And therein lies the parallel with James 5:15. If God calls us to show forth that kind of joy, He Himself will *impart* it (and He does, cf. John 15:11; 1 Thess. 1:6).

Or again, the peace which surpasses all understanding is meant to be ours (Phil. 4:7). Despite "wars and rumours of wars" we are to be "not troubled" (Matt. 24:6). "Yea, the time cometh that whosoever killeth you will think that he doeth God service" (John 16:2). Yet "let not your heart be troubled" (14:1). Is such a peace possible? Listen to the promise of Jesus in John 14:27. "Peace I *leave* with you [a bequeathment through His Cross], my peace I *give to you* [a bestowment through His indwelling]." It is another parallel with James 5:15. What we are *meant* to have but cannot originate in ourselves, our Lord *gives* us.

Christlike love, joy, and peace are meant to be ours; but we ourselves cannot produce them. If we are to express them, they must be divinely in wrought; and indeed they *are* (Gal. 5:22-23). So is it with the special "faith" which is required in James 5:15. If that special faith is required for healing, then God Himself will give it, unless for some reason it is not His will to heal at that time. R. V. Bingham wisely comments as follows in *The Bible and the Body:*

> The question of whether God intends to heal along natural or supernatural lines will be generally indicated in the consciousness of those called in to pray. God sometimes moves out in the faith that is able to claim instantaneous healing, and, when such an inspired prayer is offered, the answer immediately comes, and all other means are unnecessary; but that the accompanying presence of means and the ministry of nurse or physician is grieving to God we deny, and challenge those who hold that view to produce their Scriptural evidence.
>
> We remember being called into a farmhouse on our way to a meeting in the country years ago, to pray for a man of whom the doctors said that his only hope was in a severe operation. The medicine bottles were on the table by the bedside when we entered. The doctor had given his verdict. Two of us knelt by the bedside in simple prayer, and the "prayer of faith" was given. We had to hurry off immediately afterwards to the meeting at which we were to preach. It was several years before we met this man again, and he said to us: "If I could have secured a buggy, I would have driven after you to the meeting that night, for the Lord had perfectly healed me, and I was able to go out to my work in the fields the next day—(he cradled oats all day)—and the following day I went to the doctor to pay my bill and to tell him that the Lord had healed me, and the doctor believed it." There was no struggle by that bedside, and the medicine bottles formed no barrier to faith and no hindrance to the divine working.
>
> On the other hand, we have been present in meetings where for hours prayer has been made for an afflicted child of God, when they claimed that they were standing on "Atonement ground," and, therefore, insisted that they had the right to claim the healing, and *nothing has moved*, even though they stirred themselves up to most zealous earnestness.[3]

At this point another comment is pertinent. There are times when the Holy Spirit does not impart this vital grip to faith because the prerequisite qualifications are not present. With my inward eyes I can still see a group of Christian brethren ranged round a patient's bed to pray for healing. They had not met beforehand to seek "the wisdom which is from above" or to pool their impressions as to whether it was God's will to have them supplicate for supernatural healing. At least two of them, to my knowledge, were hardly sure whether they even believed in miracle healing. Is it to be wondered at that although they met, anointed, prayed, and struggled to believe despite doubts, the implored healing did not come?—and do not those men more or less represent too many other such groups?

Before ever the elders or their equivalents gather round a sick brother or sister, they should consult together so as to interchange impressions and then pray that the Holy Spirit may induce in them a unifying conviction as to whether it is in the will of God that they should proceed further. Invariably where there is a sincere and patient blending of hearts to know the will of God regarding the sick one, a conviction is borne in upon the intercessors as to whether it is yes or no. Then, in most cases, they should convey to the invalid and kindred what their united persuasion is. If the conviction is that healing is intended, they should then gather with prayerful confidence in the sickroom, anoint with oil in the name of the Lord, and fervently pray for healing *expecting* it. That is the true "prayer of faith," and healing is definitely promised in answer to it.

Far too many ungranted prayers for healing bring added sorrow, even anguish, to bedridden Christians, all because there has not been this prior inquiring of the Lord. No amount of fervid pleading at the bedside can take the place of it. The very realization that God is wiser than we are and that it is *not* His will to heal in *every* instance should caution us.

While we are mentioning this, let me call attention to a further factor which seems strangely overlooked. In verse 13 just preceding the words "Is any among you *sick?*" we find "Is any among you *afflicted?*" What is the "afflicted" one to do? Is he to "call for the elders"? No, the injunction reads, "Is any among you afflicted? let him *pray.*" The Greek word translated "afflicted" *(kakopatheō)* is a more comprehensive word than that for "sick" *(astheneō)*, and it may well include physical sickness. The difference between "sickness" and "affliction" is that ordinarily "sickness" is simply a product of natural cause and effect whereas "affliction" is something actually *sent* to discipline. "Sickness" is something *permitted* whereas "affliction" is something *inflicted* as an intended means of correcting, tutoring, and sanctifying us. Therefore, if a certain sickness is not purely a by-product of natural causation but an "affliction" designedly *sent*, we are obviously at cross-purposes with God in asking Him to remove it. That God Himself does sometimes send sickness is seen in the cases of Jehoram (2 Chron. 21:18), Uzziah (2 Chron. 26:19), Herod (Acts 12:23), and Christians (1 Cor. 11:30). I repeat, therefore, that in this matter of divine healing for sick ones, nothing is more important than our first seeking to know whether it is a purely natural sickness or a purposeful "affliction." In other words, we must first seek to know *the will of God*.

2 Corinthians 4:8-10

We turn now to the fourth of those New Testament passages which we submitted as either teaching or at least implying supernatural bodily healing. It is 2 Corinthians 4:8-10.

> We are troubled on every side, yet not distressed; we are perplexed, but not in despair; persecuted, but not forsaken; cast down, but not destroyed; always bearing about in the *body* the dying of the Lord Jesus, that the *life* also of Jesus might be manifested *in our body*. For we which live are alway delivered unto death for Jesus' sake, that the *life* also of Jesus might be made *manifest in our mortal flesh* (emphases mine).

These two phrases "in our body" and "in our mortal flesh" settle it that Paul here bears witness to a resuscitation or renewal of the *physical* system through our risen Lord's communication of His own life to it. That is most remarkable, for it speaks of a revivication all the while counteracting attacks of ill health or other damage to the flesh-and-blood organism.

It is a reality which evidently Paul himself was experiencing amid the wear and tear of his exhausting labors for our Lord. So perilous, costly, exacting was his traveling evangelism that he called it a "bearing about in the body the dying of the Lord Jesus," which parallels with another place where he says, "I die daily" (1 Cor. 15:31) and another where he says, "We had the sentence of death in ourselves" (2 Cor. 1:9). Every time he went forth he was, so to speak, taking his life in his hands. What with perils on land and sea, weariness and watchings, scourgings and beatings with rods, three times stoned, once left for dead, three shipwrecks, a night and a day afloat in the water, hunger and thirst, cold and nakedness (dear Paul, how you shame most of us!), it is a marvel that he did not collapse and expire long before the day he laid his head on the executioner's block. It is just as clear to any perceptive observer as it was clear in Paul's consciousness that the fearful mental and physical expenditure was being victoriously counteracted *pari passu* by the infused life of the risen Lord, healing, restoring, renewing, reenergizing.

But in telling us of this health-replenishing life imparted by our Lord, Paul did not speak of it in the *singular*. Note the plural here: "That the life also of Jesus might be manifested in *our* body" and "made manifest in *our* mortal flesh." This, presumably, was a glad reality experienced by Paul's fellow-laborers in the Gospel who traveled with him. (What fellowship in supernatural enduing must have been theirs!) Moreover, Paul speaks of it in such a way as seems to make it *representative* of a phenomenon well known to Christian believers at that time and realized in the experience of not a few.

I will not overpress that, but let me add as of peculiar interest that in *this* kind of healing or reinvigoration, the way of receiving it seems different from that which is prescribed in James 5:14-16. Here there is neither mention nor hint of any "calling for the elders of the assembly." Nor, apparently, was there any laying on of hands or "anointing him with oil in the name of the Lord"—though it *is* just possible, of course, that such procedure was practiced at different points of itineration as emergencies occurred. There is here no picture of a bedfast invalid or of some domestic sickroom—though again a little reading between the lines may possibly suggest that even Paul had his times of nervous prostration when he was grateful for convalescence in homes like Phebe's in Cenchrea. (Compare Rom. 16:1-2 with Acts 18:5: "Pressed in the spirit." See also 2 Cor. 1:8: "Pressed out of measure, above strength, insomuch that we despaired even of life.")

However, whether such surmisings are well-founded or otherwise does not affect the *fact* of this wonderful all-the-while healing and renewing which Paul derived directly from his heavenly Master. It really happened to him as also presumably to others of his Spirit-filled entourage. Does it not seem to tell us that besides our receiving some particular healing at one time or another we are meant to know the Lord Jesus as our indwelling life and health, both mentally and physically?

To me, at least, that is what seems implied; though I would fain avoid forcing it to mean more than it truly does. If the passage were the only such, I would hesitate the more; but there are others which tie in, one of which in particular we shall shortly consider. Also, it fits what Paul taught in 1 Corinthians about the Holy Spirit's "gifts of healings" among the local Christian community.

I believe that where there is full yieldedness of heart, mind, soul, and body, complimented by a grateful, constant prayerfulness and a rich, day-by-day communion with our precious Savior, we may know Him as both our spiritual life and our natural health, as our indwelling *Renewer* both spiritually and physically. I purpose later to furnish Christian testimony to such experience. Just here I am concerned only with exegetical aspects. I simply state what I think may be realized among us on the basis of what the foregoing Scripture seems to imply.

Shall I be labeled a doubting Thomas if once again I add a cautionary note? It jolts and jars me to find some preachers of divine healing asserting, on the supposed warrant of this passage which we are considering (2 Cor. 4:8-10), an impartation of the *physical* life of Christ. What next! Will foolish vagaries *never* cease? Our Lord's present body is not a flesh-and-blood organism but a supernalized physique substantially different from ours. Nor is that celestial body of His either omnipresent or communicable to others. When our Lord heals, quickens, and renews these mortal bodies of ours by His own imparted life, He does so by the Holy Spirit, His *Alter Idem* (His other self yet the same) who indeed *is* omnipresent and communicable.

Furthermore, to say, as some do, that our Lord's physical life *takes the place* of ours is a hyper-imaginative absurdity for which there is not a wisp of support in Scripture. Our Lord indwells all the truly born again. He seeks to infill us, and He does so where there is entire yieldedness. But though He may overspread us, sanctify us, and transform us, He never *substitutes* us! I recently read about a much-esteemed preacher of divine healing who said that it was his habit at close of day to lie on his bed and to exhale away his own life with its wastage and decay and inhale the renewing, *physical* life of the risen Jesus. Soon afterwards, while ministering at a convention, he was seized by pneumonia and died. Much as he was beloved, his mourners found in that coffin of his a problematical comment on his doctrine!

It is wise to read 2 Corinthians 4:8-10 in its full context. Only six verses later Paul adds: "For which cause [i.e., because of this imparted physical renewal amid labor and trial] we faint not; but though our *outward man perish* [lit. being brought to decay], yet the inward man is renewed day by day." So whatever the imparting of our Lord's life to the Christian's body may do, it does not supplant the present, normal process of physical aging and "decaying." It offsets it—may even retard it—but it does not reverse it. There is no turning the clock backward, no circumventing the plaintive sigh: "Age tells." The old machine may be made to run like new, but the old machine is still old. There may be repair or renewal of the parts, but that does not make the car a new model.

Actually, reading 2 Corinthians 4:8-10 with a careful eye to its connection would seem to suggest that this manifesting of our Lord's life in the mortal bodies of His people has to do primarily with Christian *witness bearing* and other love labors for Him (see vv. 1,5,7,11). Over against weariness, opposition, administrative pressures, and exhaustion is our Lord's supernatural healing, quickening-yet-quieting replenishment of both the "outward man" and the "inward man" (vv. 11,16). Many present-day servants of our Lord might do well to seek *that* experience.

Romans 8:11

There is only one other New Testament reference which, so far as I know, may be safely adduced as indicating direct divine renewal of the human body; and perhaps there are some who will want to disqualify even that one. The verse is Romans 8:11.

> But if the Spirit of him that raised up Jesus from the dead dwell in you, he that raised up Christ from the dead shall also quicken (give life to, vitalize) your *mortal bodies* by his Spirit that dwelleth in you (emphasis mine).

Those who would disallow this text as evidence in favor of divine healings tell us that it refers solely to the yet future *resurrection* of the saints, not to present experience. Doubtless it does have that ultimately in view; but *does* it, as they say, refer to that exclusively? I incline to think otherwise.

In both places here, where Paul writes that God "raised up" Jesus from the dead, he uses the Greek word *egeirō*, the usual word for raising from the dead. But when he adds that God will also *"quicken your mortal bodies by his Spirit that dwelleth in you,"* he changes to *zōopoieō*, which means to infuse life or vitalize. Why did Paul switch verbs? Why did he not repeat the earlier verb if he meant *only* the still future "resurrection"? My own persuasion is that when taken with its immediate context, this change to *zōopoieō* (from the noun *zoē*: life) suggests a life-infusing ministry of the Holy Spirit even now, while we are still in the "mortal body." In the New Testament there are three statements about the believer's body which should always be kept in mind.

1. The present mortal body is *dead*. Paul says so in Romans 8:10, the verse preceding our text: "If Christ be in you, the body is *dead* because of sin" (emphasis mine). What does he mean? For an

hour of grim interest, look up what the usual run of commentators say! Obviously Paul does not mean that the heart has ceased to beat and the brain has lost its last flicker of response, that the final spark of life is quenched and the body as a physical organism has expired. No, in keeping with his explanation in chapters 6 and 7 about the believer's judicial death with Christ, Paul means that the body is dead *judicially*, i.e., in the reckoning of God. When our Lord Jesus died that "death for every man" (Heb. 2:9), the whole condemned Adamic humanity was judicially put away in Him who vicariously represented it. As 2 Corinthians 5:14 says, "One died for all, therefore all died"; that is, of course, "all died" in the judicial reckoning of God. The born-again Christian is a "new creature" (2 Cor. 5:17), a part of the new humanity in Christ; but the believer's body, which still belongs to the Adamic humanity, is part of that which is now judicially "dead," by legal death sentence already executed.

2. Although the body *already* has been redeemed by the Calvary purchase price in the sense that there is no more to pay for its release from hereditary disease and death, its *actual* release has not yet been effected. That is because this present intervening age of grace is prolonged with a view to the saving of a vast "multitude, which no man can number" (Rev. 7:9). God holds the redemption title deed, sealed by "precious blood"; but as Romans 8:23 says, "Even we who have the firstfruits of the Spirit, . . . groan within ourselves, waiting for the adoption [the public attestation of our heavenly sonship which brings] . . . the *redemption* of our body."

3. Although, viewed from God's standpoint, the believer's mortal body is now judicially "dead," and although historically its redemptive translation from disease and death into immortality is not yet actualized, it meanwhile becomes a "temple of the Holy Spirit"! In the words of 1 Corinthians 6:19-20: "What? know ye not that your *body* is the temple of the Holy Spirit who is in you, whom ye have of God, and ye are not your own? For ye are bought with a price: therefore glorify God in your *body*, and in your spirit, which are God's" (emphases mine).

We can more easily imagine how astounding those words must have been to those old-time Corinthians when we remember how magnificent were the famous temples of that age! The spectacular temple of Apollo at Corinth; the architecturally unsurpassed Parthenon of the goddess Athena crowning the Acropolis at Athens; the unmatched splendor of the great Diana's temple at Ephesus (one of the seven wonders of the ancient world); and last but not least Israel's ornate, costly, fanatically revered temple of Jehovah at Jerusalem: all of these by their massive masonry and elaborate architecture were of such resplendence as to overawe. But in conjunction with all that and completing the awe-inspiring effect was the (supposed) *indwelling* of the god or goddess. They were the sacrosanct abodes of *deities*.

What thoughts must have stirred the minds of those Corinthian brethren as they read those words of the divinely inspired Apostle: "Know ye not that ye are the *temple* of God, and that the *Spirit of God* dwelleth in you?" (1 Cor. 3:16, emphasis mine)! They were temples of the one and only true God, compared with whom (as those Corinthians then knew) the idol-deities of Greek and Roman temples were grotesque absurdities.

Yet would they not marvel even more at those further words: "Know ye not that your body is the temple of the Holy Spirit who is in you?" Everywhere at that time the Gnostic philosophy prevailed that "matter" is evil and that therefore the source of all the miseries which flog human nature is the physical body. The Christian announcement "Your body is the temple of the Holy Spirit" was revolutionary. What startling suggestion it carries! That which the Holy Spirit indwells becomes itself sanctified thereby, for where He abides He *sheds* holiness. Learn and wonder: not only are the believer's mind and spirit renewed in corresponding measure to that indwelling; but the *body* also, as the outer court of the "temple," is sanctified by it!

Is it surprising then that the Holy Spirit has distinct ministries to the *bodies* of Christian individuals? Does He not prefer His human temples in best repair, even the outer fabric as well as the inner shrine? He who renovates the consecrated personality into "the beauty of holiness," does He not desire for its physical dwelling place a corresponding healthiness? Is not the New Testament ideal of Christian sanctity a holy mind in a healthy body?

If only Christians revered and *treated* their bodies as "temples" of the Holy Spirit, how different would the health of many be! How often is the temple framework dishonored and damaged by wrong eating and drinking, unhygenic habits, intemperateness, inadequate exercise, and insufficient rest! I have actually observed some Christian people bring sickness upon themselves by mistreating their bodies in one way or another, and I have also witnessed their doleful wondering why *God* "sent" it upon them! I have known others to go forward for divine cure in big healing missions and then go right back to living in ways that loudly contradict the commonsensical laws of health. We may well face it squarely: divine healing for the body was never meant to be a substitute for sanitary living or a suspension of natural cause and effect. If we would fain experience supernatural healing or renewal in our bodies, we must not contradict it by knowingly running health hazards. We must consistently honor the body as a hallowed "temple" of our indwelling Lord. If we had a more penetrating insight into this matter of divine healing, I rather think we would find that this failure in our own treatment of the body is one of the commonest reasons why in many cases divine healing does not come.

If, however, we truly *are* honoring the body as the Spirit's temple and are living in affectionate yieldedness to our Savior-King (not neglecting to obey normal health rules), then assuredly we may look to God as our Jehovah-*Rapha:* "The Lord that healeth thee" (Exod. 15:26). We also can expect the Holy Spirit to exercise His health-renewing ministry within us, in accord with Romans 8:11—not only renewing our minds in holiness, but (as the promise says) our "mortal bodies" as well.

I write all this with keen gratitude, for I have known something of that experience. Nevertheless, perhaps I should not press Romans 8:11 too far, for there still may be some who remain skeptical as to its present-day applicability. I too used to have some reservation on that score, and maybe I still would have if it were but a *solitary* reference to the Holy Spirit's activity in the believer's body. The fact is that Romans 8:11 is part of a network of such teaching; and as such, to me, it is diaphanous; i.e., it transmits rays of heavenly light on this comforting reality of health renewal by the Holy Spirit in our "mortal bodies."

OLD TESTAMENT LEGACY

We have now lingered at each clear New Testament reference to divine healing or quickening of the believer's body. There is one further feature, however, which in my judgment should be included in what we may call the Biblical "data." In 2 Corinthians 1:18-20, Paul pens a pronouncement which has an incalculably significant relatedness to this subject.

> God is faithful, so our word to you was not yea and nay [sometimes certain, sometimes doubtful]. For the Son of God, Jesus Christ, who

was proclaimed among you by us, even by me and Silvanus and
Timotheus, was not yea and nay; but in him it [the faithfulness] has
become Yea. For whatever be the promises of God, in him [Christ] is
the *Yea* [certainty] and in him the *Amen* [finality] unto the glory of
God *through us* [Christian believers].

Who can measure the reach of that statement? Who need wonder
any more why the Old Testament is so precious, so indispensable to
us Evangelicals? A minister of the non-evangelical sort remarked
some time ago, "To me the Old Testament is neither more nor less
than whatever any individual sees in it or gets out of it." I replied,
"To me the Old Testament is what our Lord Jesus said it was: the
inspired Word of God throughout; and one of its most magnetic
aspects is its unspeakable treasury of divine promises which now
become ours in Christ."[4]

In the Corinthian text just quoted, Paul enunciated a principle of
utmost importance in the divine administration of redemption. One
may say that it is almost breath-taking. He told us that in our Lord
Jesus Christ, who is the glorious "Yea and Amen" of God's redemptive purpose, *all* the promises of God made under the old covenant,
that is, throughout the Old Testament Scriptures, are now *our*
blood-sealed legacy. They are all *ours* now, in Him, and may be
appropriated with confidence!

Yes, indeed, what a treasury does the Old Testament thus become
to us! What added riches it ensures to us! Every promise is *ours*—in
Christ! Here and there, all over the New Testament Epistles, we find
this principle of property inheritance operating. For instance, in
Hebrews 13:5-6 the Lord's promise to Joshua, "I will never leave
thee, nor forsake thee" (Josh. 1:5), is appropriated with an evident
sense of perfect propriety as being now the property of each Christian; and right on the heels of that, another promise is claimed from
Psalm 118:6 as now being current Christian coinage.

Again and again Old Testament promises reappear in the grasp of
New Testament faith. Yet they are very few out of many—a mere
handful from the "grapes of Eschol." It is to all those Old Testament
promises that Peter primarily refers to when he writes, "His divine
power hath given unto us. . . . *exceeding great and precious promises*" (2
Peter 1:3-4, emphasis mine). Even the so-called kingdom promises,
made originally to the covenant nation, Israel, are now the shared
possession of us Gentile Christians; for in Christ we have become
incorporated into the true Israel. All the divine pledges given
through the Abrahamic and Davidic covenants concerning the ultimate regathering of Israel, the coming millennial reign of Messiah,

and the crowning glories of history are now ours! Nay, even more: for when that Messianic earthly rule eventually comes, we shall be in it, not only as privileged residents and subjects of the glorious King, as all others will be, but also as the blood-redeemed and glorified members of the *Ecclesia;* and thus we shall *reign with* Him! Marvel of marvels! Ten million, million hallelujahs!

As already remarked, this writing-over of all the Old Testament promises to us Christian believers has a powerful bearing on our present subject, the divine healing of the body. Readily do some of those healing promises spring to mind. I quote here only two or three of the more prominent.

> If thou wilt diligently hearken to the voice of the LORD thy God, and wilt do that which is right in his sight, and wilt give ear to his commandments, and keep all his statutes, I will put none of these diseases upon thee, which I have brought upon the Egyptians: for I am *Jehovah who healeth thee.* (Exodus 15:26)

Incidentally, notice there that the fulfilling of the promises is made contingent upon right living and obedience to the "commandments" of God's Word.

> Bless the LORD, O my soul, and forget not all his benefits: who forgiveth all thine iniquities; who *healeth all thy diseases;* who redeemeth thy life from destruction; who crowneth thee with lovingkindness and tender mercies; who satisfieth thy years with good, so that thy youth is renewed like the eagle's.
> (Psalm 103:2-5)

So evidently diseases had been contracted and permitted, or there would not have been the healings from them. Reflect also that there is nothing in these promises to preclude, much less disqualify, the "use of means"—of natural medication. Hezekiah is said to have been the godliest of all the kings who ever sat on the throne of Judah (2 Kings 18:3), but when he was "sick unto death" (20:1) God used a natural medication and caused *it* to cure him (v. 7); yet in doing so He gave him (and us) this accompanying promise:

> Thus saith the LORD, the God of David thy father, I have heard thy prayer, I have seen thy tears: behold, *I will heal thee:* on the third day thou shalt go up unto the house of the LORD.
> (2 Kings 20:5)

See also Deuteronomy 7:15, 2 Chronicles 6:28, Isaiah 57:18, Ezekiel 34:16; and hear the psalmist's testimony to the divine healing he experienced as set forth in Psalm 30:2-3.

> O Jehovah my God,
> I cried unto thee, and *thou hast healed me.*
> O Jehovah,
> Thou hast brought up my soul from Sheol;
> Thou hast *kept me alive.* . . .

With those voices ringing down from the Old Covenant days, accentuated now through the "yea and amen unto *us*" of the New Covenant, we rest our case.

INTERIM CONCLUSION

Although much present-day preaching of divine healing is, in my judgment, misfounded on a wrong interpretation of Scripture, there remains nevertheless sufficient evidence in the New Testament that a ministry of divine healing for the body is meant to be still in operation today, at least inside local Christian churches. As we have seen, there is (1) clear promise of such healing in response to faith, (2) a clear inclusion of healing in the Spirit's distribution of "gifts" among believers, (3) clear reference to such healing as being experienced by the Lord's people in those early days of the church. Therefore we should guard against letting hostile reactions against off-center extremists blind us to the true teaching of the Word. Prejudice is sometimes even worse than extremism! Yes, divine healings are meant for the church today.

NOTES

[1]Among his various peculiarities, Bullinger theorized that we cannot now apply some of the teachings in the earlier Pauline Epistles (1 and 2 Thess., 1 and 2 Cor., Gal., Rom.) because they were all written before the close of the Acts while the "kingdom" was still being offered to *Israel* and before the "mystery" (the church) had been divulged. The epistles which swing into play for the church after the Acts period, for the present age, are Ephesians, Colossians, Philippians, 1 and 2 Timothy, and Titus. That is why, for instance (says Bullinger), believers' baptism in water is nowhere mentioned in the later epistles written after the close of Acts, which is also why the "mystery" does not appear until Ephesians. But Bullinger, not uncommonly, is wrong on both counts. Water baptism is referred to in Colossians 2:12, where it *cannot* mean "spiritual" baptism (as Bullinger says), for it is a being "*buried*" with Him in baptism," whereas baptism "in the Spirit" is *never* into death and burial but into the "Spirit of *life.*" As for the "mystery" (the Church), it *is* referred to in the earlier epistles; Romans 16:25-27 refers to the church as something already taught and well-known to Christian believers.

[2]R. A. Torrey, *Divine Healing* (Grand Rapids: Baker Book House, reprint 1974), pp. 18-19.

[3]Rowland V. Bingham, *The Bible and the Body*, pp. 90-91.

[4]J. Sidlow Baxter, *Rethinking Our Priorities* (Grand Rapids: Zondervan Publishing House, 1974).

PART THREE

Divine Healing
In Present Experience

Is the Evidence Conclusive?

None are so blind as those who will not see,
    None are so deaf as those who will not hear;
Though proofs build up like solid masonry,
    And honest logic reads the meaning clear,
Unless almighty God, with deafening shout,
    Or flaming letters, speaks from out the skies,
Agnostic prejudice can only doubt
    All other kinds of proof to ears and eyes:
But if God wrote across the skies this day
    In flaming signs which *had* to be believed,
Tomorrow learned doubt again would say,
    "Our very senses must have been deceived!"

—J.S.B.

CHAPTER NINE

"We Speak That We Do Know"

We have reached the third and final area of these inquiries into divine healing of the body, and our question now is, What evidence of it is there in actual, *present-day experience?* After unprejudiced consideration of varied testimony, my own preliminary advice is that we need to exercise due caution. It is an area in which there is a strange mixture of the merely seeming with the real, of the false with the true, of sometimes loud claims with sparse proofs, of hucksterism with genuine miracle. All of us who drive cars have seen the road sign PROCEED WITH CAUTION. We need to prop that sign up just here. Our mental attitude may wisely be a blend of sincere open-mindedness and skeptical hesitancy.

It seems to me that in scientifically ascertaining the genuineness or otherwise of any cure presented as a direct divine act, there are four criteria which we must strictly apply.

1. The disease or injury must be of sufficient seriousness and duration, either organic or structural (not merely functional), and professionally diagnosed by fully qualified doctors so as to exclude all possibility of exaggeration or deception as to the patient's condition.
2. The healing must be instantaneous or in rapidly connected sequences and of such an abnormal nature as to put it beyond autosuggestion, hypnotism, personal magnetism, or any other merely natural explanation.

3. The healing must be admitted or, better still, *verified* by fully qualified doctors, including the patient's own private physician, following a fully documented case history.
4. The healing must be further verifiable after a long enough period of time to demonstrate conclusively that it was no mere remission or temporary psychosomatic reversion.

In this chapter and the next I propose to submit four instances of divine healing which measure up to those four tests. They are written by the persons themselves who *experienced* the healings, and their documentation is indicated clearly from point to point. They are selected from *very many* which are now available, and I have picked them out as representing medically and even surgically hopeless cases. The four, respectively, are miraculous healings of (1) incurable multiple sclerosis, (2) terminal metastasized cancer, (3) massive hemorrhage, (4) irremediable skeletal damage with complications due to accident. The four witnesses are all still alive, years after their miracle healing, and can speak for themselves. The last thing I did before submitting this treatise to my publisher was to contact them and hear from their own lips that they are *still* cured and in good health.

THE CASE OF MRS. MARION BURGIO

Mrs. Marion Burgio and her husband live in a quiet neighborhood across the bay from the bustling city of San Francisco. They were living a very routine life until her world collapsed in seventeen years agony of slow dying from an incurable disease.

It was in my fortieth year that I began to die. Not rapidly or all at once, but bit by bit. Slowly, across the next 17 years, my body stopped living—each section dying with agonizing pain.

I first noticed it one afternoon at the Boysen Paint Company in Emeryville, across the bay from San Francisco.

I had worked at Boysen as a printer and typesetter for many years. This particular afternoon I picked up my tweezers and reached into the tray for some extra-fine type. But something was wrong. It was almost imperceptible, yet my eyes were blurred and my hand was shaking. At the same time, I noticed a strange numbness in my hands and legs. Little did I know that at that moment death had tapped me on the shoulder.

A year passed. Then two. I had been to half a dozen doctors in the Bay area. One said I had hepatitis. Another said I suffered from spasms of the esophagus. A third doctor recommended gall-bladder surgery, which I had.

My husband Angelo, I call him "Ang," was a supervisor at the Alameda Naval Air Base. Every few weeks he would come home and say, "I heard about a new doctor. Let's try him."

One doctor prescribed glasses for my double vision. Another said the numbness in my hands was caused by poor circulation. My condition grew worse. One day I fainted at work. That night I told Ang I was going to leave my job. . . . Rosemary, our daughter, was married and our twin sons, Arthur and Don, were both working. Besides, Ang and I had long wanted another child. We agreed this would be a good time for me to quit work and adopt a baby boy. If, as one of the doctors had suggested, all I had was frayed nerves, then the change of pace might be just what I needed.

It turned out I needed far more. Several weeks after little Eugene arrived, Ang went with me to the grocery store. Waiting in the check-out line, I suddenly grew dizzy, slumping against Ang for support. As the line inched forward, I found I could not pick up my feet. I had to force them to slide across the floor. I was scared!

A top neurologist in San Francisco recommended hospitalization and I spent a month in Presbyterian Hospital. . . . Still no diagnosis. I finally called Ang to come and take me home.

Three weeks later I noticed the middle finger on my right hand looked infected. Ang took me to a new doctor on MacArthur Boulevard. He lanced the finger and then, after finishing with the bandage, turned to me.

"Is there something else wrong, Mrs. Burgio?" he asked.

I was hostile. "No, why?"

"Well, if I had treated a normal patient the way I treated you, she would have been screaming in pain. You didn't seem to feel the pain at all." He hesitated. "Could I give you a physical?" I sighed. "Okay. I guess one more examination won't hurt."

The finger healed slowly and I had to return twice before my scheduled appointment. Each time the doctor asked questions, and I knew he suspected more than he was saying. Then the day before I was scheduled for the physical, the bottom fell out of my life.

Ang went to work early as usual. Little Eugene, who was about two years old came running into the bedroom and began pulling on the covers. I yawned, put my feet over the side of the bed and tried to stand up. Instead my legs gave way under me and I fell heavily to the floor. The carpet cushioned my fall, but when I tried to stand up, nothing worked. My legs were useless—paralyzed. My arms were almost as bad. I was helpless.

I finally managed to turn over on my stomach and wriggle out into the middle of the bedroom. Eugene was standing beside the dresser, staring. "Mommy's just playing a game," I whispered, not wanting to alarm him. Then I began the slow, laborious crawl down the hall and into the family room. My hands would not work, so I had to move painfully along using my elbows and hips.

It took ten minutes to make the trip to the family room. By then I was . . . exhausted. I tried once again to get to my feet, but my muscles were useless. I couldn't even reach up for the phone.

Then, to my horror, I saw Eugene open the sliding glass doors and toddle out onto the patio. He was heading toward the wrought-iron gate that led to the busy street. I cried out, but my voice broke and faded. I started to crawl after him.

The wrought-iron gate was open. By the time I reached the patio, Eugene had disappeared. I kept crawling, pushing myself across the rough concrete on my elbows and hips. Panic swept over me as I heard the cars on the busy boulevard.

"Dear God, please help me. Help me!"

But the words were lost in my sobs. I could go no farther. I collapsed.

The clock was striking 11 when I looked up and saw Eugene coming back through the gate. "Up, Mama, up," he said.

I tried to move, but it was impossible. I tried to talk, but only hoarse tremors came out. Then I felt it. The muscles in my upper back trembled as they began to pull my shoulder blades together. "Dear God, what is this?" I cried. Then in my sudden flash of pain, I felt my neck snap back. My shoulders wrenched as though caught in a devilish vise. I began to gag as my head was forced backward.

Finally the spasms ceased. Mercifully, Eugene had disappeared into the house. For five long hours I lay on the patio, helpless in the blazing sun. "Please, God," I begged through my desperate tears, "let somebody come to help me."

It was around four o'clock when, as though in answer to my prayer, my friend, Anne Kennedy, appeared at the gate. "Marion, what are you doing there on the ground?" she cried. As she took a closer look and saw my distorted face, she gasped and ran into the house to call Ang.

Later, in the examining room, I could hear the doctor's voice. "I suspected it. Now I'm sure. Multiple sclerosis."

The nurse gave me a shot for pain and treated the raw, skinned places on my body. Later, at home, Ang took down the dictionary and read to me the definition of multiple sclerosis. "A diseased condition marked by patches of hardened tissue in the brain or the spinal cord and associated especially with partial or complete paralysis, jerking muscle tremors and sometimes intense pain."

As the months slipped into years, I lost track of the number of trips to the hospital. Over those [seventeen] years I was to learn that multiple sclerosis is a strange disease. It will take you right to the brink of death, back off and allow you, its victim, a partial remission, and then, without warning, send your body into horrible spasms.

Ang employed a full-time housekeeper and eventually a daytime nurse. We moved from our home in San Leandro to nearby Walnut Creek so I could be near our daughter Rosemary.

In the months that followed, I slipped deeper and deeper into the dark pit of despair. I knew the disease was incurable. Ang was having to spend every cent he made just to keep me alive. My old friends who used to visit me slowly drifted away. Who could possibly enjoy visiting someone so twisted and distorted, now unable to see or talk clearly, who at best could only drag herself around on crutches and utter slurred words?

One day in the doctor's office, I broke down. I was losing my hearing. I couldn't even comb my hair or feed myself. I was totally dependent upon others.

The doctor said, "Mrs. Burgio, there is nothing more that I can do for you. You are beyond medical help."

"I wish I were dead," I wept.

In June our family received an invitation to attend the golden wedding anniversary celebration of Fred and Helen Smith, former neighbors in Oakland whom we had not seen in 11 years. My enthusiasm for going anywhere was at an all-time low, but Rosemary convinced me I should go. "We'll make it a family affair," she said, "and it will please Daddy."

Helen, a striking woman with friendly blue eyes, was at the door with a warm welcome for all of us as Ang rolled me up the sidewalk in my wheelchair.

"Oh, Marion," she said as she bent over to kiss me, "I'm so happy you came. I just know you are going to be healed."

Puzzled, I looked up at Ang. Neither of us understood what she could possibly be talking about. However, during the evening Helen told us all about the miracle services held by Kathryn Kuhlman. . . .

Helen was very enthusiastic about this new dimension she had found in her religious life, but Ang and I just couldn't take it all in—prayer meetings, healing services, and what she called "the power of the Holy Spirit." . . .

A few weeks after the party, my disease exploded with all the fury of a hurricane and it was back to the hospital for me. . . . My vision was badly impaired, my hearing almost gone, and the muscles in my throat had deteriorated to the point where I could not swallow food. The sad look on my husband's face was becoming too much to bear.

It was during this time of deep depression that Helen Smith and another friend came to visit me at the hospital. While there, Helen asked, "Do you mind if I say a prayer over you?" I looked at Ang in puzzlement. He just shrugged as Helen placed her hands on my stomach and began to pray softly. . . .

As she was praying, from far off I heard the sound of music. Everything had been distorted for so long, yet this music was beautifully clear. It was the sound of a choir accompanied by stringed instruments. . . .

I was released from the hospital two weeks later. The doctor told Ang there was nothing more that could be done and it would be better for me to spend my last days at home. Three days after I got home, I received a card from Helen. Ang read it to me.

"Dear Marion:

Glad you are home again. Hope you are feeling better. You are going to be well again. Praise the Lord. Both of you will enjoy the tape I am sending you today. You will find great help and inspiration from it. Hold on to your faith and believe. In case you go to Kathryn Kuhlman's meeting at the coliseum, I'll be there in the choir praying for you. Accept your healing when the time comes. God bless you, dear. Remember, you are being healed. Get there early, about 3:30 p.m. Wheelchairs go in first.   Helen"

"Do you understand her?" I said to Ang when he finished reading.

"Not really," Ang replied.

He examined the small cassette tape that had arrived in the same mail. "It's by Kathryn Kuhlman," he said. My hearing ability was so distorted at this stage that I could not get very interested in listening to a tape by Kathryn Kuhlman. . . .

Five days later, on July 28, we received another card from Helen urging me to go to the meeting. . . .

The next evening the phone rang. I heard Ang say, "Yes, Helen,

I'm taking the day off and I'm going to take Marion to the meeting."

When he hung up, I began to cry. "Please, Ang, I don't feel like going. . . . I don't want to go."

The next day was the worst day of my life. I was twisted far more severely than ever before. My hands looked like claws and I was shaking like a vibrator. Even before I got out of bed, I took three pain killers, but they had no effect.

"I'm not going!" I cried.

Ang was firm. "We have nothing to lose, honey; let's go see what it's all about."

The trip to the coliseum was horrible. I cried all the way, begging Ang to take me back home. When we arrived at the coliseum, one of the ushers tried to help Ang with my wheelchair and I went all to pieces. "Oh, don't touch me . . . please don't touch me! I just want my husband to take care of me."

She moved back and stood by helplessly while Ang tried to calm me down.

Finally, we were settled in the huge coliseum, which was filling rapidly as the choir was rehearsing on the platform. Soon, every available seat was taken.

All around us were people in wheelchairs and on stretchers. I could not comprehend the amount of human suffering that had come together in that one place. Yet there was something else present—something intangible—*hope*. Everyone, or at least nearly everyone, seemed to have it on his or her face. It was as though each person was straining for some unseen hand to reach down and touch him or her. My heart ached for everyone and I began to pray, asking the Lord to help them.

Suddenly the choir began to sing again. This time the great crowd joined them. That song! "Ang!" I cried out. "It's the same song and the same choir I've been hearing ever since Helen's prayer.". . .

All the people around me seemed to have their arms raised as they sang. I asked myself, "What kind of meeting is this anyway?" I looked over at Ang and even with my double vision, I could see he had his arms up also. . . .

I wanted to scream. Everyone seemed so happy—even those in wheelchairs—yet I remained miserable and confused.

I felt Ang's hand on my arm. "Here she comes. This must be Kathryn Kuhlman."

I strained to see, but my eyes simply would not focus on the platform, which was at least some 70 yards away. All I could see was a bright glow—like an aura. . . .

"What's she doing?" I kept asking Ang.

He tried to describe what was happening. She introduced certain guests. She told a few stories. There was more singing and then she began to speak. To me the sounds were all jumbled. The only word I heard plainly was "Bible."

"Ang," I whispered, "I think we better get out of here . . . I feel funny."

He ignored me. His eyes were riveted on the platform.

Just then a woman dressed in red moved slowly down the aisle beside us. Her daughter was in front of her and her husband was walking behind her. As she got opposite our row, she fell to the floor.

"Oh, dear God," I moaned, "help her." Her family was bending over her, crying and trying to help her to her feet. I began crying also as I realized what my own family must have been going through as they had tried to help me.

When I looked up, I noticed another girl, a young woman, lying on a wheelchair stretcher farther down the aisle. She was dressed in a plaid suit, but it was obvious her body, like mine, was the twisted victim of multiple sclerosis.

"Dear Lord, help her, too," I prayed.

Later the woman in red passed by my wheelchair. *She was transformed* (emphasis mine).

"Ang!" I cried out. "She's been healed!"

I could not tell all that was happening or even understand what was being said, but I knew it was the same woman. No longer was she hobbling—she was almost running. Her face was radiant!

It was then that the struggle within my own body began. Suddenly my knees began to shake. I tried to hold them with my hands, but things were happening too quickly. My feet were being pulled out of the foot rests of the wheelchair and pressed against the floor. It seemed as though two great forces were at work within my body— one pushing me down and another pulling me up. I felt myself being lifted up, but the downward force was too great and I fell back into the chair.

Ang was alarmed at my movements and said, "Marion, what's wrong? What is happening to you?"

I couldn't answer, for I was literally being pushed right up and out of my wheelchair. It was as though the chains that had bound me had suddenly broken. I was on my feet! Standing! And as I stood up, my twisted hand just stretched right out. I couldn't believe my eyes—my hand was straight and normal!

Just as quickly as I had stood up, I began to walk. I didn't know where I was going or why—but I was on my way. Past Ang. Past the place where Eugene was sitting. Down the aisle and toward the platform. Ang, in a state of shock, was close behind me.

The next thing I remember was Kathryn Kuhlman's voice. "You're healed, honey! Just walk across the stage."

And then it dawned on me that I was walking, sometimes half-running, in front of thousands of people. I felt bathed in God's love! He was real! He had come to me! He loved me enough to minister to me personally and, glory of all glories, to fill me with His beautiful Holy Spirit!

"Thank you! Thank you!" I exclaimed to Miss Kuhlman.

Her face was smiling. "Don't thank me," she said. "I'm just as surprised and happy as you. Thank Jesus. He's the One Who healed you."

"I thought you were a farce," I said, crying with joy. "I came only to please my family and my friends, Helen and Fred, who sing in your choir."

Amazed at myself, I realized I could talk! My speech was normal! My eyes, too. I could see clearly! My legs were working! The pain was gone! I could breathe! Just as Helen had said it would happen, I had been healed!

I came off the platform unaware that the Lord had yet another joy in store for me. I looked up and there was the girl in the plaid suit. Walking! She had been healed also! The tears started all over again. What joy to know that the two people I had prayed for—the woman in red and the girl with MS—had both been touched by God. And so had I. The trip home was far different from the trip to the coliseum. We sang all the way. The first thing I did was call Rosemary. "I'm healed!" I shouted.

"Oh, Mama, you've gone bananas," Rosemary chuckled. . . .

The next morning, for the first time in ten years, I jumped out of bed and pulled open the window blinds so the summer sun could come streaming into the bedroom. I headed for the kitchen to fix Ang some coffee while he dressed.

Half an hour after Ang left for work, Rosemary came rushing through the door. I was in the kitchen drinking coffee. She stood there with her mouth open. "Mother! Mother! What's happened to you?" she cried in disbelief.

She was like that for the next two hours as I told her everything. All she could do was weep and shake her head. Everyone who came wept unashamedly in the presence of the miracle our Lord had wrought.

Monday morning I went to Doctors' Hospital for my regular X-ray appointment. The technician who had taken my X-rays for the last two years looked at me strangely.

"You must be Marion Burgio's twin sister," she said.

I laughed. "No, Betty. I'm not Marion's twin. I'm Marion."

She grabbed me and pulled me into a side room. "What happened to you? Last week you were dying. Now look at you!". . .

Just at that moment the door swung open and the doctor walked in. He stared at me but said nothing—just motioned me to get ready for my X-rays. I undressed and leaned up against the slanted X-ray table. The doctor stood watching.

"Don't you have any pain?" he asked.

"No," I said evenly.

"Haven't you had pain?"

"Oh, yes, constantly. But not any more."

"When did the pain go away?"

"Last Tuesday night."

He asked no more questions, just kept turning me and snapping X-ray pictures. Through the thick glass window I could see Betty watching.

Finally she could take no more. She called out from behind the lead shield. "You remember Mrs. Burgio, don't you, doctor? She was here twelve days ago with multiple sclerosis."

The doctor's expression never changed. "You had an ulcer, too, didn't you?"

"I did, but I don't have it any more."

"H'm, how do you know?"

"I don't have any more pain. I eat anything I want. I don't have to take medicine any more."

He cleared his throat as if he wanted to ask more, but had decided to keep silent.

It was sheer joy to be able to dress myself without assistance. I was so wrapped up in the realization of what I was doing for myself that I did not hear the receptionist when she returned:

"You may go home now, Mrs. Burgio. I don't think we'll have to see you again."

More than anything, I wanted to tell the doctor about the miracle service. But he was gone. I walked out into the hot August sun. A fresh breeze was blowing off the bay; the sky was so clear I could almost see into tomorrow. . . .

As I walked to my personal physician's office, I was wondering how he would react. After all, he had treated me for almost 13 years and the last time he saw me, I was completely helpless.

He was standing in the hall talking to the receptionist when I entered the waiting room. I rang the buzzer on the desk and stepped back. He glanced up at me and started to turn away. My heart went out to him as he turned and looked again.

"Mrs. Burgio?" he asked timidly.

I just grinned.

"Where's your wheelchair?"

"I don't need it any more."

"But your canes . . ."

"I've put them aside also."

He looked at his nurse. "The hospital just called about her X-rays. I told them they had made a mistake . . . that they had the wrong person. Now I'm not sure." He was silent for a moment. "Get all of Mrs. Burgio's files and bring them to my office."

I sat in the examining room waiting for the doctor to finish looking at my files. Finally he came through the door and closed it behind him.

"I suppose you're going to tell me your MS is healed."

"Right!" I grinned.

He had me sit on the side of the table while he tapped my knee with his little rubber hammer. For more than ten years there had been little or no knee reflexes. Now my leg jerked at the slightest touch of the hammer.

"I just don't understand," he admitted.

"Do you believe in miracles?"

He looked at me blankly. "No, I don't."

Once again he checked my reflexes, twisted my arms and legs and listened for long moments with his stethoscope.

"I'm completely baffled," he admitted. "It's as if you had been born again."

"That's it exactly, doctor." I laughed. "I *have* been born again."

And then I told him the full story of my beautiful miracle healing. He listened patiently, then spoke.

"You've been my patient for thirteen years," he said quietly. "I am so glad for you."

My heart felt a deep twinge of sadness for him as I said, "Doctor, you cared for me all those years—that is true. I could not have asked for better medical care. I will always be grateful to you for that. But the Lord healed me. And the glory for that goes to God."

His eyes were serious as he studied my face. I knew that he was a learned medical doctor, and that my knowledge was limited; but I also knew I had something he didn't have. He knew it also.

"While I don't understand it, I wish I had a little of whatever it is that you have, to give to my other patients," he said thoughtfully.

"All you have to do is reach out, doctor," I said, "and God will touch you, too."

His eyes were moist as he took me by the elbow and helped me to the floor from the table. He walked to the door of the examining room with me and lingered for a moment.

"Doctor," I said, "is it true that multiple sclerosis is incurable?"

He paused, then answered, "Medically speaking, there is no known cure."

"Is it true that I am healed?"

He nodded his head and gently bit his lower lip. *"You are not only healed, Mrs. Burgio; you are a new person!"*

"Then to God be the glory," I said. I gave him a little hug, opened the door and walked out into the bright day.[1]

POLICE CAPTAIN LEVRIER TESTIFIES

John LeVrier is a captain in the Houston Police Department, Houston, Texas. Since his remarkable healing some years ago, I have both seen him and heard him speak in public before an audience of 7000, when he gave every evidence of robust health and radiant joy.

I have been a policeman since I was twenty-one years old. I started with the Houston Police Department back in 1936 and worked my way up to the rank of Captain of the Accident Division. In all those years I had never been sick. But in December, 1968, when I went in for a physical examination, things changed.

I had known Dr. Bill Robbins since he had been an intern and I was a rookie cop. He used to ride with me in my prowl car when I first started on the force. Following what I thought was a routine physical exam in his office in the St. Joseph's Professional Building, Dr. Robbins pulled off his rubber gloves and sat on the end of the table. He shook his head. "I don't like what I find, John," he said. "I want you to see a specialist."

I glanced at him as I tucked my shirt in my pants and buckled my gun belt around my waist. "A specialist? What for? My back hurts some, but what cop's back. . . ."

He wasn't listening. "I'm going to send you right on up to see Dr. McDonald, a urologist in this same building."

I knew better than to argue; and two hours later, following an even more thorough examination, I was listening to another physician, Dr. Newton McDonald. He minced no words. "How soon can you go into the hospital, Captain?"

"Hospital?" There was just a tinge of fear in my voice.

"I don't like what I find," he said deliberately. "Your prostate gland should be about the size of a hickory nut, but it's the size of a lemon. The only way I can tell what is wrong is run a biopsy. We can't wait. You ought to be in the hospital no later than tomorrow morning."

I went straight home. After supper Sara Ann put the three children to bed. John was only five, Andrew seven, and Elizabeth nine. Then I broke the news.

She listened quietly. We'd had a happy life together. "Don't put it off, John," she said evenly. "We have too much to live for."

I looked at her, leaning up against the edge of the kitchen counter, so young, so pretty. I thought of our three beautiful children already in bed. She was right, I did have a lot to live for.

Three evenings later, after extensive hospital examinations (including the biopsy), I sat propped up in bed at the hospital, eating dinner. The door to my room opened. It was Dr. McDonald and one of the doctors on the hospital staff. They closed the door and then pulled up chairs beside my bed. I knew busy doctors didn't have time to chat socially and I felt my pulse begin to throb in my throat.

Dr. McDonald didn't leave me guessing long. "Captain, I'm afraid we have some distressing news." He paused. The words were hard to utter. I waited, trying to keep my eyes focused on his lips. "You have cancer."

I saw his lips move and form the word, but my ears refused to register the sound. Over and over I could see the word on his lips. Cancer. Cancer. Just like that. One day I'm as strong as an ox, a veteran of 33 years on the police force. The next day I have cancer.

It seemed like an eternity before I could respond. "Well, which way do we go? I guess you'll have to take it out."

"It's not that simple," he said, clearing his throat. "It's malignant and too far advanced for us to handle it here. We're referring you to the doctors at the M. D. Anderson Tumor Institute. They're known all over the world for their research in cancer treatment. If anyone can help you, they can. But it doesn't look good, Captain, and we would be lying if we held out any hope for the future."

Both doctors were sympathetic. I could tell they were moved, but they knew I was a veteran police officer and would demand the facts. They gave them to me as frankly, yet as gently, as they could. Then they left.

I sat looking at the cold food on my tray. Everything seemed lifeless. The coffee, the half-eaten swiss steak, the applesauce. I pushed it away and swung my legs over the side of the bed. Cancer. No hope.

Walking to the window I stood looking out over the city of Houston, a city which I knew better than the back of my hand. It was cancerous too, filled with crime and disease like any big city. For a third of a century I had been working trying to stop the spread of that cancer, but it seemed like an endless task. The sun was just setting and its dying rays caught the spires of the church steeples rising above the rooftops. I'd never noticed, but Houston seemed to be filled with churches.

I was a member of one of them, the First Baptist Church. In fact, I was an active deacon in the church, although my personal faith didn't amount to much. . . . Now here I was, face to face with death, groping for something to stand on. But as I put my feet down into the water there was no bottom. I felt as if I were sinking. . . .

I walked back to the bed and sat on the edge, staring into the gray-black dusk that seemed to be closing in on me. How would I tell her, and the kids, that I was going to die?

The next day the doctors from the M. D. Anderson Institute came in. There were more tests. Dr. Delclose, the doctor in charge of my case, really got honest with me. "All I can tell you is you had better be prepared to see an awful lot of doctors," he said.

"How long do I have?" I said.

"I can't give you any hope," he said frankly. "Maybe a year, maybe a year and a half. The cancer is very extensive in your entire lower abdomen. The only way we can treat it is with massive doses of radiation, which means we'll have to kill a lot of healthy tissue at the same time. However, if we are to prolong your life at all, we must get started."

I signed a release and they started cobalt treatment the same day.

I believed in prayer. We used to pray for the sick every Wednesda night at the First Baptist Church. But we prefaced our prayer for healing with the words, "If it's Your will, heal."... I believed that God was certainly able to heal people, but I just assumed that He wasn't in the miracle-performing business today.

Thus, when I went into radiation, my body shaved and marked off with a blue pencil like a side of beef ready for the butcher's cleaver, the only prayer I knew to say was, "Lord, let this machine do what it was designed to do."... The cancer was in the prostate area and had to be treated from all angles, so the huge cobalt machine circled the table, the radiation penetrating my body from every side.

The treatments lasted for six weeks, one a day. I was released from the hospital and allowed to go back to work, coming in each morning to receive the cobalt.

Four months passed after I had been diagnosed. Easter was approaching and Sara mentioned that it looked like it would be happier than Christmas. Maybe the cobalt had done its job, or even better, maybe the doctors had made a mistake. Then, just 120 days after the first diagnosis, the pain hit.

It was a Friday noon. I had promised to meet Sara at the little restaurant where we often met for lunch. She had already arrived. I grinned, laid my policeman's cap on the window sill, and slipped into the booth beside her. As I sat down I felt like I had been stabbed with a white hot dagger. The pain surged through my right hip in excruciating spasms. I was unable to speak and just looked at Sara in mute agony. She grabbed my arm.

"John," she gasped, "what is it?"

The pain slowly subsided, leaving me so weak I could hardly talk. I tried to tell her; then, like the tide moving in over the salt flats, it returned. It was like fire in my bones. My face beaded with perspiration and I pulled at my collar to loosen my tie. The waitress who had come to take our order, sensed something was wrong. "Captain LeVrier," she said with concern, "are you all right?"

"I'll make it," I finally said. "I've just had a sudden pain."

But we decided not to eat. Instead we went straight to the hospital and Dr. Delclose immediately set up more X-rays. As they were preparing me I put my hand on my right hip and could feel the indentation. It was about the size of a silver dollar and felt like a hole under the skin. The X-rays showed it up for what it was: the cancer had eaten a hole all the way through my hip. Only the outer skin was covering the cavity.

"I'm sorry, Captain," the doctor said with resignation. "The cancer is spreading as expected." Then in measured tones he concluded: "We'll start the cobalt again and do everything we can to make your time as painless as possible."

The daily trips to the hospital began all over again.

Sara tried to be calm. She had worked in the Police Department before our marriage and had been exposed to death many times. But this was different. I didn't know it at the time, but the doctors had told her that I probably had no more than six months to live.

I kept on working, although I was growing weaker and weaker. . . . One afternoon Sara picked me up from work and said, "John, I've been thinking. I've been out of circulation a long time. What would you say if I went back to work?" . . . It began to dawn on me what she was doing. She was getting things in order. It was time for me to do the same thing. But before I could, a new development took place—surgery.

"It's the only way to keep you alive," the woman surgeon said. "This type of cancer feeds on hormones. We are going to have to redirect the hormone trend in your body through surgery. If we don't do this, you are really going out fast."

I agreed to the surgery but within another 120 days the cancer reappeared on the surface. This time in my spine.

I first noticed it on a Saturday afternoon in June. Sara had taken the children to a Vacation Bible School picnic and I was home, trying to set out a little potted plant in the flower bed. By now I was so weak I could hardly bend over, but I thought the exercise would help. I had dug a small hole in the ground and bent over to pick up the potted plant when the pain, like a million volts of lightning, surged through my lower back. I fell forward into the dirt.

I never dreamed such pain could exist. No one was around to help me so I dragged myself, partially on my hands and knees, partially on my stomach, up the steps and into the house. Then, for the first time, I let myself go. Lying on the floor in that empty house, I wept and moaned uncontrollably. . . . There followed another series of cobalt treatments with more hopeless looks from the doctors. I had received the death sentence. . . . As the summer ended we packed the family into the car and set out on what I thought was to be my last vacation. I wanted to make it a good one for the children. . . . Sara and I both believed it would be our last summer together as a family.

I returned to Houston and tried to patch up loose ends. But when life is frayed beyond splicing, it's impossible to pick up the strings.

All you can do is let them dangle and wait for the end.

One Saturday morning, in the early fall, I walked into the den and turned on the TV. Our pastor at the First Baptist Church, John Bisango, had a program called "Higher Ground." John had come to Houston from Oklahoma where his church had been recognized as the most evangelistic church in the Southern Baptist Convention. What had happened in Oklahoma was beginning to happen in Houston as this dynamic young pastor began to turn that huge church right side up. I was thrilled with his ministry.

Too weak to get up, I sat slumped in the chair as the program ended. "I believe in miracles," a woman's voice said. I glanced up. I wasn't impressed; very few Baptists are impressed about a woman preacher. But as the program progressed and this woman, Kathryn Kuhlman, talked of wonderful healing miracles, something inside me clicked. "Can this be for real?" I wondered.

The show closed. . . . Suddenly I saw a familiar name: Dick Ross, producer.

I knew Dick.

I had kept in contact with Dick across the years. . . . I picked up the phone and called him.

"Dick, I've just watched the Kathryn Kuhlman show. Are those healings real?"

"Yes, John, they're real," Dick answered. "But you'd have to attend one of these meetings at the Shrine Auditorium to believe it for yourself. Why do you ask?"

I hesitated, then spoke it out. "Dick, I've got something terribly wrong with me. I have cancer. I've already had it break out in three areas of my body and I'm afraid the next time it will kill me. I know I sound like I'm grasping at straws, but that's what a drowning man does."

"I'll send you the books," Dick said.

Sara and I both read her books and became avid watchers of the TV program. "Where have we been all our lives?" Sara asked. "I've never even heard of her before, yet she's world famous."

In February I knew my time was running out. Sara and the children encouraged me. "Daddy," Elizabeth said, "you go to California and we'll stay home and pray. We believe God will heal you."

I looked at Sara Ann. Her eyes were moist as she nodded and said, "I believe He's going to heal you, too."

On Friday, February 19, I flew from Houston to Los Angeles. Old friends in Los Angeles loaned me their car and I found a motel in Santa Monica. But as a policeman and as a Baptist, I wanted to size up Miss Kuhlman before I attended the meeting on Sunday.

(Captain LeVrier here tells of meeting Miss Kuhlman and of accompanying her to the auditorium on Sunday.)

We went in through the stage entrance and Miss Kuhlman said, "Now, you just feel free to roam about this place until you see me meet with the ushers. When I meet with them, I want you with me."

I agreed and wandered off through the vast auditorium. The ushers, hundreds of them who had driven for many miles to volunteer their time, were busy setting up chairs for the 500-voice choir, roping off the section for the wheelchairs, seating those who had come on chartered busses, and preparing the room for what was about to take place. Even as I walked through the auditorium I could almost taste the expectancy. It was like electricity. Everybody was whispering in hushed tones, like the Holy Spirit was already present.

Later the doors were thrown open and the people came pouring down the aisles like lava down the sides of a volcano. I fought my way up the aisle, pausing to look at a whole section filled with people in wheelchairs. I couldn't get my eyes off their faces. Some of them were so young, yet so twisted. I wanted to cry again. "Oh, Lord, am I selfish wanting a healing when there are so many people here, some of them so young?"

As I stood looking, I heard, maybe for the first time in all my life, God's inner voice saying, "There's no shortage in my storehouse."

With new strength I made my way to the back and slowly, painfully, climbed the stairs to a seat on the first row of the balcony.

There was still time before the meeting started. The huge choir had taken its place on the platform and was doing some last minute rehearsing. As usual, I spent my time sizing up the various people who were sitting around me.

I introduced myself to the man beside me. "I'm Dr. Townsend," he said.

"Are you a medical doctor?" I asked, astonished that medical doctors would attend a healing service.

"Yes, I am," he said, pulling out one of his business cards. "I come because I get a great blessing. I just like to see the mighty working power of God." Then he introduced me to his family. "I've brought my dad here from out of state," he said. "This is his first meeting.". . .

The service started. A beautiful girl, a fashion model whose face I had often seen on the cover of Sara's women's magazines, shared a brief testimony of what Jesus Christ meant in her life. I had been in many evangelistic meetings, but this one was different. Maybe it was the sense of expectancy. Maybe it was the sense of awe. Whatever it was, this was different from any other meeting I had ever attended.

Miss Kuhlman was speaking from the platform.

"Father," she was whispering, so low I could hardly hear it, "I believe in miracles. I believe that You're healing today like You were when Jesus Christ was here. You know the need of the people here, all over this huge auditorium. I pray that you will touch them. In the name of Jesus I ask it. Amen."

Then there was silence.

Suddenly she was speaking again, her voice coming rapidly as she received knowledge of what was happening in the auditorium.

"There is a man in the upper balcony, on my extreme right, who has just been healed of cancer. Stand up, sir, in the name of Jesus Christ and claim this healing."

I looked up. She was pointing to the opposite side of the balcony. It was phenomenal. I could only stare in amazement, yet I felt the excitement building inside of me. This was real. I knew it was real.

"Do not come to the platform unless you know God has healed you," she emphasized. . . .

The healings she was reporting seemed to be mostly in the balcony. They moved across from the right to the left.

"Two people are being healed of eye problems."

"A woman is being healed right now of arthritis. Stand up and claim your healing."

"You are seated right in the middle of the balcony," Miss Kuhlman said. "You came today to receive your hearing. God has restored it. Take your hearing aid off. You can hear perfectly."

I looked. A woman in her forties was standing to her feet, pulling hearing aids out of both ears. The doctor sitting next to me was weeping and saying, "Thank you, Jesus." One of the personal workers was standing behind her whispering. I thought the woman was going to shout as she threw up her hands, praising God. She could hear. . . .

Suddenly Miss Kuhlman was pointing at the left balcony, right where I was sitting. "You have come a long way for your healing for cancer," she said. "God has healed you. Stand up in the name of Jesus Christ and claim it."

It was so far from the stage to the balcony. She had no idea I was up there. But her long, slender finger was pointing in my direction.

One of the things I had learned as a Baptist was to operate on faith, not feeling. I said, "O Lord, of course I want to be healed. But how do I know this is for me?"

Instantly that same inner voice, the one I had heard downstairs when I was looking at the wheelchair people, said, "Stand up!"

I stood. Without a feeling of any kind, I simply stood in obedience and faith.

Then I felt it. It was like being baptized in liquid energy. I had never felt such strength flowing through my body.

A woman approached me. "Have you been healed of something?"

"I have," I declared, wanting to leap and run all at the same time.

"How do you know?" she asked.

"I've never felt so gloriously well. I hardly had enough strength to get to this seat and now, ooooh, I feel so good." All the time I was stretching and bending, doing things I hadn't been able to do in more than a year. "I feel like I could run a mile," I said.

"Then run right on down to the stage and testify," she said.

I did. But on the way I began to wonder. "What if there's someone here from Houston? I'm going to bound up there on the stage and she's going to put her hands on me and I'm going to hit the floor. What will they think?"

But I didn't care.

Moments later I was standing beside Miss Kuhlman on the stage. She just walked over to me and said simply, "We thank you, blessed Father, for healing this body. Fill him with the Holy Ghost."

Bam! I was on the floor. . . . because of the new healing energy surging through my body, I bounced right back to my feet. The next time she didn't even touch me. She just prayed in my direction and I heard her say, "Oh, the power . . . ." And I was on the floor again. But even there, Satan atacked me. He came on like a roaring lion. "What makes you think you've been healed?"

Miss Kuhlman had already turned her attention to someone else. I rolled over and came up on my knees, my head in my hands, praying. "Oh, Father, give me the faith to accept what I sincerely believe you've given me."

I opened my eyes and coming to the platform was a little girl about nine years old. I had never seen anyone so happy. She was running and skipping, barefooted. She danced all the way across the stage, right by Miss Kuhlman who reached out to catch her but missed. She turned and started back. Again Miss Kuhlman reached for her but she danced out of reach. By that time the child's mother was on the platform. She was holding a pair of shoes with heavy steel braces.

Unable to catch the dancing, skipping child, Miss Kuhlman turned to the mother. "What do we have here?"

The mother was sobbing. "This is my little girl. She had infantile paralysis when she was a baby and has never walked without these braces. But look at her go now."

The huge congregation broke into a mighty roar of applause.

"How do you know God has healed her?" Miss Kuhlman asked.

"Oh, I felt the healing power of God going through her body," the mother almost shouted. "I took the braces off and she began to run."

Right behind her was another mother, holding a two-year-old child. "What's this?" Miss Kuhlman asked.

"God has just made my baby's foot whole," the mother said, her voice shaking so hard she was hard to understand.

Miss Kuhlman reached out and took the baby's foot in her hands. "Was this the foot?"

"Yes, yes it was," the mother blurted out.

"But I see no difference in this foot and the other."

"But look at this," the mother said, holding a built-up shoe. "This child was born with a club foot. There have been many operations. Had you been massaging her foot the way you are turning it now, she would have screamed in pain."

Miss Kuhlman said, "On the platform with me are a number of doctors. They know me. Is there a doctor in the audience who doesn't know me and doesn't know these children, and would you come up and examine them?"

A man stood up.

"Are you a practicing physician, sir?" she asked.

"I am," he said.

"Where do you practice?"

"St. Luke's Hospital here in Los Angeles," he said.

"Would you please come up and examine these children?"

The doctor came to the platform. "The first thing I say is that this little girl, running and jumping on these toothpick legs, is a miracle. It's a miracle she can even stand on them, much less jump with joy." Then he took the infant's feet and held them together. "Miss Kuhlman," he said seriously, "I can see no difference in this child's two feet. I think this mother can throw away the therapeutic shoe."

I needed no more proof. I staggered back stage, found a coin telephone, and called Sara in Houston. The line was busy. I asked the operator to break in.

"I can't do that unless it is a matter of life and death," she said.

"That's exactly what it is, operator," I said. "And you can listen in if you want to."

Suddenly Sara was on the phone. I tried to talk but all I could do was sob. I've never cried so hard in all my life, holding the phone and standing back stage at the Shrine Auditorium. Sara kept saying, "John, John, have you been healed?"

I finally got the message through. I was healed. Then she began to cry. I hoped the operator was listening.

In the motel I did all kinds of exercises—sit-ups, push-ups, things I hadn't been able to do in more than a year. And I did them with ease. Even without a medical examination, I knew I was healed. All that night I kept waking up, not to take pain pills (for I stopped all medication that morning before going to the service), but to say out loud in the darkness, "Thank you, Jesus. Praise the Lord!"

Then came the reunion with Sara and the children. They were waiting at the Houston airport when I arrived. Forgetting the crowd of people getting off the plane with me, I rushed to them, hugging Sara so tightly I literally picked her off the floor. She gasped at my strength. Then I grabbed the boys, first Andrew then John, picking them up and holding them over my head. We were all talking at once.

"Your face, John," Sara kept saying. "It's full of color and life."

"I knew you would be healed," Elizabeth was saying. "I prayed for you every day at 9, 12, and 6."

"Us too, Daddy," little John piped up. "Us little guys been praying too. We knew God would heal you."

It was too much, and this veteran police captain stood in the middle of the Houston airport and cried. . . .

Shortly afterwards I returned for a physical examination. I made an appointment with two doctors from the M. D. Anderson Institute on the same day.

The first doctor to see me was the one who had performed the surgery. I gave her a copy of Miss Kuhlman's book, *I Believe in Miracles*. She glanced at the book, listened as I told her my story, and then looked at me like I was crazy.

"Let me tell you something," she said. "The only miracle that has happened to you is a medical miracle. That's all. The only thing that's keeping you alive is your medication. You quit taking it and see how long you'll live."

I smiled. "Well, I haven't had any medication since the 20th of February, more than a month ago."

She was very shocked and angry. "You've done a very foolish thing, Mr. LeVrier," she snapped. "It won't be long before that cancer breaks out someplace else and you'll be done."

Such a strange attitude, I thought, for a scientist.

I left and went to Dr. Lowell Miller's office, chief of the Department of Radiation Therapy at Hermann Hospital. I hoped his reaction would be more positive, but after the last encounter I was determined not to tell him a thing about the miracle. He could just find out for himself.

His nurse asked me to go in the dressing room and prepare for a physical examination. She gave me one of those funny little white robes to put on, the kind that covers almost nothing in the front and is wide open in the back. I slipped off my pants to get dressed, and then noticed a strange thing. Like many long-time policemen, I had developed a good case of varicose veins in my legs. In fact, they had been so bad I wouldn't wear Bermuda shorts in public, for I was ashamed of the knots on my legs. Of course, when you're dying of cancer you don't worry about varicose veins, but in the bright light of the examination room I looked at my legs for the first time since returning from Los Angeles. Not only had the Lord healed me of cancer, He had healed the varicose veins also! My legs were as smooth as a young teenager's. By the time Dr. Miller came into the room I was bubbling over with praise.

Unaccustomed to seeing his cancer patients in such a joyful spirit, Dr. Miller stepped back. "My, what in the world has happened to you?"

That was all I needed to launch into the whole story of how Jesus Christ had healed my cancer.

"Now look," Dr. Miller said. "I'm a Christian too, but God has given us enough sense to look after ourselves."

"You'll get no argument from me on that," I said gleefully. "That's the reason I'm here to be examined. I'll submit to any exam you want to give. But I'm telling you, you won't find anything wrong."

"Okay, let's go," the doctor said. And what followed was the most thorough physical examination I had ever had.

When he finished he said, "You know, I wish my prostate felt as good as yours." Then he went down my spine, beating on me, vertabrae by vertabrae. "Remarkable," he kept repeating. "Remarkable."

He sent me to X-ray and then said, "I'll call you in a day or so after I've compared these pictures with your old ones. But from all indications you've been healed."

Three days later the phone on my desk of the second floor office in the Houston Police Department rang. My secretary said it was Dr. Miller.

"Captain," he said, "I have good news. I can find absolutely no trace of cancer. Now, I want to ask you one other question. Do you ever bring talks?"

"You mean about my police work?" I said.

"No," he said, "not about police work. I want you to come out to my church and tell the people what God has done for you."

That opened the door, and I've been going ever since, all over the nation, telling hopeless people about the God who has no shortage in His storehouse of miracles.[2]

NOTES

[1]Kathryn Kuhlman, *Never Too Late* (Plainfield, N.J.: Logos International, 1975).
[2]Kathryn Kuhlman, *Captain LeVrier* (Plainfield, N.J.: Logos International, 1973).

"Ye Shall Be Witnesses Unto Me"

I scarcely ever guessed before
  How real my Lord could be,
Till trouble leapt inside my door
  And hurled its blows at me:
That Jesus ever sees or hears
  How little did I care,
Till anguish swept away in tears
  My castles in the air!
Amid beguiling sunny hours
  My sense of need was rare,
Till sorrow wilted all my flowers
  And stripped my garden bare:
Then, in my withered paradise,
  Mid disenchantment grim,
When nothing earthly could suffice
  I learned my need of *HIM*.

Drab sky ahead, lost joy behind,
  While vain regret assails,
At last, in *JESUS,* now I find
  The love which never fails:
I'm learning, too, as now I sit
  A pupil in His school,
Whate'er God's wisdom may permit,
  His love can overrule:
His kindest, loveliest purposes
  To bless us, so it seems,
Oft wind by strangest processes
  To joys beyond our dreams:
So now in His great love I rest,
  His life enfolds my own;
He's working out some purpose blest
  To me, as yet, unknown.

—J.S.B.

CHAPTER TEN

"Ye Shall Be Witnesses
Unto Me"

Following up the thoroughly investigated and attested divine healings reported in the preceding chapter, we now furnish a couple of further examples similarly remarkable, equally well corroborated, and provenly permanent. I would like it to be realized that these are selected, not because they are more dramatic than others or more extraordinary or because there are not others available. They are representatives of many, for it seems as though there is nothing less than a divine *movement* among us in these days, reemphasizing the reality of the Holy Spirit's healing power. So far as America is concerned, there certainly seem to be gladdening tokens of spiritual quickening in many areas. Over against the sickening incursion of new and deadly evils, our God is raising up new and powerful witness to the saving power of the Gospel. In larger numbers than hitherto, souls are being saved and lives transformed—and bodies miraculously healed. Yes, I think that the many wonderful miracle healings today are to be seen as just one aspect of a spiritual movement. In these latter days the heavenly Wind is blowing afresh, and the invisible fire of the Holy Spirit is falling upon many.

MASSIVE G.I. HEMORRHAGE WITH SHOCK
INSTANTANEOUSLY HEALED

Such is the title of one chapter in H. Richard Casdorph's recently
published book *The Miracles*.[1] Perhaps it may seem a superfluity on
my part to say it, but H. Richard Casdorph, M.D., Ph.D., in medical
status is outstanding. One only needs to glance through the *Cur-
riculum Vitae* appended to his book to know this. I rather gather that
at first, with true medical caution, he was skeptical as to the reality of
miraculous healings; but careful investigation of the documented
facts and direct consultation with those who were "healed" fully
convinced him that such divine interventions today are real enough.
I am here submitting only one "case" from his carefully selected ten.
Casdorph wrote as follows.

When Paul Trousdale gave the commencement address at Pep-
perdine University June 13, 1975, newspapers across the country
and in Honolulu took note of it. More than 25,000 quality homes and
many commercial complexes in California and Hawaii bear the
stamp of Paul Trousdale. This prominent builder and civic leader
has gained a reputation for superior work. He was chairman of
Trousdale Construction Company, which he established in 1946,
until 1969, when Lear-Siegler Inc. bought him out and he became a
consultant for them and later a member of their board. . . .

A graduate of the University of Southern California, Mr. Trous-
dale is a member of the board of regents of St. John's Hospital in
Santa Monica, trustee of the Eisenhower Medical Center in Palm
Springs, and a member of the associates of the University of South-
ern California, California Institute of Technology, and the Univer-
sity of Hawaii. He also serves as a trustee of Webb school, a trustee of
USC and, since his healing, as a member of the board of Christ
Church in Los Angeles.

I obtained copies of Mr. Trousdale's medical records from St.
John's Hospital in Santa Monica. He was admitted there December
12, 1973, and dismissed January 4, 1974. He was suffering from
gastrointestinal hemorrhaging which required many blood transfusions during the first few days of his hospitalization. The bleeding
and blood transfusions continued until his instantaneous healing.
He was markedly anemic upon admission with a hemoglobin of 8.4
(normal 14-17.0) recorded on December 27, 1973. Thereafter, the
hemoglobin ranged from 8.4 to 9.8 in spite of repeated blood transfusions. After his healing, the hemoglobin gradually rose to essentially

normal values by the time he left the hospital.

Mr. Trousdale today is a handsome man with a large athletic build. He appears considerably younger than his sixty-one years. In spite of his history of vigorous health, on Christmas Day, 1973, he fainted for the first time in his life. He fainted twice more during the night and was taken by ambulance to St. John's Hospital in Santa Monica. There physicians quickly realized he had lost a great deal of blood internally and started blood transfusions. After four days of this conservative therapy he was still bleeding continuously. His doctors ruled out diagnostic x-rays under the circumstances and were planning exploratory surgery to find the source of the bleeding. During the night of December 28th, Mr. Trousdale seemed to have suddenly lost blood pressure, broke out in a profuse sweat (diaphoresis), and, possibly, lost consciousness.

When he opened his eyes the following morning he found that his wife had called the Reverend John Hinkle to his bedside. They prayed and a miracle of healing occurred. Mr. Trousdale had been raised, baptized, and confirmed in the Episcopal Church. However, during the preceding six months he and Mrs. Trousdale had been attending services conducted by John Hinkle at Christ Church in Los Angeles. Hinkle had taught them that the Lord Jesus Christ, through the Holy Spirit, appears and touches the lives of some of us in miraculous ways.

Hinkle told Trousdale that Jesus and the Holy Spirit had healed the internal bleeding and that no tumor, ulcer, tear, or scar would ever be found, because the Lord had completely healed him. Paul closed his eyes and repeated a prayer after the minister. As he did he saw Pastor Hinkle on the right side of the bed praying and Jesus on the left side. A warmness ran through his body and he had a sense of well-being as never before. He extended his hand toward Jesus and felt a warm, firm handclasp in return.

Paul immediately wanted to go home. His physicians wisely insisted that he remain for diagnostic studies which, as Pastor Hinkle predicted, were all negative, revealing no obvious source for the massive bleeding which had necessitated the transfusions. On December 31st, a barium study of the upper gastrointestinal tract with small bowel follow-through was entirely normal. The doctors were at a loss to account for the patient's bleeding. They could see no abnormality at all of the esophagus, stomach, duodenum or small bowel. On January 3rd, a barium enema showed some diverticulosis of the sigmoid colon (a common finding in Americans), but no other significant abnormality and no source of bleeding.

Following his release from the hospital, Mr. Trousdale has remained healthy, and subsequent examinations have not revealed any abnormality. He has resumed his active professional life *but he* is a *changed man spiritually* (emphasis mine).[2]

A FOURFOLD MIRACLE

Mrs. Ann Gunther lives in Louisville, Kentucky. She was trained as a nurse and later became a teacher of nurses. From childhood she had in chronic form a rare and deadly disease which, as she grew to womanhood, developed into its acute stages. Two of her three children were born deformed: also two of them fell victims to the same deadly disease which afflicted their mother. For nearly twenty years Mrs. Gunther lived on death's threshold, fighting to hang on to what little life she had left. Then something happened which changed everything, as she is still testifying years later, and which she confirmed to me just before this book was published.

I could feel myself falling, pitching forward down the aisle of the little chapel at St. Joseph's Infirmary in Louisville. It was a frantic, desperate feeling, as if all my muscles had melted. . . . A student nurse, I was in my first year of clinical training. . . . I tried to reach out and grab the end of a pew, but my hands had no grip. I staggered forward against the nurse in front of me, then collapsed heavily to the floor. . . . With the help of two nurses they finally got me out into the infirmary and onto a bed in a vacant room.

"You're pushing yourself too hard, Ann," one of the doctors said after my strength had returned. "I'm going to keep you in bed for a few days so you can rest."

When I was a little girl of thirteen, Mother had enrolled me in a Saturday morning ballet class in Louisville. Even way back then I tired easily. I could seldom get through an entire dancing session. My legs would just stop working, and I would have to sit down while the other girls performed their *arabesques, jetes,* and *pirouettes.*

Mom took me to a doctor in our suburb of Shively, outside of Louisville. He noticed I also had double vision and sent me to an eye doctor who made a thorough examination. The eye doctor couldn't find any occular problems and advised Mom to take me to a neurologist. However, back in 1945 a neurologist was hard to find, so the matter was dropped. Besides, the condition seemed to come and go. For a few weeks I would be fine, then the exhaustion would return—along with the double vision and shortness of breath. . . .

Rest helped. In fact, it became a necessary element in my life. Other children could take part in athletics or go out for cheerleading, but my time was spent confined to my room after school, resting and studying. I wanted to be a nurse—the finest nurse in the world. Thanks to a full scholarship to Nazareth College I was able to concentrate on getting my degree in nursing. But physical activity was out. My body just would not stand the strain of exercise.

One morning I was climbing the stairs to a third floor chemistry lab when I collapsed. I didn't faint; my muscles just refused to hold me up. I knew everything that was going on, each rolling fall, each jarring bump until I landed in a heap on the landing of the stairs.

I was ordered to remain in bed all that day, and a doctor gave me a physical examination. Again I heard the words, "You're working too hard. You're physically exhausted. You need to slow down.". . .

By the time I got to my clincial work at St. Joseph's Hospital, physical exhaustion had become a way of life for me. My last year there I married, but this only increased my problems. Thirty-seven months after the birth of my first child, I found myself with two more babies (the two youngest born with severe birth defects) and a husband who because of chronic physical, emotional, and spiritual illness could no longer cope with or be expected to help with rearing our family.

Joey, our middle child, was baptized in the nursery of the hospital by a nurse because the doctors did not expect him to live. Denied oxygen at birth because of a horrible cleft palate, he had also suffered brain damage. Yet he lived. . . . He had no palate at all and no gums on one side. Besides this, he couldn't drink milk or milk substitutes, was covered with rashes, was underweight, and couldn't retain food. The allergist found 105 things his body could not tolerate. I had to prepare a liquid from mashed potatoes, which meant coming home each day after work, mashing this mush so it would go through a lamb's nipple, and then spending another two hours trying to feed him.

Then Ronnie was born with a cleft lip. We started into a long series of plastic surgery operations—first on Joey to restore his mouth, nose, and face, and then on Ronnie. Joey's condition was most severe, however, for the doctors confirmed he not only had brain damage but was permanently deaf in one ear with minimal hearing in the other.

The year after Ronnie was born, my discouraged husband left us. This was indeed painful.

The doctors conceded that the birth defects could have been caused by my exposure to X rays. Prior to Joey's birth, while I was carrying him, I would return to my nursing position as often as I could, even if for only a few weeks at a time. I desperately needed the money. However, during this time I spent much time in the X-ray department, and the overexposure to the radiation had taken its grim toll.

For several years I was head nurse at . . . a psychiatric hospital in Louisville. Later I took a teaching position at St. Mary's School of Nursing. The job was perfect for me. I didn't have the long hours on my feet and was assigned a position as an instructor in medical nursing, teaching young nurses.

But the satisfaction of the new job did not help my physical condition. . . . I was steadily growing weaker and weaker.

Finally my supervisor took a hand. I had returned one afternoon to my office. She waited until I was at my desk before she entered.

"I just saw you come down the hall," she said with a concerned look on her face. "You could hardly walk from that classroom to your office."

"I don't believe that you are simply run down," she said. "There is something wrong with your muscles. I want you to see a neurologist."

The doctor was a young neurologist who had just come from residency. He was up-to-date on all the new discoveries in medicine, and I felt secure in his care. I spent considerable time with him on my first appointment as he thoroughly reviewed my medical record and gave me a complete physical examination. Then he gave me some pills to "pep me up."

"Call me tomorrow afternoon," he said definitely. "I want to know how you feel after taking this medicine."

The next afternoon I was feeling worse than ever. I wasn't even able to go to work. I called the doctor from the house. "I feel much worse," I complained.

That evening, after taking the other little white tablets, I really felt better—fast. I knew then what he was doing. He had set me up on the first medication to rule out fatigue from abnormal stress.

The following day I returned to his office. He told me I would have to come back once a week until he could regulate the new medication. "It has rather potent side effects," he said cautiously. I asked no more questions. He told me to take the pills once every thirty minutes during my waking hours. I was determined to be a good patient, ask no questions, and take my medicine as ordered.

Well, that attitude lasted about two weeks. My medical curiosity was boiling inside. It was a Tuesday afternoon. I was in the medical library at St. Mary's preparing a lecture for the next morning when I saw some neurological medical books which had been pulled from the stacks and left on the table. I knew I had a muscle condition which responded to drugs. I had also quizzed the hospital pharmacist and knew the name of the drug. With the help of the books and the latest medical journals, I discovered there was only one kind of neurological condition that responded to this particular medication—myasthenia gravis.

That night after the children were in bed, I went back to my nursing school notes on neurology. I found a small paragraph dealing with myasthenia gravis, a rare, progressive disease. In my own handwriting, scribbled at the bottom of the page, were the words: "Patients usually die within two years. No hope. Incurable."

The next morning I returned to the medical books. I wanted to learn everything I could about this killer that had invaded my life. Myasthenia gravis is an electrical breakdown in the nervous system of the body. Every move of every muscle is controlled by an impulse from the brain which runs down a nerve much as an electrical current runs down a copper wire. This electrical (nervous) impulse is transmitted to the muscles through a chemical known as acetylcholine.

In myasthenia gravis there is an imbalance in this chemical. When fatigue occurs the nerves gradually cease to send this juice over to the muscles so they can flex. All the generalized voluntary muscles in the body are affected: the muscles in the throat . . . the eyelids, swallowing, and worst of all, the lungs. Without a respirator you cannot breathe, for your lungs refuse to inhale air. You die within minutes.

Perhaps that is what happened to my father, I thought. Mother said he had just "gasped for breath" and died. Four of his brothers had died in infancy of "crib death"—that mysterious disease which has no known cause. Since the cause of myasthenia gravis is in the chemical transmission at the time, this would not even show up in an autopsy, for there is no pathology in the muscle itself. That is why the disease is so difficult to diagnose and treat.

Further reading revealed that some forms of myasthenia gravis are passed on from parent to child—for several generations. I shuddered, thinking of my three children at home.

Carol, now four years old, didn't seem to play normally. She tired easily, complained of weakness and whined because she was so exhausted. Surely, what had killed my father, and was now killing me, wouldn't be passed on to Carol also. Yet . . .

That afternoon I was back in the doctor's office. "You don't have to tell me what you suspect," I said. "I already know." . . .

"Okay, you're a nurse. You know that a diagnosis is very difficult at this point. It is important that you not be discouraged. Whether this is myasthenia gravis or not, at least we're bringing it under some kind of control." . . .

I took the medication for six months, and it provided enough relief so I could work and take care of the children. A woman had moved in with us as a live-in housekeeper, which helped considerably. It also enabled me to do something I had put off for several years—begin a Saturday morning course at Spalding College in Louisville, working toward a master's degree in nursing. This was partly the doctor's idea for "supportive therapy," partly out of my own financial need to improve my pay scale by getting the graduate degree. . . .

Six months later the old symptoms began to return. This was cause for hope. My medicine was useless *unless* I had myasthenia gravis. If I had the disease, the medicine would give me strength. If I did not have it, it would have no value.

I called the doctor. "The medicine's not working any more. Perhaps I don't have myasthenia gravis," I said happily.

"Do you have any kind of infection?" he asked.

I admitted I had a bad cold. He then told me the medicine does not always work in the presence of an infection. This could mean I might have to be put in a respirator in case my lungs ceased to function. . . .

Sensing my near panic, the doctor suggested it was time to have his diagnosis confirmed by another physician. He mentioned a physician in Indianapolis, a specialist in myasthenia gravis. . . .

Grasping at straws, and hoping against hope that I did not have MG, I made an appointment with the doctor in Indianapolis. It took only a few moments in his office before I understood why the other physicians described him as an expert. After carefully checking my medical records, he strapped me in a special chair—a chair that had electrical connections that ran to a graph machine. Much as an EKG measures impulses from the heart, this chair measures the strength of the muscles of the body. When I leaned backwards it recorded my back muscles. When I squeezed a little ball it measured the muscle strength in my hands and fingers. Chin muscles were tested by raising my head.

Next came two hypodermics. I had read up on the procedure and knew what was coming. I would receive two hypos several minutes apart. One of them would be a placebo, a shot of water in the vein. If I had MG this would cause no change in the ergo-graph. The other would contain a special drug, *tensilon,* designed to give temporary relief to a myasthenic, but it would not affect an ordinary person. When I received that hypo the graph would react radically because of my new strength.

Of course, I did not know which hypo was the water and which was the tensilon. But the doctor did, and the ergo-graph recorded it. I definitely had myasthenia gravis.

The doctor asked me to follow him into his office where he calculated my responses from the graph and regulated my medication. He then told me what to expect in the future. Infections, even minor ones, would put me to bed for weeks. He cautioned me not to fight my condition, saying I would live longer if I didn't panic when I went into a crisis.

"Is it right that I have only a couple of years to live?" I asked.

"You're a nurse, Mrs. Gunther," he said gently. "And you're a teacher of nurses. Therefore I am going to talk straight.". . .

Taking a seat behind his desk, he pulled off his glasses and leaned forward. "No doctor has the right," he said in a soft voice, "to limit your life like that. Besides, there are several categories of myasthenia gravis. The brittle myasthenic might live as long as two years before he goes into a crisis. The intermediate myasthenic could live ten or fifteen years if his medicine is regulated properly. It all depends on how many times you experience a crisis condition in which your lungs fail and you must have a respirator. Your heart can stand only so much strain, and life expectancy isn't good after two crises."

He then told me I fit into the "borderline brittle" category. In other words, my days were numbered.

The doctor was right about expecting the crises. They started soon afterwards, building in intensity. The first one came soon after I returned from Indianapolis. I couldn't get my medicine regulated. In the beginning I was taking one pill every fifteen minutes, which meant I always had to carry a full supply with me wherever I went. To leave the house without my medicine could mean death on the sidewalk. To forget and take too many pills could send me into a spasm similar to that which soldiers exposed to poison gas might experience on a battlefield. It seemed as if every waking second was spent struggling to stay alive.

My first major crisis occurred one night away from home. I had become active in the local MG Foundation and had been invited to speak to a group of people at the mall on Shelbyville Road. I seldom went out at night, usually being in bed by eight o'clock. My eyes were bad, and sometimes I would see four headlights rather than two. Glasses were no good, so I had stopped driving except during the daylight hours.

It was a rainy night in June. Lois, one of the nurses at St. Joseph's Hospital, had picked me up for the meeting and was now driving me home. The stately poplars that lined the dark streets were hidden by the pelting rain which beat against the windshield like scattered shot. I leaned back in the seat beside her, listening to the steady whoosh-whoosh of the windshield wipers. How tired I felt. The car seemed awfully warm and it was hard to breathe. Suddenly I realized my lungs were not working. When I tried to inhale nothing happened. Only by opening my mouth and swallowing desperately could I force air into my lungs. I was suffocating!

I groped out and felt Lois' arm, afraid to move my head from its locked position. My mouth stretched open, gasping, trying to suck in air. She had already noticed. She had heard the horrible sucking noise coming from my throat.

Jamming the car in gear, she swerved around two cars waiting for a red light and with horn blowing, headed toward the emergency room at St. Joseph's. The beat of the windshield wipers syncopated with my wild gasping for breath. Over and over I repeated the doctor's words in my mind. "Don't panic. Relax. Don't fight it." But when your body is starving for air, panic is only a blink away. I knew my bloodstream was being deprived of life-giving oxygen. I was dying.

Skidding on the dark, wet streets, Lois finally pulled into the lighted portico outside St. Joseph's. Moments later two male attendants were lifting me onto a stretcher and bursting through the doors. I could feel the wheels bumping along the uneven floor as they raced me into a cubicle where a positive respirator was strapped around my chest and face. I felt the machine begin to lift my body at regular intervals, pumping air into my lungs. I gulped it readily.

Two nurses were working, massaging my hands and feet. "Her nails are blue," I heard one of them say. I wanted to talk, to tell them

I was alive, but the mask over my mouth and nose kept me silent. I looked up into the face of a strange doctor. He was adjusting the machine which was pumping my chest, causing my lungs to expand and contract mechanically. A needle was in my arm and I felt my body relax. Gradually my lungs were beginning to work again.

"Take her up to ICU [Intensive Care Unit]," the doctor said. "We'll keep her on the respirator all night. Keep the injections going every thirty minutes. I think she's going to make it."

The room was swimming before my eyes. I tried to think of the children. It was Ronnie's fifth birthday. He would be terrified when I did not return home. But my mind refused to focus. I knew I was being moved along the corridor on the stretcher. Attendants on each side were supporting the IV bottles and the respirator equipment. . . .

It was a week before I was released from the hospital. The doctor explained I had a viral infection and a low grade fever which had counteracted the medicine, making it virtually ineffective. Not aware of how serious any infection could be, I had allowed myself to become fatigued. The chemicals which carried the involuntary messages from my nerves to my muscles had stopped working.

"Muscles," said the doctor the day he dismissed me from the hospital, "work only because the brain tells them to work. When the message doesn't get through because of a faulty connection, they don't do anything. Your lungs stopped getting messages to inhale and exhale. Like any piece of machinery that is no longer being told what to do, they just ceased functioning until the messages were restored. If this happens and there is no respirator or iron lung close by, you'll quickly die of suffocation, or your heart will fail."

"What if I'm home alone when it happens?" I asked, feeling desperately helpless.

He repeated the specialist's advice: "Don't panic. Relax. Your brain is functioning normally and will keep shooting impulses to the lungs. If you relax, some of them will get through. But if you fight it, the chemical reaction will be negative and you'll be gone."

The night after I got home, I gathered the children around me. In simple words I tried to explain that at any time I might have another crisis. I would need their help.

"I'll phone the doctor," Carol said.

"And I'll remind you to take your pills," little Ronnie chimed in.

Joey, struggling with his words, reached out and took my hand. "I'll hold your hand, Mommy, so you won't be afraid."

Joey knew what fear was, but he knew nothing of the fear of suffocating. "Don't panic." The words ran over and over in my mind. But how can you keep from going into a panic when you can't breathe? Only God could help me now.

The four of us held hands. "Children, I need your prayers," I said, trying to hold back the tears. Then speaking to God I said, "Lord, without You we are lost."

The house was silent. But in my heart I felt peace. God was there listening.

My condition gradually deteriorated. My weight was down to ninety-eight pounds. It seemed my body was building up resistance to the drugs. The doctors in Louisville recommended cobalt treatment. . . .

Every day, for three months, I entered the hospital for the radiation treatment. My neck was marked with a big purple pencil and each morning, for a split second, the technician would send deep X rays into my thymus. Within a week my body began to swell and I turned puffy all over—bloated. The inside of my mouth was sore from the effects of the radiation. The skin on my neck was burned and began to wrinkle. At the same time I was horribly nauseated. Yet the doctors felt that even though the outcome was uncertain, it was better to try the X ray than to sit around doing nothing.

It was a year later when I had my first cholinergic crisis, caused from an overdose of the medication. The doctors had warned me that too much of the medicine would kill me quicker than not enough.

I had stayed home from work that day because the children were sick. They were always sick, it seemed. And I had a splitting headache. I knew I shouldn't take any other medication as long as I was taking my doctor's prescription, but the head pain was so great I thought I would chance a couple of aspirins. I was in the kitchen and had just taken two of my own pills when I realized that instead of taking two aspirins, I had mistakenly taken two more pills.

Immediately my mouth began to fill with saliva. My stomach and intestines were cramping. My eyes felt like the sockets were just there—but no eyeballs. My vision went out of proportion. All in moments.

Carol heard me cry out and ran to me. I had collapsed on the kitchen floor.

"Call the doctor," I stammered.

"Oh, my goodness!" he said when I told him what was happening. "How long ago did you overdose?"

"About 15 minutes ago," I said, my mouth now frothing furiously. "You've got about fifteen minutes left," he said. "Take the atropine immediately."

Atropine was an antidote which I kept on hand in case of an overdose. It is the same antidote used against the curare poison which South American Indians use to tip their arrows. In fact, a cholinergic crisis is very similar to the effects of the curare poison.

The doctor told me how much of the antidote to take, and Carol prepared the hypodermic as I lay on the kitchen floor. I managed to get the needle into the top of my leg. The doctor was still on the telephone. "If the conditions don't subside in ten minutes," he said, "get to the emergency room immediately."

I lay back on the floor, my head in Carol's lap, and prayed. The conditions did begin to subside. The cramping eased and the saliva in my mouth stopped running. I knew I could help things by wearing the drug out of my system, so I began to crawl. I dragged myself on my knees all over the house, using up the extra chemical I had put into my body. Carol crawled with me, holding up my head which dangled uselessly. Gradually my body returned to its former state. I determined that night never to take another aspirin. Better to suffer the pain of a headache than run the risk of a cholinergic crisis.

Mrs. Gunther here tells of what she calls "the final blow." Her dear young daughter, Carol, was found also to have the same dread disease. Her son, Joey, after thirteen operations, was pronounced totally and permanently deaf in his left ear, in addition to his brain damage and cleft palate troubles. Then came the further heart-rending grief: her boy Ronnie, after various operations, was declared also to have myasthenia, like his mother and sister! All this was in addition to Mrs. Gunther's own deteriorating condition. Was there ever a darker night of seemingly hopeless trouble?

By now Mrs. Gunther was unable to work most of the time, which brought still further trial by way of a financial crisis. She could no longer climb steps. She could not even use her hands to pump up a blood-pressure cuff on a patient's arm. Fortunately, Social Security benefits were arranged because the doctors declared her condition to be one of "total disability."

There they now were: all four of them were slowly dying by degrees. Yet that very ordeal bound them close together and set them not only weeping together but praying together for God to help them—and He did. But first He had to prepare them for a miracle, as Mrs. Gunther now tells us. She was persuaded by Nell Adams, a member of the Myasthenia Gravis

Foundation, to go to Pittsburgh, to one of Kathryn Kuhlman's healing meetings. That, remember was after nearly twenty years since the first acute outbreak of her incurable disease, and when two of her children were now in their teens.

The next day I called Nell Adams. She had patiently stayed away, ceasing her pressure for me to go to another miracle service. . . .

"You told me Miss Kuhlman conducted miracle services in Pittsburgh on Friday mornings," I said. "Where are they held?"

"In the First Presbyterian Church," she answered, and I could hear the joy bells tinkling in her voice. Her patience had paid off.

I talked to the children. They all felt as strongly as I did. They didn't even object to driving all the way to Pittsburgh in our old car.

Nell loaned me her copy of Miss Kuhlman's book, *I Believe in Miracles*, so we could know more about this unusual but consistently fruitful ministry. I then bought a copy of *God Can Do It Again*. The more I read, the more I believed God did not want us sick.

We read all the way to Pittsburgh. Carol and Ronnie would take turns reading aloud while I drove. On two occasions even Joey read.

I had not been driving much, and the long trip was really an adventure in faith. I would drive with my left foot on the pedal because my right leg was almost useless. For a month I had been dragging it behind me as I walked. My eyes, too, were giving me real problems, and by the time we reached Pittsburgh we were all exhausted.

We spent the night at a downtown hotel, just a block from the stately old graystone church where the services are conducted.

It was still dark at five o'clock the next morning when Carol woke us, shaking our beds and pushing us into the bathroom.

"One of us has to be healthy enough to hold a place in line," she said, her eyes sparkling with excitement. "I'm going on down. You all come as soon as possible. God is going to do something special today for all of us." With that she was out of the room.

"Oh, baby," I thought, "I hope you're right."

Ronnie was so sick and weak that morning that Joey and I had to support him down the dark street past the Mellon Square parking garage. The line in front of the building was already two blocks long, extending down toward the heart of town into the cold, gray mist of the early dawn. The city was just coming to life for a new day, and I could not grasp the full impact of seeing all these people waiting in front of the church—waiting for a miracle.

Carol was waving. She had saved us a place. We stood and stood, crushed, it seemed, by the press of the crowd.

We took turns helping Ronnie stand; but when the doors were opened, we almost lost our grip on him. The surging mob forced us up the steps and literally propelled us down the aisle into the big church.

We found a pew together, about half way down. Moments later we realized the building was full. . . . Balconies, choir loft behind us, and a huge overflow auditorium in front of us behind the pulpit area—all were packed with people.

Again I was overcome by a desire to praise God. The singing started and I lost myself in it. The crowd, no longer a pushing mob, was welded together into one body through praise.

Fifteen minutes after the singing began (it seemed as if it were seconds) I began to feel heat. It was November, and I of course assumed the heat had been turned on in the building. Yet I grew hotter and hotter—uncomfortably so.

Ronnie was sitting beside me, and during a tiny break in the singing, just as Miss Kuhlman was coming up to speak, he leaned over and whispered in my ear, "Mom, are you hot? I'm burning up."

"Oh, no," I thought. "Surely we're not both going into a crisis right here in the church—at the same time."

I put my hand on Ronnie's forehead. He *felt* cool. I looked at the other people around me. No one seemed to be hot. Some of the women had sweaters draped over their shoulders. But I felt as if I were in a furnace.

Miss Kuhlman was speaking, but the heat was so intense I couldn't listen. I wanted to get out, to get a breath of fresh air, but I felt I needed to stay, unsure of what was going on. Again I tried to concentrate on Miss Kuhlman. She was talking about the Holy Spirit, about miracles. I had come all this way, but the burning was so intense I could not listen. I felt Carol's hand on my arm.

"Mom, Joey and I are burning up. What's wrong?"

Now I was frightened. What was this? Then, as quickly as I thought it, the heat disappeared. It had been on us for an hour, and now it was gone. Not only did it leave, but I felt a cool breeze wafting across my face, my thighs, all the way down to my feet. It was as though a window had been opened and a fresh breath of cool air was rippling across my body, encasing me in a gentle breeze.

I glanced at Ronnie, then at Joey and Carol. They felt it too. They were grinning in relief.

I turned back to the platform. A lady had been healed of multiple sclerosis and had come to the platform to testify. Then almost interrupting her as she talked, Miss Kuhlman moved quickly to the microphone, her voice ringing with excitement.

"Somebody," she said, her words coming rapidly, "somebody who drags her right leg has been healed. You're seated RIGHT DOWN HERE!" She was pointing directly at me. "Stand up! Claim your healing!"

Nothing, not even a mountain on my shoulders, could have kept me seated. I knew she meant me. I leapt to my feet!

Then I realized my children were standing too—Ronnie on my right, Carol on my left. All three of us had been healed!

Instantly, it seemed, there was a woman in the aisle leaning over the others and whispering, "Have you been healed?"

"Oh, yes!" I sobbed. "We've all been healed. I know it. We've been healed of myasthenia gravis."

There was an audible gasp from the people around us who heard what I said. All around me I could hear people whispering softly, "Praise God! Thank You, Jesus!" A man and a woman in the pew behind me, total strangers, were weeping. The man was so overcome he had his face buried in a handkerchief. A woman in front of us turned and touched my hand, as though she were touching something very sacred, very holy.

I had never felt so much love, so much thanksgiving, so much praise. I felt like a lost child who had been the object of a great search by her family, who had wandered in out of the woods and been caught up in the arms of her father. I looked around. Almost as great a miracle as my healing was the miracle of love. This was my family. These people whom I had never seen before, who were reaching out to me in love, were my real brothers and sisters. And God was my Father. No longer was I bound to an earthly inheritance which passed disease from father to daughter and on to my own children. I had been cut loose and was spiritually joined to another Father—my true Father, a Father from whom I would never inherit death or disease—only life and health. The very genes and chromosomes in my body were being changed as I was adopted into the family of my new Father. And with that transaction came healing and health to my lineage—my children.

Ronnie was the first up the aisle, lifting his legs high as he walked. Only an hour before he could hardly stand. Now he was filled with life—new life.

The three of us waited on the platform for Miss Kuhlman to interview us. Others who had been healed of a variety of diseases were in front of us. But instead of letting us come to the microphone, Miss Kuhlman suddenly turned and headed toward us. No words were spoken. She just pointed in our general direction and said, "Oh, the power of God is all over this place."

And we all fell down. I mean all of us: Ronnie, Carol and all the other people standing around us. One second we were waiting in line and the next we were all on the floor. I didn't faint. I wasn't even aware of falling. It was like one of the myasthenia gravis attacks when suddenly the nerves stop transmitting sensations to the muscles and everything stops working for a moment. Whatever it was, it wasn't MG, for this time we were back on our feet. We were refreshed. Then before we knew it, we were back in our seats.

Joey was waiting. His eyes were brimming with tears and he grabbed my hand. "Mother, I can hear! I can hear!"

One of Miss Kuhlman's helpers was back in the aisle. No doubt he had noticed the commotion we were causing. Indeed, no one in our area was paying any attention to what was happening on the platform. They were all watching us as I hugged Joey close to my chest and Carol and Ronnie held on from the outside, crying and laughing.

Then we were all back on the platform again. I explained to Miss Kuhlman about Joey's deafness—total deafness in his left ear, with minimal hearing in his right. The doctors had said there was "no hope, ever" for his hearing. Now he could hear!

Miss Kuhlman checked his hearing and then turned to me. "And you, also, and the other children. All healed of myasthenia gravis. How do you know?"

I explained that I was a nurse, that I was the state coordinator of the MG Foundation. I had my pills in my purse which I was to take every thirty minutes. But it had been four hours and I was feeling wonderful. Instead of going into a crisis, I had been healed.

Miss Kuhlman lifted her hands in praise, and suddenly we were all back on the floor—all four of us this time. We climbed to our feet and fell back again; the power of God was so great. Heaven was outpoured in our midst.

It was almost three o'clock when we returned to our car and headed toward Louisville. We had missed lunch, but it didn't matter. Our whole family had been healed. Who could think of food at a time like that? And who could think of medicine? We were so filled with the glory of God that there just wasn't any thought of medicine. And we've never taken a pill since.

We arrived home at midnight and Ronnie hit the back door running. When I got into the kitchen, I found him down on his stomach on the floor—doing pushups.

Medically speaking I knew I was going to need proof. I knew there were remissions in myasthenia gravis, although I had never known of one like this—and certainly not three at the same time. I decided to wait and let God test it out for me.

Three days later the first test came. I caught a severe case of flu. Ordinarily such an attack would have put me in the hospital in a respirator. Yet despite the raging fever and body pains, I remained strong. I recovered in two days and was back on my feet. God's healing was quite complete.

The doctor just shook his head when he examined us. Happy, but noncommittal, he said none of us was any longer showing symptoms of myasthenia gravis.

I didn't expect him to testify to our miracle. I would do that. Simply confirming that all the symptoms were gone—for all of us—was enough for me.

The final test of my healing came a year later. I was having some severe female bleeding and my gynecologist insisted I have an immediate operation. He did not know of my healing from myasthenia gravis and expressed great concern that I would have to go under anesthesia, which is the ultimate test for a myasthenic. Very few advanced cases come out of surgery alive. I drove myself to the hospital, signed myself in, and went into surgery alone. The operating room was ready for me, equipped with respirator and all the necessary drugs to bring me back to life in case my lungs stopped while I was on the operating table. But God had breathed health into me. I was safe. I came out of the recovery room much faster than an ordinary person, got up the next morning and drove myself home.

I said to my amazed doctor, "God did this just to show all these medical people whom I have known so long that I have been healed."

He looked at me and grinned. "Indeed you have," he said with farewell pat on my shoulder. "Indeed you have."

I know that physical healing should never be seen as an end in itself. I believe God heals our bodies to bring us to a far greater end than physical health—that of glorifying Him. This has been demon trated in my life and the lives of my three children many times over.

As great as my healing has been, as grateful as I am for the touch of God on the bodies of my children, far greater is the wonderful assurance that I am part of His Bride, awaiting the soon coming of the King.

As a nurse, as a teacher of nurses, my healing does not make me believe any less in medicine. In fact, it has helped me understand the entire healing process much better. I see doctors, nurses, hospitals and drugs as a part of God's great healing process. But I also see beyond—to a loving heavenly Father who longs to restore . . . gifts of healing, to the Church.

There will always be a need for doctors and nurses. The greatest book on miracles—the book of Acts—was written by a physician, Dr. Luke. Yet I now understand there is more, far more, than those of us who have spent our lives in medical science can comprehend with the mind. This "far more" is the power of the Holy Spirit. And no one is more grateful than I am—than we are—that God is restoring this power to His people.

Incurable? Hopeless? These words have been crossed out of my medical vocabulary. I have four living affidavits to attest to the power of God to do the impossible: Carol, Joey, Ronnie, and myself. How big is God?
BIG ENOUGH!

Notes

[1]H. Richard Casdorph, *The Miracles* (Plainfield, N.J.: Logos International, 1976).
[2]Ibid.

A Testimony From "Down Under"

CHAPTER ELEVEN

A Testimony
From "Down Under"

Mrs. Morag McDougall of Melbourne, Australia, was a victim of medically incurable heart disease for no less than twenty years; again and again almost dead from recurrent and debilitating cardiac crises. Nothing but supernatural intervention could avail to cure her; and that is just what happened—a miraculous healing, instantaneous, complete, to the astonishment of all her friends, and most of all to her own doctor who, after careful test, now pronounced her "a remarkably well woman." The full story is in the booklet, 10,000 Miles for a Miracle, *published by Bethany Fellowship, Inc., Minneapolis, Minnesota.*

My housecoat around me, I cracked the front door and peered at the early morning mist. Behind me, Jack, dressed in his usual conservative brown business suit, gently wrapped his arms around my waist. I loved the feel of his freshly shaved cheek. He was ready for his day at the office.

Moving around me and out the door, he brushed his lips across mine. "See you at dinner, dear," he smiled. "And happy anniversary."

Fifteen years of marriage to the busiest, yet most wonderful man in all Australia, I thought as I watched him get in his car and pull into the street of Ascot Vale on his way to work. Still a young man, he occupied a most important position in the petroleum business on the

231

continent. Even so, his vigorous drive was combined with a deep faith in God. Despite the grief we had suffered when our blind child had died, and despite our son Bruce's affliction, some of which could have been caused by brain damage, these had been fifteen years of happiness.

There was a scent of spring in the air. It was September in Australia, and before long the summer winds would blow, and the people of Melbourne would shed their jackets and head for the beaches and tennis courts. But this morning, as the sky turned from rose to pale yellow and then light blue, everything was springtime.

But deep inside me, like a cloud passing the sun, there was an uneasiness. Perhaps it had to do with that fainting spell Wednesday as we were on our way to church. I had never felt that way before. It was as though my veins had simply squeezed tight and all the blood that normally surged through my system disappeared. In that brief instant I had the sensation of dying. The men carried me to the church but I was soon on my feet again. Then there was Jack's worried look after it was all over as he insisted I see a doctor.

The sound of the boys' voices brought me back to the present. Rob was eight—the picture of good health. Bruce, in his thirteenth year, was one of those special children that had to struggle all the time just to keep up: those horrible seizures since he was three. And then the day when he was playing under the baby's pram—back when little blind Johnny was still alive. The doctor had put Bruce in eyeglasses shortly before, and still unaccustomed to them, he had raised up and smashed the glass into his eye. When I got to him he was crying and rubbing his eye with his fist, grinding the slivers of glass deeper and deeper into the eyeball. The doctors wanted to remove the eye, but I insisted God would perfect him also. They left it, though he was totally blind in that eye.

But no time to reminisce. The day was upon me. Get the boys off to school, then visit the doctor.

The boys off to school, I started straightening up around the house. Why did I tire so easily? Why this nagging feeling that something was wrong? I was taking the last of the breakfast dishes off the kitchen table and wiping the counter with a damp towel when I became aware of a strange sensation in my left arm. Heat. That's what it was. A spreading warmth from my shoulder to my fingertips. *Odd,* I thought. But I finished with the kitchen and started down the hall when the tingling suddenly changed into fire. Searing! Burning! I gasped in agony as scorching pain ran the length of my arm. I tried to move my hand, but the arm was powerless, paralyzed, hanging at my side with liquid fire.

"Dear God!" I choked out as I stumbled into the bedroom. "Oh please . . ."

Gradually it subsided and, strangely enough, I dozed off. When I awoke, moments later, the sun was streaming through the big bay window in the bedroom. Tiny dust particles, like elves on a golden staircase, were dancing up and down the sunbeam.

"Think, old girl," I said aloud. "Try to remember what happened." But I could not. My mind simply blocked out the ordeal as though it had never taken place.

I finished my housework and walked two blocks to the tram. Melbourne is the second largest city in Australia, and our suburb of Ascot Vale is one of the many smaller communities that surround it. It was a short train ride into the city.

My first stop was the clinic where several doctors had their offices. After a quick examination the young doctor said, "Just nerves, nothing to be alarmed about."

"Sorry," I argued, "but my husband insisted I see a specialist."

"But that can't be arranged for two weeks," the doctor replied.

Back home that afternoon, I went through the motions of preparing the evening meal. Since the war, beef was plentiful in Australia, and Jack's gentle hug as he came in and smelled roast was all the reward I needed. At dinner Jack reached over and squeezed my hand, then bowed his head and asked grace. "Lord, I thank you for these fifteen years. . . . May we have many more. . . ."

The boys were up from the table, leaving Jack and me alone for a few moments. He was in a hurry to attend a Sunday School teachers' meeting at Flemington Presbyterian Church that night, but I needed to talk. I reached over and touched his hand.

"Jack, this morning . . . the strangest thing . . ." He listened as I described the pain.

"You had better go down to the doctor in the morning," he said.

"I was there this morning," I told him. "He said it was just nerves. I have to wait two weeks to see the specialist."

"Then I want you to go back in the morning and tell them it's not nerves. Something must be wrong."

Jack was on his feet, reaching for his coat. "It was a good dinner," he said. "And you are a good wife. I want to keep you around for a long time, so just take it easy tonight. I'll be home early."

The children were in bed when it returned. Like a dark intruder it came into our home. There was nowhere to hide as it sank its ugly talons into my body. It started the same way as before—tingling, then warmth, then searing pain in my arm, spreading across my neck and into my chest.

Surely, Jack will be home soon, I kept thinking. But the minutes dragged into centuries as the pain raged through the top half of my body.

I looked up and saw Jack standing in the door of the bedroom. His face paled as he saw me twisting on the bed, my head drenched in perspiration. Without a word he grabbed the phone and called the clinic. A young doctor, a locum, was on duty. By the time he had reached the house I was fighting for each breath. The doctor gave me an injection, checked my heart and took my blood pressure. He then motioned for Jack to follow him into the other room.

When they returned Jack bent over me. His eyes were red and swollen. *That's funny,* I thought, *Jack crying? I must be worse than I think.*

"Your husband tells me you are a very sensible person," the young doctor said.

I tried to grin through pain.

The doctor placed his stethoscope against the upper part of my chest. "You have had a heart seizure, Mrs. McDougall. We are going to get you to the hospital and do everything we can for you. But I do not want you to move a muscle until the ambulance arrives."

I was in and out of consciousness by the time the ambulance pulled into the driveway. Vaguely, as through a foggy glass, I could see the boys' faces peering from their bedroom window—the fright in their eyes reflecting in the eerie red glow of the flashing light on the ambulance. Then the doors shut behind me and I slipped into blackness. I knew that just beyond that misty shadow was the silhouette of death—so close I could almost reach out and take his hand. How easy it would be to go with him. But if I did, who would care for Bruce? . . . I hung on, determined to live.

I was six weeks in the Royal Melbourne Hospital. Dr. Maurice Etheridge, who was to become a dear friend over the years ahead, was my heart specialist. He explained I had barely escaped death during a coronary occlusion—a clot to the heart.

"You've cleared a big hurdle," he said when he dismissed me. "You came as close to dying, yet living, as anyone I've ever known."

I was alive, and although I left the hospital with what the doctor called an "enlarged heart," I was able to return home and resume a partial routine. The doctor assured me, however, that I would *always* be on medication, that I could never again exert myself physically, and that the condition could return any time—with even more serious results. Although I didn't ask, I knew what he meant by that. I could drop dead at any moment.

For two years I struggled, vainly, to regain my former strength. Nothing seemed to help. Sometimes there would be weeks which passed when I couldn't even get outside of the house. Gradually, though, as I read my Bible, I discovered that although it is God's intent for a person to get old and die, nowhere does it seem to be God's intent for people to get *sick* and die—especially to linger on with a debilitating disease. Yet I was getting sicker and sicker.

Even while I was pondering all this in my heart, I had another serious attack. I had been in bed most of the day with a throbbing headache. Towards evening I had arisen to fix the dinner meal for the family. Rob, who was eleven by then, had been home all day with a cold. By dinner time, however, he was feeling better and joined the rest of us at the little table in the kitchen.

Winters in Melbourne, which last from June until September, are usually rather mild. However, I had been cold all day and by dinner was actually shivering. Jack had pulled a small radiator (heater) up close to my chair at the kitchen table when suddenly I began to feel great flashes of heat through my body. I tried to speak, but nothing came out. I knew my mouth was moving, but I heard no words. I raised my hand to motion Jack to move the radiator away from my chair, but when I did I felt myself falling.

Everything went into slow motion. I could see Jack rising out of his chair, could see the look of panic on his face. I saw the terrified look on Bruce's face and the tears appearing in Rob's eyes—all as I fell toward the floor. Then there was pain—pounding, pulsating, stabbing through my head. I knew I was having a stroke.

I tried to speak, to ask Jack to call the doctor. But instead of words, all I heard coming from my lips were slurred, animal-like sounds. My right side was dead—no feeling. Jack tried to help me into a sitting position but I could not move my right arm or leg; it was as if they belonged to somebody else. Rob and Bruce half-carried, half-dragged me to the couch. I could not get my eyes off my right arm. How strange it looked, dangling there by my side. I reached over with my left hand and grabbed the wrist, pulling my arm up onto the couch beside me. It was like holding somebody else's hand. There was no feeling, no sensation whatever.

I could hear Jack in the kitchen, dialing the phone. The first doctor said he could not possibly come; he had a clinic full of people. Another doctor was on his way to a hospital emergency. Jack finally reached the specialist, Dr. Etheridge, who agreed to come at once. By that time the first effects of the stroke had subsided, and I could feel some sensation returning to my arm and leg.

Dr. Etheridge examined me, called it a "spasm," then gave me an injection and some medicine. He first insisted I go to the hospital, but when I objected he allowed me to stay home, providing I would remain bedfast for at least ten days.

The effects of the stroke wore off, but my heart condition grew progressively worse. Over the next *fifteen years* I became a semi-invalid, in and out of the hospital, often confined to the bed for days at a time.

Many times I wakened at night to find my heart beating wildly as though it were trying to force blood through a closed passage. On at least two occasions, when I was hanging out clothes during the hot months of January and February, my legs buckled under me as my tired heart seemed to quit. On these occasions I would have to go back to bed for a week or more, and twice the doctor put me in the hospital for observation. My blood pressure soared and dipped—to dangerous extremes—and I realized my condition was rapidly deteriorating. Dr. Etheridge finally insisted I return to the hospital for treatment. "We must do something further," he said.

Doctors at the Royal Melbourne Hospital later put me through a new series of tests. Among these was a strange examination where the doctors attached wires to my body which led to some sort of television screen. I gave them reports as they pushed buttons. It took a fair while and the next day Dr. Etheridge came into my room to make his report.

The aorta valve, he said, was narrowed down until only a small amount of blood could pass through. "It is like a pipe that has formed a crust on the inside. It must be replaced immediately."

"Are you suggesting an operation?" I asked.

"Not suggesting," he said soberly. "I am telling you it is imperative."

"Will the operation cure me?" I asked.

"We don't know," he said, pacing the room at the end of my bed. "We might open you and then have to sew you right back up again. It might be that the tissue has been irreparably torn. At best, it is risky business."

"Look," I said, "I think Jack and I should pray about this."

Dr. Etheridge nodded. "Of course," he said. "But you must not wait long. You are critically ill and any sudden shock could kill you."

Neither Jack nor I felt God wanted me to have the operation, so we trusted that there would be no sudden shock to force me back into the hospital.

We were wrong. Within weeks from the time I left the hospital, my very soul was wrenched from me. Rob died! My son, the pride of my life, the father of my precious granddaughter—dead. There was no warning. He was the picture of health. The typical young Australian, strong, muscular, tall, and handsome as they come. One day he was with us, the next he was gone.

The shock and grief proved to be too much for my tired heart. Susan (Rob's widow) and Caitlin (the baby) visited us, and one night, just after Susan had taken the baby upstairs and put her to bed, I felt my lungs begin to tighten up. I was losing my breath. Standing in the hall between the dining room and the living room, I tried to call out to Susan. I could not. All I could do was slump against the wall, praying she would hurry down from upstairs. The world was rapidly closing in on me, like an evening fog that swirls in from the sea and smothers the ships in the harbor. I was backed into the corner of nothingness, strangling, gasping for air.

"I'm going to have an attack," I choked out as Susan came down the stairs. I staggered forward and pointed to the phone.

"Do you want me to call Dr. Etheridge?" Susan asked, alarmed.

I nodded. She dialed the doctor, but before she hung up, Jack walked in the back door. He knew, without asking, what was wrong. Hadn't he seen me, many times, in the same condition? I was standing against the wall, bent double from the waist, my lungs fighting for each breath.

Moments later Dr. Etheridge rushed in. He listened to my chest with his stethoscope, took my blood pressure and then said, "Don't move. I'm going to call an ambulance. You have an accumulation of fluid in your lung cavities. Edema. You're literally drowning and I've got to correct it immediately. I'm going for a hypodermic. I'll be back before the ambulance arrives."

Things were reeling by that time. I could hear some of the words; the rest drifted off into space. I knew Jack was pacing back and forth in front of the window. Bruce had left the room, weeping. The pain, raging through my chest, was worse than it had ever been. I was dying.

Dr. Etheridge was back. He stabbed the needle into my flesh . . .

then the ambulance . . . and the flashing red lights outside the house
again . . . and the swaying ride to the hospital . . . the weird wail of
the siren . . . the mask over my face as the attendant gave me
oxygen . . . and finally the intensive care unit of the hospital.

Months passed, and it was only the lingering presence of little
Caitlin that kept me in touch with reality. When Susan announced
that she was going to remarry and move to Los Angeles, taking
Caitlin with her, I thought the end had surely come. Tired and
weary, the candle of hope flickered and almost went out.

It was Mrs. Olive Reekie, I believe, who gave me my first copy of *I
Believe in Miracles*. "That's what I need," I told Olive after I had
pored through the book in one evening. "I need a miracle."

Olive had come by the house and we were sitting over a cup of tea.
I had been in bed all morning, and was able to get out only for a few
hours each afternoon.

"Pittsburgh is so far away," I said sadly. "If Miss Kuhlman
would come even as close as California, I would jump a plane. I
could then go see little Caitlin and be healed at the same time."

Olive blinked and half rose from her chair. "Morag, don't you
know? Kathryn Kuhlman has meetings once a month in Los
Angeles."

I had a shocking rash, like a bad case of eczema that covered great
parts of my body. The Collins Street skin specialist, perhaps the
leading dermatologist in Melbourne, had hospitalized me for it on
several occasions. "You won't die from the rash," he had concluded,
"but it will be with you forever. All we can do is ease the discomfort
with an ointment."

Dr. Etheridge pointed out that the rash alone was bad enough to
keep me home, not to mention my heart condition which was bound
to be aggravated by the strain of flying ten thousand miles.

Oddly, despite the doctor's objections, Jack felt I should make the
trip. "If God is speaking to you, dear," he said, "then I shall not
stand in His way. I am believing with you that you will return to
Australia healed."

Ten days later Bruce and I were winging our way to Los Angeles.
Bruce had lost his job several months before. His blind eye and
unpredictable blackouts plus his overall condition made regular
employment difficult. Jack felt that even though Bruce was now past
thirty, he would be better off living with us where we could take care
of him. I was glad to have him along, hoping he, too, might receive
some kind of miracle.

Susan and her new husband, Steve, met our plane at the airport on Friday afternoon. We spent Saturday touring Beverly Hills with them. We stopped for lunch in a small restaurant off Wilshire Boulevard and after we ordered, Susan said, "Look in that window across the street. Isn't that a notice about this lady you've been speaking of, Kathryn Kuhlman?"

I turned and looked. There was a notice in the window of a shop saying, "Booking for Kathryn Kuhlman coaches." I could hardly wait to finish my meal.

The man in the shop explained that they had regular buses from this area of the city that went to the Kathryn Kuhlman Miracle Services. In fact, he said, there was a meeting scheduled for tomorrow afternoon at the Shrine Auditorium just south of the business district.

"Oh, can you reserve two seats for me on the coach?" I asked.

"I'm sorry," he said shaking his head. "There is no more room. All our seats are taken."

"Look," I said, "just tell me how to get there. That's all I want to know."

I turned to Bruce. "Let's take a chance. The doors open at one o'clock so we had better get there early."

Early was the word. The next morning we were at the Shrine Auditorium at 5:45 a.m. There was already a crowd of people queued up around the front doors. It was going to be a long wait and I was concerned about my heart. Seldom on my feet for more than a few minutes at a time, now it seemed I would have to stand for almost seven hours. I turned to a woman standing beside me: "Does anybody ever die waiting to get into these meetings?"

She laughed. "I've been coming to the Miracle Services for some time. We always get here about sunup to get a place close to the door. Many of those who arrive early are desperately ill, but I've never known of anyone dying. The power of God surrounds this place on the day of the Miracle Service. He protects all those who come in faith."

The hours passed. Suddenly the doors swung open and we were inside—seated in the second round of the balcony. It was like nothing I had ever experienced before. The crowd was warm, friendly, and most informal. Yet in spite of the friendly buzz of conversation, there was a holiness about the place. This giant auditorium, filled with more than seven thousand people, was vibrant with life. The mighty choir was on stage, rehearsing.

As we sat and listened, I sensed something special about even the rehearsal. God was moving through those voices and I had to fight back the tears even as I listened. God was there.

It never was clear to me when the meeting started. Most of our Australian churches have a formal call to worship, perhaps even a processional. But here in the big auditorium the love and praise just seemed to flow together and suddenly I was aware that Miss Kuhlman was on stage.

A spirit of praise seemed to sweep the mighty auditorium. The people rose, as one, and erupted in joyous acclamation of sound and harmony. All around me they were spontaneously coming to their feet, arms raised toward heaven, voices blending together in marvelous symphony. The entire room was filled with music. It swelled up from the main floor, vibrated off the walls and ceiling, and lifted my inner being to heights never before experienced.

Slowly it died, until only the soft strains of the organ, barely heard, whispered through the room. Softly, just above the sound of a breath, I heard Miss Kuhlman's voice: "There is power in the name of Jesus . . ."

All around me I heard that name, that matchless name, being whispered from muted lips of thousands. "Jesus . . . Jesus . . . Jesus."

"There is a beautiful presence of the Holy Spirit here this afternoon," Miss Kuhlman was now saying. "The same Holy Spirit who fell upon those early believers at Pentecost is here today."

A sacred, holy stillness descended upon the meeting.

"There is a child being healed," she whispered. "He's in this section." She gestured to her left at the wheelchair section. My eyes followed the direction of her extended arm and I saw that young boy, that crippled, twisted young boy, rising out of his wheelchair.

A gasp went up from the audience. All over the auditorium people were rising to their feet, stretching their necks to see. The boy and his mother were out in the aisle, walking forward. A cheer, starting as a low rumble, grew with intensity and swept through the crowd.

The boy's steps seemed to grow stronger as he moved down the aisle. Miss Kuhlman met him at the front edge of the platform and escorted him to the microphone.

"This applause is not for me," Miss Kuhlman said to the young lad, "nor is it even for you. These people are applauding Jesus."

After questioning the boy and even having one of the doctors on the platform step out and examine him, Miss Kuhlman reached out to pray for him. Even before she uttered her first word, the boy crumpled to the floor.

My heart sank. *Oh no, it wasn't real. It was all emotion. He tried and got as far as the platform, but now he's fallen to the floor. How awful!*

But no one else seemed alarmed. Miss Kuhlman was standing on stage, her hands raised, praising the Lord. The ushers, the members of the choir—all were standing around looking at the boy and thanking God. One of the men helped the boy to his feet. He wasn't staggering. His legs were firm and strong.

"What happened?" I asked the man beside me, who had been to the meetings many times before.

"He went down under the power," he said.

"Under the power? What a strange phrase."

"Not so strange," the man whispered as the young boy left the stage with his mother. "It happens all the time when Miss Kuhlman prays for people. She says she doesn't understand it, and neither does anyone else. It's the same thing that happened in the Bible when people came face to face with the power of God, and fell to the ground."

It was too much to comprehend.

There was another healing in the wheelchair section. A lady whom I had noticed outside the building earlier had come forward. While in the wheelchair she had to breathe from an oxygen tank, which was attached to the chair. Now she was coming across the stage, pushing the wheelchair in front of her—the oxygen tank hanging uselessly to the frame. Behind her was a great line of other people who had been healed and were coming to the stage to testify.

I lost track of time as one after another the people came forward. It was so much different from the tent meeting I had attended in Melbourne. There they had brought the sick forward and the evangelist had prayed for them. Here the people came forward *after* they were healed. Miss Kuhlman prayed for no one to be healed. In fact, several times that afternoon she definitely said she was not a healer. She had no power herself, she insisted. All she did was conduct the service and God did the healing.

The meeting was drawing to a close. Neither Bruce nor I had evidenced any personal healing, but we had been blessed beyond all expectation. An announcement was made for a future meeting in December, less than a month away. I knew we should remain in the States in order to return once more.

Susan and Steve found us a beautiful room in Encinitas, down the coast from Los Angeles, where we could relax and enjoy being in this beautiful section of America. Three days later Bruce and I had returned to the room after breakfast. I was sitting quietly in a chair near the window reading my Bible when Bruce interrupted me.

"Mum, show me your hands."

"What's all this?" I answered, laying aside my Bible.

"Your hands," Bruce insisted. "Look at them."

I gasped. The rash was gone. How long it had been gone I had no idea. Perhaps it had disappeared during the night. Perhaps it had been while I was reading my Bible. But it was gone.

I hurried into the bathroom and examined other parts of my body. The ugly, red rash, which had become so much a part of me that I had forgotten about it, had disappeared. Not a trace was left. The rest of the day, indeed for many days thereafter, I spent the majority of my time praising God for this miraculous deliverance. Surely, I felt, it was the first sign that God intended to heal my heart also.

We moved back up to Los Angeles and returned to the Shrine Auditorium for the December meeting. Once again arriving before six o'clock in the morning, I found my new friends Orpha and June, in the queue.

As before, I was caught up in the presence of the Holy Spirit which seemed to permeate every corner of that great building. The meeting had scarcely started when Miss Kuhlman, in her warm, informal manner, began polling the people in the audience to see where they were from.

My heart was beating rapidly as people called out their home states. *Should I shout out "Australia"?* I wondered. Then, even before I had a chance to say anything, I heard something else. It was a rushing, gushing sound of wind whirling through the auditorium.

I looked up, expecting to see the huge drape which covers the ceiling, billowing in the wind. Nothing was moving. I looked at the stage; perhaps it was coming from there. The drapes were hanging motionless. No one else seemed to notice it.

I turned to Bruce. "Do you hear it?" I said.

"Hear what, Mum?" he asked.

Am I losing my mind, hearing sounds that aren't there? I wondered. I turned to Orpha who was sitting on the other side. "Can you hear that noise?"

She shrugged and said, "What noise?"

"It's a rushing noise, like the sound of the wind."

Orpha looked deep into my face. "Do you still hear it?" she asked.

"Yes, it's all through the building."

Orpha's lips grew white and she said with shaking voice. "It's the Holy Spirit. It's your healing. Let's join hands and pray."

Miss Kuhlman was still taking a poll of the states as Orpha, June, Bruce, and I joined hands down the row and began to pray. I felt a wonderful peace. At the same time there was a pumping sensation throbbing in my chest. I closed my eyes and could visualize the blood, long held in check beyond that blocked valve, now surging through the healed organ, pulsating out into my lungs and through my body. Along with it came an exquisite inner calm.

I relaxed in my seat and heard nothing for the next twenty minutes. It was as though I had dropped off to sleep, although Orpha later suggested I was really "under the power."

Then, as the voice of Jesus called dead Lazarus to rise and come forth from the tomb, I heard Miss Kuhlman's voice, rousing me from my reverie.

"There is someone in the center section, a dozen or so rows back, who has received a healing for a blockage in the chest—perhaps a blockage to the heart."

I was on my feet, waving my arms. "It's me!" I shouted. "Oh, thank God, it's me!"

Gone was my Scottish reserve, my Presbyterian dignity. Gone was the fear of ridicule, the shame of public opinion.

I dived for the aisle, tromping on people's feet, banging against their knees as they tried to move aside for me to get out. Behind me I could hear Bruce. "Mum, Mum, I can see colors out of my blind eye. My sight is returning!"

I reached back, grabbed his hand, and pulled him along with me. We barged out of the row of seats and into the aisle. An usher met us and tried to block our way.

"What have we here?" he asked kindly, determined not to let me get to the platform unless my healing was genuine.

I was unable to reply, unable to articulate. I guess my Australian accent was bad enough without having all my words jumbled together in excitement.

"It's me," I said over and over. "I am the one Kathryn Kuhlman was talking about. I'm healed."

I finally made him understand that I had received healing of my heart. Even as I stood there in the aisle, it was becoming more and more evident. The old tiredness, which I had lived with for twenty years was gone. I could feel my blood flowing freely through my body. I could breathe, long deep gasps of air all the way down to the bottom of my lungs. And the rattle in my heart, that awful rickety sound which used to wake me at night, was gone. *I was healed.*

The usher escorted me to the stage where a medical doctor pulled me aside for a few minutes and talked to me. He asked question after question but, like the usher, had a difficult time understanding me.

"Have you a husband?" he finally asked.

"Yes, back in Australia."

"Do you mean you came all the way from Australia to America to be healed?"

"On a wing and a prayer," I laughed.

I had almost forgotten about Bruce, who was standing behind me. I grabbed his hand and pulled him toward Miss Kuhlman. The doctor was telling her something about my aorta valve . . . Australia . . . Bruce . . . and suddenly I was on my back on the floor. For a moment I had a vision of Elijah, ascending to heaven in a whirlwind, and then it was like the emerald South Pacific at dawn, stretching for limitless miles beyond the horizon, calm and glassy, with only a slight ripple on the beach.

Someone helped me to my feet and I saw Miss Kuhlman's face in front of me, smiling. She reached out again and I slipped back into the serenity of that ocean of peace.

Strong arms lifted me back to my feet. I tried to speak to Miss Kuhlman, but I felt myself once again being immersed—slipping into the gentle tide of the Holy Spirit.

"Don't touch her," I heard Miss Kuhlman's soft voice from some place far away. "That's the power of God."

I do not know how long I remained on the platform, but some minutes later I was aware that two men were helping me to my feet. Bruce was in front of me, as we went down the steps to the main floor. He had removed his glasses and his face was wet with tears. Even though he could not see clearly out of his blind eye, it was miracle enough for him that he could see colors and shapes through it already.

To this day I cannot remember how we got back to our room in downtown Los Angeles. I remember stepping off the bus about a block away from the Oasis Motel and feeling so joyful that I began to skip and sing. "Oh, God is good, oh, God is good, praise the Lord, for the Lord is good."

I wanted to call Jack in Australia, but I knew he was in Sydney that day on a business trip. It made no difference: we were scheduled to leave early the next morning on a flight back to Melbourne and he would meet us at the airport. I could surprise him then.

I settled in my seat on the Pan Am 747. The captain announced we would be flying through a hurricane and warned all the passengers to buckle in tight and not be afraid. I smiled, leaned back, and prepared to go to sleep. Nothing frightened me any more. *I was whole!*

A Grateful Personal Testimony

The meadows laughed so gaily,
  The flow'rs wore fairest hue,
The genial sun smiled daily
  From skies of fleckless blue:
Life seemed a magic rhapsody
  Of field and flower and sky;
Then whispered I naively,
  "Heaven's favorite am I."

The sky grew sombre, fright'ning,
  Dark tempest swept around,
Mid thunder-peal and lightning
  It lashed me to the ground:
No more the lulling symphony,
  But gasping, heart-wrung cry,
As in bewildered agony
  I moaned to Heaven, "Why?"

Once more came beauty gleaming
  Thro' meadows, flowers, skies,
But now how lovelier seeming!
  I saw through chastened eyes!
My heart, to heav'n upreaching,
  In mellower strain now sings;
I've learned the secret teaching
  Which only suffering brings.

                              —J.S.B.

CHAPTER TWELVE

A Grateful
Personal Testimony

With upspringing gratitude a godly psalmist, three thousand years ago, addressed his friends and neighbors as follows: "Come and hear, all ye that fear God, and I will declare what he hath done for my soul" (Ps. 66:16). Royal David, too, sang with a leaping heart, "O LORD my God, I cried unto thee, and thou hast *healed* me. . . . thou hast *kept me alive*" (Ps. 30:2-3, emphases mine).

There is a two-sided value in such testimony. It honors our Lord, and it stimulates the faith of His people. So although my precious wife and I keenly dislike talking about ourselves, this chapter is a testimony concerning our own experience of divine healing.

Away back in ancient Galilee, when a delegation asked John the Baptist who he really was, he made no claim to be a prophet or some special messenger of the Lord. He did not even give himself a personal identity but simply said, "I am a *voice*"—meaning a voice speaking for another, whose "shoe latchet" he was not worthy to unloose (John 1:23,27).

That is what my Ethel and I would fain be here: just two voices, two voices blending as one in testimony to Him whose lovingkindness has set us singing, "My cup runneth over!" We invite those who have ears to hear: "O magnify the LORD with me, and let us exalt his name together!" (Ps. 34:3).

In the Day of My Trouble I Sought the LORD (Ps. 77:2)

Late in 1973 we returned home after a lecture tour covering parts of Greece, Turkey, Patmos and other Aegean islands, Crete, Rhodes, Syria, Lebanon, and Israel. (I had been one of the lecturers.) We had been home only a few days when my wife said, "Sid, I have disturbing news for you: I have cancer." I could scarcely believe my ears; but she had indeed said it, and her grave look told me that she really meant it.

"Oh, Ethel, are you quite sure? If so, how long have you known?—and why did you not tell me sooner?"

"Yes, I'm pretty sure. I knew it well before we went on the tour, but I did not want it to interfere with your ministry."

The very next day I accompanied her to our doctor. As soon as he saw the evidence he groaned, "Oh, Mrs. Baxter, this certainly seems like cancer. Let me call in the surgeon at once; he is only a couple of doors away." One look by the surgeon was enough to confirm it; and his big regret was that the growth had apparently now traveled right into the armpit and the lymph system. There and then a date was fixed for the operation—mastectomy, for metastic carcinoma.

As we came out from our interview with the surgeon my mind was dazed. I felt as though I would fall to pieces, for it seemed a foregone conclusion that I was to lose my lifelong companion. Her father had died of cancer. So had her eldest brother. So had her next-younger brother. My Ethel and I had been little neighbors when we were only a few years old. We had grown up together. We had gone to the same school. She had never had any sweetheart but me and I none but her. Our union of heart and memory went right back to early childhood. The thought of the dark, empty blank without her was dismaying beyond words. I knew the Lord would somehow prove all-sufficient, and there was no rebellion in my heart; but I was all too human, and it seemed to me as though the sun was suddenly being blotted out of my sky.

The date of the operation was December 12, 1973. My dear one braved it trustfully and survived it successfully. In fact she healed from the surgery remarkably well. However, healing from the mastectomy was one thing: complete cure from cancer in her system was a very different matter. Bit by bit we learned afterward that there was far more and far worse.

She was put on a course of treatment by radiation. This rather surprised us and aroused our suspicion that more cancer was there, and it surely was—more than we then knew. She came through the several weeks and twenty installments of radiation with only minor accompaniments of irritation such as radiation often provokes; but, alas, there was now a paralysis of the left vocal cord which left her voiceless; even whispers were a struggle.

By that time another worrying symptom was her rapid loss of weight. She was becoming a mere shadow of her former healthy womanhood. Along with that, it was cutting to my own heart to see in her that strange fear which so often grips the cancer victim.

It was decided by the doctors that she should be put on a chemotherapy course of treatment, i.e., on a hormonal and chemical therapy program. But as a prior requirement to that they arranged for an operation on her vocal cord. We were told that the throat operation would be a "quite minor" one and that Mrs. Baxter could probably leave the hospital in the evening of the same day.

Instead of leaving the hospital the same day, she came the nearest to dying (so it seemed) that she had ever been and had to remain in the hospital some days. She started having gagging spasms. She could scarcely swallow either solids or liquids; and if the slightest speck of anything got on the trachea (windpipe), she would choke, unable to breathe. Apparently the radiation had so dried her up inside that the chest and throat muscles did not have normal flexibility to expand and contract. As the surgeon said, "Even at best, radiation is a mixed blessing." It was awful to see my dear one suffer so. Ten or a dozen times during those days I held her in my arms during critical chokings, expecting any second to be her last.

Then came the chemotherapy. I am only stating what everyone now knows when I say that the drugs used in chemotherapy are lethal. That is the very word the doctor himself used in telling me about them—"*lethal.*" She was put on Stilbestrol, Cytoxan, and weekly intravenous injections of Fluorouracil and Methotrexate. From the start there were distressing side effects which I will not here describe, but what alternative to chemotherapy was there?

One day I chatted with the doctor for a few minutes, in Ethel's absence. "Will this treatment cure her?" He slowly shook his head and then explained that there was a whole cancer "mass" in her mediastinum (the space between the lungs) and that there were cancerous nodes up the left lung. It was quite inoperable. Attempted surgical removal would kill her.

"How long has she?" I asked him. He paused, then slowly replied, "Eight months, maybe; or it could possibly be a couple of years."

I knew then that there had either to be a miracle or a funeral. Up to that point, although I had prayed fervently that God would heal and restore Ethel, I had meant that He would use the surgery and other natural means to do so. But now, since all such earthly skills were confessedly impotent, I was cast on God alone for *supernatural* intervention.

Day after day, early and late, I sought the dear heavenly Master whom for fifty years I had loved, adored, and preached. I knew that many others were praying as well. Yet somehow I could not find Him in the way I needed and wondered why He should seem so distant.

Then, very early one morning, about three weeks after my special praying had started, He was there, in my study! I knew it. He was really there. I did not see Him—yet I did! I did not hear Him—yet I did! I did not touch Him—yet I did! Many of you will know what I mean. As clearly as could be, He said to me in deep-down heart language, "All right, Sid. You think I have not been listening; but I have. I know your need of Ethel. I have kept you waiting for a purpose which you will soon know. Sid, if you can take it in simple faith, the healing is yours."

Yes, I knew instantaneously that He had said it; and amid my tears of grief and joy, in simple faith I "took" it. That instant, though neither Ethel nor I had the slightest physical evidence of it then, the whole cancer mass disappeared—as was verified two days later.

The second day after that early morning experience, we had to be at the doctor's for the weekly examination. As it was the seventh such, she had to have another X-ray that day, along with special clinical tests to check on what side effects the chemotherapy drugs might be having. The first inkling that anything inside Ethel had happened was when the doctor saw the blood report. He glanced at it, then picked up his phone and said, "You've sent the wrong one." The reply came back: "No, that's Mrs. Baxter's." After that Ethel went with him and a lady doctor into another room for the clinical examination.

So far as I can recall, it was some ten to fifteen minutes later that the doctor came to me in the waiting room and said something like this: "Well! Dr. Baxter, I would like to have a chat with you about your wife, but I cannot stay now as I am due in the theater for surgery. We are certainly surprised—very pleased, of course, but puzzled. That large cancer mass about which I told you and the cancer nodes up the left lung—*they have all completely gone!* My colleague will show you the X-ray taken some seven weeks ago and the new one taken this morning."

Well, we saw the two X-rays side by side, and there was no mistaking: *the new one was thoroughly clear!* Can you imagine our feelings? We wept, we sang, we praised, we winged hosannas to heaven. I was back in Psalm 30.

> O LORD my God, I cried unto thee,
> And thou hast healed me
>
> Thou hast turned for me my mourning
> into dancing;
> Thou hast put off my sackcloth,
> and girded me with gladness.
>
> (Psalm 30:2,11)

"In My Distress I Called Upon the LORD" (Ps. 18:6)

And now let me "declare what the LORD hath done" by way of bodily healing in my own experience. On the first day of January 1955, my dear wife and I left Liverpool, England, for what we intended to be a two-year Bible-teaching itineration here in the U.S., never dreaming that we would ever make our residence here. Yet somehow after the first few months of ministry here, we knew by spiritual instinct that our heavenly Master meant us to stay on; and we are still here, twenty-three years later.

Everywhere we were received with characteristic American cordiality; and if I may say so with nothing but humble, grateful praise to God, everywhere our expounding of the Word seemed frought with heaven's blessing. There were far more open doors than we could enter; and there ensued ten years of practically non-stop peregrination through most of the states, among various denominations, in churches large and small, at summer conferences and united conventions. At the same time we managed to keep up with a fairly heavy correspondence, gave interviews on and off radio or television, visited other countries, wrote books, and in general kept "up to the eyes" in eager doings for our Lord. Many souls were born again; and many Christian believers testified to such enrichment that our hearts sang to heaven, thanking our Lord that He could use such unworthy vessels. It was a decade of wonderfully rewarding ministry.

The Unexpected Happens

Then, exactly ten years after our emigration to the U.S., the unexpected happened; and it did so in a suddenly prostrating way. All thought of further travel ministry seemed knocked out in one fell blow. I had to be hurried to the hospital in Santa Barbara with acute diabetes.

I call it the "unexpected" because there is no other instance of diabetes in our Baxter family, either in my father's or my mother's line. In my own case it was unwittingly self-induced. Let me explain.

For years my dear wife preferred not to eat breakfast, except perhaps a nibble now and then. So during those earlier years of continual travel, I would say in a morning, "I think, dear, I won't go into the hotel coffee shop for breakfast without you. We'll have a cup of tea here in our room and then an early midday meal."

About that time someone gave me that best seller *Vermont Folk Medicine*, written by Dr. D. C. Jarvis. In my opinion it is a strange mixture of medical knowledge and naivete. Apple cider vinegar and honey are the two wonders on which it majors. Honey is extolled as nature's purest sugar and quickest energy imparter, the finest conditioner for athletes, and so on. Not having studied diet at all up to that point, I was "taken in."

"Why, this is the very thing to keep me physically at 'concert pitch' for all the travel and public ministry! It won't matter one bit, my missing breakfast, if I make it up with plenty of honey," so I convinced myself.

Each morning I would have one or two cups of tea, each containing a big teaspoonful of honey. We started buying five-pound containers of honey, and I got into the habit of having one or two teaspoonfuls in each cup of tea—several times a day. By that time, also, we had learned not to book series of meetings up North in the wintertime but to keep South and then go North in summer. Thus all through the year I was on a sweet rather than a savory diet.

My! did I have energy! Did I get corpulent! My jacket and collar buttons were all pulling! My wife teased me that when I appeared on platforms, I looked like a prosperous farmer! So it went on for a few years. I was a walking sugarplum. Then trouble struck.

We were holding meetings in Pomona, California. An elderly lady who followed us around whenever we were within a convenient radius invited us to her home. She commented appreciatively on my pleasant plumpness, to which I responded, "Yes, I'm very well, thanks to plenty honey." "Honey!" she gravely exclaimed. "You stop that honey, young man! It nearly killed my son!" The remark was smilingly shrugged off, but later we wished we had asked her *how* honey had played traitor. Also, I wished I had known my Bible a bit better. Twice in one chapter we are warned: "It is not good to eat much honey" (Prov. 25:27, cf. v. 16), even though honey merits all that Jarvis says about it!

When we got home to Santa Barbara after the Pomona series, disturbing developments occurred. My healthy-looking plumpness fell away, and my flesh sagged. I began to have a pasty look. I had an insatiable thirst and could not help drinking, drinking, drinking at the cold water tap; yet all the while I seemed to be drying up. I went thin and looked haggard. "Oh, Mrs. Baxter," a neighbor volunteered, "your husband has all the symptoms of diabetes!"

Yes, I had brought on diabetes. For five years and more I had so continuously over-sugared myself that at last my bewildered little pancreas had cried, "Sid, old boy, I just cannot take any more! I'll have to spill all this sugar over into your system!" The result: Diabetes mellitus!

I certainly had it; and a crisis point came early one morning. Languidly I dragged myself out of bed, feeling as parched as a desert. When my Ethel asked me what I would like for breakfast, I said, "My mouth and throat are so dry, I think the only thing I could manage is a small salad." As it turned out, even a tasty salad was no use. Not a morsel could I swallow. I had no saliva at all. I was dehydrated.

Even then I foolishly resisted my wife's appeals that we contact a doctor; but later that day, as I became more distressingly ill, she took the law into her own hands and called the Santa Barbara Medical Clinic. Still later the doctor called back with an emergency message. The urine test had revealed not only that I had diabetes but that I had it very badly. I was critically ill and must be brought to the Cottage Hospital without a moment's delay. The fact was, as we later learned, I had reached the line just beyond which would have been coma and death.

It costs me something to confess, but I will frankly admit that just before going to hospital I had one of those desolating emotional flops, which at some time or other floor most of us. The whole facade of fond hopes and cherished plans dropped from my ministry. Indeed, the whole structure seemed to collapse around me. Any further vigorous ministry seemed a forlorn hope. I saw myself a pallid-faced invalid or at best a diabetic going round with an insulin needle carefully dieting, and not really safe for travel ministry. Even dehydration could not prevent a flow of tears. Deep down it was not that I feared either sickness or death, but the sudden shock and sense of bleak frustration crumpled me.

Yet I went to the hospital smiling (forgive the seeming self-compliment), for as I cast myself wholly upon our Lord Jesus, His presence with me flamed into vivid new reality. I knew He was with me, and I found myself praying that He would make me a means of communicating Him to others while I was in the hospital.

How can I ever forget those two weeks in that hospital! Something happened there which I could never have guessed beforehand. The Lord met me and did something new in my life.

As soon as I entered, of course, I was given insulin treatment; and careful tests were taken daily. True enough, I had become badly diabetic. The tests confirmed it. But by this time I had resignedly leaned my weary head on my heavenly Father's bosom. I had wrestled my heart into complete surrender to His permissive will for me. I knew that the God who bled for me on Calvary could never mock me, that He was sympathetically sharing with me, and that He would somehow overrule to my eternal good the calamity which He had allowed to lay me low. And He *did*. Let me tell you about it.

Who Believes in Visions?

When I was just a young Christian, in my late teens and early twenties, I used to envy those Christians who testified to having "*visions* from the Lord." It seemed to me that theirs must be a superior, aerified kind of spirituality. As time slipped by, however, I revised my thinking. Observation caused me to suspect that in most cases the visions were a product of excitable imagination; for apparently they served no real purpose and tended to beget a dreamy kind of religion rather than solid Christian character. At any rate, I myself have never been the type to have visions. I considered it extremely unlikely that ever the Lord would speak to *me* by such a means, but while I was in hospital that is just what He did!

Either the second or third morning, when I was emerging from sleep into that hazy semiconsciousness before one becomes fully awake, I had a vision. There was a bright amber background, then, in the forefront, a Bible—opened to Psalm 103; and next a hand appeared with the index finger pointing to verse 3: "*who forgiveth all thine iniquities.*"

What those words conveyed to me at that moment I could hardly get over to you vividly enough. They seemed to say, "Sid, what does it matter basically whether you live or die, whether you are well or ill, compared with knowing that you are *saved*, that you have a full, free, final, and forever forgiveness, a forgiveness which is not merely a pardon but a loving welcome to the heavenly Father's heart, and that you have a ministry for Him in that fair realm beyond the grave?"

"Who forgiveth all thine iniquities"—the words were like a glistening rainbow overarching me all that day.

The next morning, just at the same time and in the same way, there again was the same vision—the amber background, the Bible opened to Psalm 103, and the hand with the pointing index finger. But now the finger moved to the next clause in the psalm: *"Who healeth all thy diseases."* Never had those words seemed so wonderful. They stood out with a neon glow. I looked and looked and looked. They were before my inner eyes all day. I knew, I knew, I *knew:* God was about to *heal* me!

The third morning, there it all was again: the amber background, the Bible opened to Psalm 103, and the pointing hand; but now the finger had moved to the further clause: *"So that thy youth is renewed like the eagle's."* Even as I came out of the vision, I was still overcome with wonder. I knew that God was telling me not only that He was going to heal me but that I was going to be renewed into even better health than ever hitherto. I recalled that the eagle is a long-lived bird and that (besides its annual molting) when it is near a hundred years old, it casts *all* its feathers, from head to talons, and has a complete re-feathering. So far as I know, the eagle is unique in that respect; and that, of course, is why the psalmist used it for his illustration: "Thy youth is renewed like the *eagle's.*"

As I kept looking at the promise, something else flashed into my mind. In a lecture which I had recently prepared, I had made a point of the difference between a "climacteric" and a "climax." My dictionary definition of a climacteric is "A period or point in human life in which some great change in the constitution of health takes place." Just underneath it adds, *The Grand Climacteric:* the sixty-third year; supposed to be a critical year for *men"!* And there I was, in *my* sixty-third year! It was *my* "grand climacteric" all right!—and God was meeting me then in a strangely wonderful way, with forgiving love, healing power, and gracious health renewal! He had laid me low that He might lift me up reconditioned for new service.

Soon "signs" began to appear. During the hours following the second vision, I had insulin shock; that is, my blood sugar level suddenly dropped from way, way up down to the low fifties. One of the doctors was called. From then on my insulin injection was reduced. Two days later my sugar level plummeted again. The doctors were puzzled. The insulin injections were further readjusted.

Some days later I left the hospital, with diet charts, insulin gadgets, and instruction booklet; but deep down I knew they would not be needed. Nor were they. The Lord had told me He wanted me to do another ten years of travel ministry. During all those ten years there was no recurrence of the trouble. We traveled, preached, lectured, wrote books, put more time in than ever, and had even more tokens of divine blessing on our ministry of the Word than ever before. Often I would marvel at the stick-at-it energy which I had. In the pattern of Isaiah 40:31, I found myself mounting up with wings as eagle's, running without weariness, walking without fainting; and I remembered the vision:

> Who forgiveth all thine iniquities,
> Who healeth all thy diseases,
> Who satisfieth thy years [elderliness] with good;
> So that thy youth is *renewed* like the eagle's
> (Psalm 103:3,5, ERV)

I had no need to be on any kind of diet. My cuisine was full and varied. There really *was* "renewal." However, having had that brush with the dread disease which assails so many in these days, I took the precaution to cut out all refined sugars and to study diet with a view to continuing fitness—for I do not believe that divine healing allows any of us to play fast and loose with commonsense dietary and hygenic rules of health.

At this moment of writing, it is thirteen years since that upset during my grand climacteric(!). My prayer and confidence is, in Pauline phraseology, "that the life also of Jesus might be made manifest in [my] body" (2 Cor. 4:10) so that to my last breath on earth I may serve and praise my royal Savior-Healer. It is with a deeper sense of gratitude than ever, nowadays, that I sing the grand old favorite:

> *Praise, my soul, the King of Heaven,*
> *To his feet thy tribute bring;*
> *Ransomed,* healed, *restored, forgiven,*
> *Who, like thee, his praise should sing?*

But Strange-seeming Mysteries Remain

Yes, with vivid empathy I can join with David in Psalm 40: "He brought me up also out of an horrible pit, out of the miry clay, and set my feet upon a rock, and established my goings: and he hath put a new song in my mouth, even praise unto our God." Yet what enigmatical mysteries remain! How can I tell you? In one of his strangest-seeming providences, our dear Lord allowed my precious Ethel to suffer weariness and pain for some days and then took her to be with himself in the heavenly home, only four years after her wonderful healing.

How we had loved each other through the years! At the time of her translation we were just about to celebrate our golden wedding anniversary. Right through our long wedlock our love for each other had grown not only deeper but fonder. I can truthfully say that to the very end my dear queen never walked into my study but I thrilled. And now (oh, grief beyond expression) she was gone, inexorably gone, never to walk again from room to room in our dear little home. To think of her yonder, actually looking into the face of Jesus, seeing "the King in his beauty," living in the transfiguring radiance of his face, experiencing the exquisite rapture of heaven, how could I help but reverently thrill and adore, and even indulge a little envy? But here on the earthward side, oh, the pain of the parting, the sense of bereftness, the bleak blank, the stab of fear in thinking of the lonely future!

Yet I must not omit to give my testimony to this: from the time of her going our wonderful Savior became more wonderful to me than ever hitherto. He matched my emergency with his all-sufficiency. Since then, in my daily trystings with him, He has somehow been nearer, clearer, dearer, than ever before. I thought I would never sing or smile again: but He has turned my fear to faith, my sighing to singing, my grievous loss to spiritual gain, my bereftness into richer communion with Himself. He has taught me to "sing Hallelujah through my tears": and if I may reverently say so, here on earth Jesus never looks so beautiful as when we see him through our tears. It is then that we see most of all what He can be to us.

From that time onwards our Lord began to speak to me in a comforting new way through the promises and assurances of his written Word. Time would fail to tell how this and that and the other passage have leapt into brilliant new meaning. It has reminded me of something which happened when I was just a youth. One night soon after I had got into bed and was about to fall asleep I was startled by a strange, bright light underneath the bedclothes, quite near to my face. I wondered what on earth it could be. At first it seemed like two sharp, bright eyes, then it became a ring of glowing points, and then a disc of opalescent light. A moment later I chuckled to realize what it was. I had forgotten to take my wristwatch off, and it had a luminous face—that is, a face which became luminous in darkness. Oh, there are so many promises of Scripture which become luminous with new meaning in our times of darkness! That is what I found after my bereavement.

Then, as the days became weeks and months, I began to realize that there was a golden lining to the frowning cloud. I began to detect *reasons* why our Lord had taken my dear one. For one thing, I discerned how kind it was to my Ethel that *she* should have been taken first, rather than *my* having been taken, leaving *her* in widowhood—which would have been beset with trying circumstances which I will not here take space to detail. The more I reviewed the situation, the more confirmed I became that there was divine wisdom and *considerateness* in what had happened. There were other reasons, too, which became clear, but they are secrets between God and my own heart. I became increasingly aware, also, of God's presence enveloping me, and of his strength supporting me, and of his putting a new something into my ministry not there before. Cowper's stanzas kept singing their way into my mind:

> Ye fearful saints, fresh courage take,
>   The clouds ye so much dread,
> Are big with mercy, and shall break
>   In blessings on your head.

> Our finite minds so often err
>   And scan God's work in vain:
> God is his own interpreter,
>   And He can make it plain.

In the preceding chapter I give the testimony of Mrs. Morag McDougall, the Melbourne lady who was miraculously healed of heart disease. What a testimony that is, and documented beyond all gainsaying. By interesting coincidence, her instantaneous healing occurred roughly about the same time as my dear wife's divine healing of cancer; and she, too, passed to heaven about the same time as my Ethel. In both cases the question arises: After such a remarkable healing, why should death of the body be allowed to occur so soon afterward? Yes, there seems plenty of mystery about that: yet both were now elderly, and both of them lived long enough after their healing to give wide and effective testimony to it, to the praise of our dear heavenly Physician.

I am not saying that these considerations clear up the seeming mystery, but they do throw *some* light into it. It should be remembered that even at best, miraculous physical healings are but for the few years we live in these mortal bodies. God is far more concerned about our *spiritual* education and our preparation for the high destiny which is ours through Christ in the larger, higher life beyond this. God is absolutely sovereign, with a sovereignty immersed in fatherly love. He knows what is best—both when to heal and when not to heal; both when to leave us here and when to take us there. Meanwhile, with worshipful gratitude for every answered prayer for healing, and with trustful resignation to that loving wisdom which never errs, we must rest in our Lord's sympathetic assurance to Simon Peter in John 13:7, "What I do thou knowest not now; but thou shalt know hereafter."

Conclusion: Final Reflections

I believe that God would still have us follow the example of the apostle Paul, and pray for the sick; and I know of multiplied instances where God has had mercy, and raised up the sick when no human aid could have given healing. I believe that Paul would join us in saying "Amen" to the prescription of the apostle James: "Is any sick? Let him pray."

Yet there is nothing in the Scripture which teaches Christians that God looks with disapproval upon the use of natural means in the time of sickness, or that it is necessary to lay aside the use of means before God will answer prayer in the supernatural realm. Moreover, we can show that while certain teachers of healing in our day denounce the use of means as contrary to a life of faith in God, almost all of them in the time of sickness or infirmity have used means in some form or other, or else they have died before their time.

—Rowland V. Bingham

This must still remain axiomatic in all our thinking and teaching on direct divine healing of the body: Our Lord has definitely promised to *save* all who come to Him for salvation, but He has *not* promised to heal all who now come to Him for bodily healing.

—J.S.B.

CHAPTER THIRTEEN

Conclusion: Final Reflections

We have now traversed the three areas indicated at the outset of these studies: (1) divine healing through the centuries, (2) divine healing as it is preached today, (3) divine healing in present-day experience. Realizing how much more might have been included, I readily grant the incompleteness and other imperfections clinging to our treatment of the subject. Yet I hopefully believe that enough has been said to validate our conviction that a continuance of direct divine healings may reasonably be expected today inside our local Christian churches. The actual fact is that such *are* happening today in significant increase among Christian groups.

But what about the big *public* gatherings for miracle healings *outside* our local churches? That many startling healings have been happening in them is beyond all gainsaying. How are *they* to be classified? That prompts some final reflections.

Where have these studies brought us? Four things emerge: (1) Direct divine healings have occurred right down through the centuries when Christian groups have fervently returned to New Testament teaching. (2) Such healings are Scripturally promised to the Lord's people and are clearly included in the Holy Spirit's "gifts" to the Church. (3) Such healing miracles are plentifully happening again today. (4) A hitherto *unknown* development now appears in the modern healing *movement* through which direct divine healings are coming, not only to evangelical believers, but to many others. With those four findings established, perhaps we are now ready for some thoughtful conclusions and recommendations.

Some Perplexing Problems

At once we find provoking enigmas attaching to *public* healing ministries today, like strange blotches on a human body, indicating that something is wrong with the system. This is true of even the largest and best known such as those of Oral Roberts and Kathryn Kuhlman. There is one persistent problem: Why are some healed and others *not?* That question indeed may be asked in intensified form: Why, comparatively, are so *few* healed and so many not? We thank God for all genuine divine interventions to heal and that in the aggregate they are an impressive number; but for everyone cured, scores remain *un*healed.

This has been a sore problem, not only to thoughtful onlookers, but to those who have been preachers and actual *channels* of divine healing. As representing the many, let Kathryn Kuhlman be quoted: "Why are not all healed? The only honest answer I can give is: I do not know; and I am afraid of those who claim that they do know. For only God knows; and who can fathom the mind of God?"

Is there, then, any satisfying answer? It seems to me that there are three main considerations which throw light on it, especially the third.

The Sovereign Wisdom of God

First and most obviously, the yes and no are decided by the sovereign *wisdom* of God. The divine will which decides is never merely arbitrary. Whether or not we grasp it, there is always benign motive. God is far more concerned with educating *souls* for eternal destinies than in healing mortal bodies for a few extra but quickly expiring years on earth.

In India two blind women entered a missionary hospital. One of them went out later with her sight restored yet with no response to the Gospel and still unsaved. The other woman remained incurably blind; but in her blindness and heartbreak of disappointment she suddenly found the light which no darkness can quench and the joy which transfigures deepest grief. She found Christ and went out eternally saved. Which of those two women was the more blessed or the more deeply *healed?* God's first concern is always the cure of *souls*.

The same loving wisdom operates just as decisively among afflicted Christians. However unsympathetic God may seem at times, in reality He is "very present" and "touched with the feeling of our infirmity." Unless Christ and the Scriptures are a lie, when God does not heal us bodily, He suffers *with* us inwardly. If only we could always perceive it.

> Ill that He blesses is our good,
>   And unblest good is ill;
> And all is right that seems most wrong
>   If it be *His* wise will.

But especially in these days, when there seems to be almost an epidemic of physical healings in some places among both believers and others, we must recognize this sovereign wisdom of God. Many such miracles are not just "mercy healings" (as Kathryn Kuhlman rightly called some of them); they are *proof* healings, i.e., proofs that true Christianity is of God. Such being so, we may well praise God and pray for more, yet always recognizing that in such cases God will sovereignly *select* persons through whose healing He can most usefully demonstrate the divine origin of the Gospel. However much we may or may not know as to why some are healed and others not, we *must* allow for this discriminating sovereignty of God.

Illumination by Parallel

We get illuminating confirmation of that selective sovereignty by comparison with what happens in large evangelistic campaigns. Moody and Sankey were the Spirit-guided innovators of modern "mass evangelism," followed by Torrey and Alexander, then others. At present, in the Billy Graham campaigns we have the most elaborately organized mass evangelism ever contrived. Heaven be praised for all who have become saved by our Lord Jesus in such campaigns; but what about all the others who have *not* even though they attended?

Often there seems a baffling contrariness in what happens. Here is a person who has been prayed for by friends and pressed to attend; yet the earnest Gospel message leaves him strangely untouched. Here is another who just meanders in curiously, without the slightest concern for his soul, but is suddenly stricken with alarm over his sin and is one of the first to be converted. How many of those converted are the seemingly unlikely! How many of the seemingly likely go out unresponding!

Come to think of it, does not this puzzling feature keep reappearing, not only in evangelistic campaigns, but throughout our more usual church ministries? Some come under the power of the Word quite evidently through the moving of the Holy Spirit on them while others, sitting under the same presentation of saving truth, seem afflicted by hopeless deafness or incapacitation to "lay hold on life eternal."

In all of this we are right back up against that (to us) insoluble mystery of divine sovereignty and human free will coexisting without either of them being violated. Man is free within amply wide enough latitude for him to be consciously independent and responsible at all times. Yet high over all is the super-control of Him who *allows* man this wide freedom.

Therefore, what we see happening in *healing* missions today is not peculiar to them. This recurrent spectacle of some being strikingly healed while others who seem perhaps to be likelier or worthier qualifiers are silently by-passed is paralleled far and wide in other connections. Admittedly that does not solve the problem, but it may well allay our feeling of helpless *surprise* at it. It is one further expression of an overall divine pattern of procedure. Back of what *we* see outwardly, there are divine purposes for human individuals which are all the while moving on through processes beyond our understanding but all of which are motivated by unerring divine love and wisdom for our utmost well-being.

Building on Unsupportable Assumptions

But we come now to what, in my own judgment, is the clearest reason why some are healed and others are not. I believe that the modern *public* healing movement is founded on a subtle *fallacy*. Its preachers are basing their message on propositions which seem Biblical enough superficially but which on careful examination are found to be misapplications of Scripture. Let me here state and then justify a principal conclusion to which these studies have been leading. The main reason for the enigmatical zigzag of "some healed but others not" is as follows:

> *The modern public healing movement is operating on a partly faulty basis inasmuch as it is applying to the public at large Scriptures which pertain exclusively to local Christian churches and born-again Christian believers.*

Let me underscore a remark already made. Although divine healing is promised to individual believers, and although "gifts of healings" are promised to local Christian groups, nowhere in the New Testament can I find that healing for the mortal body is to be preached as a component in the Christian message to "whosoever" or as an adjunct to the Gospel of salvation through Christ.

In an earlier part of these studies have we not seen how wrong it is to presume that because our Lord worked numerous healing miracles long ago, they are meant to continue today? Have we not seen also that we have no valid reason to expect the post-Pentecost miracles of the Apostles to be perpetuated down to the present? There is no Scripture statement that either our Lord's miracles or those of the suspense period covered by the Acts were to continue throughout subsequent history.

Reflect again: our Lord's miracles were *credentials* of His Messiahship to *Israel*, and the Pentecostal miracles of the Apostles were "signs" again mainly to Israel. The healing miracles among the Gentiles, through Paul, were also special attesting "signs and wonders"—supernatural apologetics adapted to conditions as they then *were* rather than to conditions which now *are*. Largely, they were not healings of born-again believers *within* local Christian churches, for at that time neither the organized Church as a whole nor local Christian churches had been established. There were no New Testament Scriptures much less a completed and logically structured Bible; there was no world-girdling, well-established, tried-and-proved Christianity.

Today we *do* have a completed Bible, a world-girdling Christian organization, accumulated "Christian evidences," and generations of Christian experience. The whole situation seems so different from Apostolic times that many thinkers, as earlier mentioned, have asked, "Do we really *need* miracles today as they were needed way back then?" We may reasonably ask again, How *can* the healing miracles of today be a continuation of those performed by our Lord and the Apostles since *all* who came then were healed *without exception* whereas today the thorniest problem is "Why are only some healed and many others *not?*"

With nothing but cordiality to all concerned, I give it again as my considered opinion that the modern public healing movement is operating, at least in part, on misapplied Scriptures. It has no real right to base itself on the healing miracles either of our Lord or of the Apostles. As for the New Testament Epistles, *their* promises of supernatural healing belong *only* to born-again believers within local Christian churches; and therefore the modern healing movement has no right to make *those* provisions the basis on which to offer healing to the *public* at large.

WHAT, THEN, OF THE MIRACLE HEALINGS ACTUALLY OCCURRING IN BIG HEALING GATHERINGS TODAY?

Yes, that is the further question. The fact that many wonderful miracle healings are occurring today in great public healing rallies who can deny? Only those deny who have not been and seen. With my own eyes almost jumping out of their sockets, I have seen the dumb from birth given speech, the stone-deaf given new hearing, the long blind suddenly given clear vision, terminal cancer instantaneously cured (and later medically attested), crippled arthritics released and straightened on the spot, wheelchair victims of multiple sclerosis wheel their own chairs away, not to mention other such wonderful healings.

Let us get this bluntly straight here. To use a common English slang, those outside critics who still keep decrying all these miracle healings as fakes are "talking out of the back of their hats." Despite the problem "Why some, not others?" many genuine healings are taking place. What is more, for some decades now they have been happening on a scale never known before since sub-Apostolic days. In confirmation of that statement, let me recommend the following publications by Kathryn Kuhlman:

> *Captain LeVrier Believes in Miracles* (Bethany Fellowship, 1974)
> *God Can Do It Again* (Pyramid Publications, 1974)
> *How Big Is God?* (Bethany Fellowship, 1974)
> *I Believe in Miracles* (Pyramid Publications, 1969)
> *Never Too Late* (Bethany Fellowship, 1975)
> *Standing Tall* (Bethany Fellowship, 1975)
> *10,000 Miles for a Miracle* (Bethany Fellowship, 1974)
>
> I also recommend *The Miracles* by H. Richard Casdorph, M.D., Ph.D. (Logos International, 1976).

The above instances of extraordinary miracle healing are all just as carefully substantiated as they are touching and thrilling; and they are but a few choice sheaves from a large harvest field of present-day evidences.

Yes, the extraordinary healings certainly *are* happening today in connection with large public ministries. But if (as I maintain) they are *not* happening in fulfillment of New Testament promises made exclusively to Christian believers, and if the modern public healing movement has no right to make those promises its basis for offering healing indiscriminately, then how *shall* we classify those miracle healings happening in such public ministries?

I know of only one Scripture passage on which the modern *public* healing movement may with some justification base itself. It is that controverted passage in Mark 16:15-18.

> Go ye into all the world, and preach the gospel to every creature. He that believeth and is baptized shall be saved. . . . And these signs shall follow them that believe; In my name they shall cast out demons. . . . they shall lay hands on the sick, and they shall recover.

Those "signs" evidently *were* meant to have a place in Christian witness to the public. They are not to be confused with the Holy Spirit's "gifts" *inside* the Church. They are meant to operate *through* the Lord's people to the public *outside*. Of course, the very fact that our Lord called them "signs" may indicate that they were intended only for the Apostolic period; for "signs" are intendedly temporary only. Yet over against that is the fact that those "signs" were still given on a wide scale long after the Apostles and first-century Christians were all gone. As I have already suggested, may not those "signs" have been meant to break out again and again at subsequent periods of special emergency or challenge?

Remember, however, those "signs" are not themselves the Gospel. They are only an accompaniment of it, if and when they occur. Our Lord certainly did not give us any prescript to *preach* them. Yet inasmuch as there is no Scripture which says they were ever rescinded, may we not even today *expect* them—to meet the challenge of these age-end decades?

Well, I believe that today we *are* seeing another fulfillment of Mark 16, which means that the public healing miracles, often among unconverted persons, are not only "mercy healings" (as Kathryn Kuhlman called them) but new *apologetics* attesting the divine origin of the Gospel. Perhaps there is even more to it than that, as I will try to show.

A Unique Latter-Day Phenomenon

Frankly, I believe that today we are face-to-face with a unique *latter-day phenomenon*. Mark 16:15-18 is being fulfilled in an unprecedented way. God is doing a new thing to match the times. The modern public healing movement is *not* fulfilling New Testament promises given exclusively to the Church (except in the sense that many of those who receive healing are Christian believers *from* local churches); it is fulfilling something else. The time has come, so I deem, when we must make a sharp distinction between the healing ministry of the Holy Spirit inside a local Christian church and the miracles He is doing in public gatherings of the present-day healing *movement*. We are dealing with something which has never happened before. Let me clarify this.

Although down through the A.D. centuries miracles of divine healing have recurrently broken out among groups of Christian believers, they have been *confined* to those different groups at those different times. In other words, they have been solely *within* "the household of the faith." They have never become a movement *through* believer-groups to the outside world. They have been in fulfillment of the New Testament promises to the true Church: "gifts of healings" by the Holy Spirit to the saints. Much less have there ever been in the Church's history organized Christian healing campaigns to the general public. The outreaching healing movement of today is something *different*.

The nearest thing to it is what happened during the first century or two, when a brand-new Christianity was pushing its introductory conquests among the nations. Its healing miracles, along with other "signs and wonders," were God-given evidences of its divine origin. Obviously, those were not miracles *upon* Christian believers but *by* Christians upon *others*, with a view to their becoming converts to the new faith.

Yet even then there was nothing closely comparable to the healing movement of these latter days, with its crusades and centers *specializing* in supernatural healing. What we are witnessing today is something peculiar to the twentieth century, especially to this second half of it. To exemplify this let me now refer to the ministry of Kathryn Kuhlman.

A "New Dimension"

To use a common current expression, a "new dimension" appeared in this latter-day divine-healing phenomenon through the ministry of the recently deceased Kathryn Kuhlman. In my considered opinion she was one of the most significant figures in the recent history of evangelical Christendom. She was no scholar and never claimed to be. Nor was she even a trained preacher: she never claimed to be. But she was a superbly effective evangelist and won thousands to the Lord. She was not the kind who go to a town for ten days or two weeks and then move on. Right from the early days of her evangelizing exploits she preferred to continue in a town or city for weeks or months. In fact, her preference all the way through was to work *in* and then *from* a settled center. Such a procedure, however, meant that besides sustained evangelism there must be Bible teaching for young believers and others, a by-product of which was that she developed a captivating style as a popular-type Bible teacher.

Apparently it was after a crisis experience of enduement by the Holy Spirit that divine healings began to appear in her meetings. It was not because of any preaching or stress on the subject. The healings occurred unannounced, then became frequent, then increased to such proportion that special place had to be made in the program for those wonderful doings of the Lord. Gradually at first, then more rapidly in her fifties and sixties, she became one of the most notable figures in evangelical Christendom.

She would *never* allow herself to be called a "faith healer." She rightly considered the title misleading. I myself have heard her say, as she often said, "*I* have no power to heal; it is all of the Lord. I do not have any *'gift'* of healing. All I know is that the power falls, the Holy Spirit fills the place, and the healing miracles begin."

Now about the new feature which appeared with Kathryn Kuhlman. There was no coming up of anyone from the congregation to the platform, to have the "laying on of hands," or to have the preacher say with loud authority, "I command this sickness to depart, in the name of JESUS." There was no contact between anyone in the audience and the Lord's servant on the platform before the healings took place. The miracles happened in the *audience* during the meeting, usually from a certain *point* in the meeting when the power seemed to sweep down among the people. Never have I seen in meetings where there was such union of trembling adoration and irrepressible shouts of gratitude to God or where the healings were more carefully screened against any kind of artificiality. The platform was kindly but firmly guarded against anyone coming there until *after* being healed; and, once on the platform, a healed person, besides being allowed to declare the nature of the miracle, was interrogated with a view to a certifying of it.

Coinciding with that "point" in the meeting when the Spirit began moving with healings among the audience, Kathryn herself would plainly become enswathed by His power. She would suddenly say, "There is a man in the gallery to my right with spinal trouble. You are wearing a brace for it. You have worn it several years. If you will take it off, you will find you are healed." Or it might be, "Down there to my left, in the wheelchair section, is a woman with crippling arthritis. You have been for months now in that wheelchair, but this minute the Lord is completely healing you." Now and then she would mention some uncommon ailment most specifically and actually point right at the afflicted person in the vast audience.

Once the healed persons began gathering on the platform, the power seemed to envelope Kathryn herself yet the more. Those who came near her would crumple and fall to the floor. My memories of it are fresh. A young Roman Catholic woman had been healed of some stubborn malady. Kathryn could not make out something the young woman was trying to say; so as two Roman Catholic priests happened to be among the platform visitors, she asked them to come forward and help. The two priests essayed to do so; but as they passed near Kathryn, they were swept off their feet, and down they fell "under the power." Several times I saw her call doctors forward to examine some miraculously healed luxation of a joint or some straightening of a crooked limb; but as they passed near to Kathryn, the power caught them and they fell flat on the platform. So it went

There are *big meanings* wrapped up in Kathryn Kuhlman's ministry. This was no "gift" confined to one chosen spokesman of the Lord. It was something which Kathryn herself neither possessed nor understood. I have been in her meetings. I have heard her down-to-earth expositions of the Word. I have keenly observed the change of expression that came over her face as she drew to the end of her message, a look of sudden new intensity as the Holy Spirit somehow began to inform her that certain persons with certain ailments were over here or over there, in the balcony or down in the wheelchair section. Then the healing power would break loose and the miracles would begin. Then, also, the "power" would atmosphere Kathryn, after which those who came near her would buckle up and sink to the floor. I have indeed seen it all; I have marveled and have adored the Lord who was so evidently in the midst. I have also met Kathryn about half-an-hour after such a meeting, in the little room offstage, and have found, even so soon afterward, the supernatural aura departed, leaving Kathryn just an engaging but ordinary person.

Some of the most astonishing movings of the Holy Spirit occurred in connection with her ministry; yet they occurred in such a way as to emphasize that it was independent of Kathryn herself. For instance in his biography of her entitled *Daughter of Destiny*, Jamie Buckingham tells how in 1966 she was guest speaker at a ladies luncheon held in the Deauville Hotel, Miami, Florida. Over a

thousand women packed the room. Kathryn was duly introduced, but she never had chance to preach. Just as she rose to bring
her message, there was a rustle of noise at the rear of the room, "like
wind blowing through the trees."[1] Then came a sound of chairs
scraping against the floor while at the back of the room there were
outbreaks of laughter and excited cries of surprise. The healings had
already started! "Women began streaming to the front of the
crowded room, tears running down their faces as they testified of
healings which had occurred instantaneously the moment Kathryn
stood to speak."[2]

Similarly extraordinary features clung around her great monthly
assemblages at the Shrine Auditorium, Los Angeles, and at other
places. Often there would be sudden healings of persons while they
were being driven in cars or buses *on their way* to the auditorium!
Others would be completely healed while among the crowd outside
waiting for the doors to be opened! Still others would be healed in the
meeting before ever Kathryn appeared on the platform!

There were even stranger accompaniments. Dr. Ralph Wilkerson,
who heads a great evangelical witness in Anaheim, California, with
continual miracle healings similar to those of the Kathryn Kuhlman
ministry, videotaped one of the services which she held for him at
Anaheim. When he showed the film later to a ministers' meeting,
even more healings suddenly broke out through the watching of the
tape! Jamie Buckingham tells of the time when the film of her miracle
service in Jerusalem was shown later at his church in Florida, and
now suddenly, as the people quietly stood for a moment of prayer,
"there was the sound of scraping chairs and falling bodies. . . .
Almost one third of the congregation, it seemed, were stretched out
on the floor or slumped in chairs. . . . It was one of the most powerful
demonstrations of the Holy Spirit I have ever witnessed."[3]

I repeat, there are big meanings wrapped up in it. This coming of
the Holy Spirit directly upon *audiences* instead of operating as formerly through some human instrument has brought a new dimension into present-day public ministry of healing. It swings big new
possibilities and likelihoods into view in answer to prayer. It has not
appeared before so far as I know. Even back in that first century A.D.,
this kind of thing does not appear to have happened. What is its chief
significance for us at the present moment? Surely it means this:

*Such an unusual manifestation of miracle healing in such a new way is
the clear, bold signature of the Holy Spirit upon the present-day public
ministry of divine healing.*

God is doing a "new thing" in these days in answer to the abnormal insurgence of evil. As the present age draws to a close, Satan is more brazenly unmasking himself. Filthy forms of sin which hitherto have skulked in the shadows now parade with vulgar publicity. Witchcraft, spiritism, Satan worship, antigodism, demon possession, sexual libertinism, anti-Christian philosophy, drug addiction, sodomy, violence, and such are rioting today with a naked defiance and clever self-justification never known before. The usual kind of intellectual Christian apologetics seems powerless to penetrate it, for it laughs religious ethic and logic in the face. It is directly energized by Satan and demon intelligences in a latter-day upsurge. There is a peculiar need for a *new* Christian apologetic to match the hour, a new dynamic demonstration that the Christian Gospel is "the power of *God*"; and I believe that God is giving it.

I say again that this new *public* healing movement of the divine Spirit is *not* to be confused with His intended healing ministry *inside* our local Christian churches. The "gifts of healings" among born-again members of Christian assemblies are clearly *promised* in Scripture; but this new phenomenon of public audience miracle healings is something which is *not* forepictured even in Mark 16. Do we not see in it our Lord's "new thing" for this present hour of abnormal, Satanic challenge? The Holy Spirit's "gifts of healings" among believers and Christian churches are a ministry of divine compassion and edification; but, as we have said, the divine miracles occurring in *public* healing ministries and among many who are not avowed Christians are meant to be unanswerable *evidences* to all men that true Christianity is of God.

Of course, there is some inevitable overlap between the Holy Spirit's healing ministry inside local Christian churches, on the one hand, and His surprise visitation with miracle healings among the larger *public*. There is overlap because many who get healed in public divine healing missions are believers; also, some of the large healing campaigns are held inside church buildings. Yet these two different healing activities of the Holy Spirit should not be confused. They are not one and the same. The one is confined within the churches; the other is largely *outside* the churches. The one is clearly promised in the written Word; the other is nowhere predicted (unless we press again Mark 16) but is an unprophesied work of the Spirit. The one within the churches will go on right to the end of the Church age; the other may prove to be only an emergency visitation to match a present crisis hour.

Yes, there is real reason why we should differentiate. The healing "gifts" of the Holy Spirit will remain continually accessible to local Christian groups right up to our Lord's return whereas the Kathryn Kuhlman large-scale type of healing phenomena may prove to be only a *temporary* manifestation—though that does not make it any less wonderful or any less needed. It should be the prayer of all Christian hearts that such miracle-attested ministries of the true Gospel might yet become a high tide of *salvation* rolling in upon the shores of our national life.

But if, as we have said, this reappearance of miracle healings in this unprecedented way is *not* the promised "gifts of healings" within local Christian assemblies and is *not* foredescribed in Scripture, how can it prove to be anything *more* than a flash in the pan? What scriptural reason have we to expect such an extraordinary visitation in these days? Many tell us that according to Scripture, things are to go from bad to worse now, until Antichrist appears, the man whose cryptic identity is 666. Surely, they say, there is no indication of any major movement of God's Spirit between now and our Lord's return.

To that we may well reply, Where does Scripture foretell the mighty evangelical liberation which we now call the Protestant Reformation? Where does Scripture foretell that glorious spiritual awakening, the Methodist Revival, which saved Britain from something akin to the French Revolution and spilled over with wonderful blessing along the Eastern Seaboard of the U.S.? Where does Scripture foretell any of the other similarly epochal visitations of spiritual revival during the anno Domini centuries? The answer is, Nowhere. Yet they *came*, thank God, and took the Lord's languishing "seven thousands" by lovely surprise. Moreover, as already noted, there is indeed much reason why we may expect some singular intervention of our Lord today over against the accentuated machinations of Satanic evil in our twentieth-century society. When the enemy "comes in like a flood," need we wonder that in corresponding power the Spirit of the Lord will "lift up a standard against him"?

DIVINE HEALING IN OUR LOCAL CHRISTIAN CHURCHES

That brings us to another aspect of present-day healing miracles. If the big healing movement now in evidence seems mainly *outside* our local Christian churches, what about supernatural healing ministry *inside* them? Is not God speaking to all of us evangelical ministers and congregations today by what He is doing in outstanding healing ministries to the crowd? I, for one, believe that He is.

Should there not be a resuscitated ministry of supernatural healing in *all* our truly evangelical churches?

Let me speak frankly. I have no connection with the so-called Charismatic movement nor with any miracle-healing center nor with any Pentecostal group. In conviction I am thoroughly evangelical and by denominational affiliation Baptist—though for the past twenty years my itinerating Bible ministry has been quite interdenominational among our various Protestant and evangelical churches. I would not necessarily decline to speak at a meeting under the auspices of the Charismatic movement—if invited; though I would never knowingly do so in any way which would compromise our precious, vital, evangelical *doctrines*. For in my judgment one of the urgent needs today is for a new reaffirmation of those saving truths in differentiation from Liberalism on the one hand and from Romanism on the other.

It is heartening to see so many Roman Catholics coming into evangelical meetings these days. We love every one of them as human individuals, from the pope and the cardinals downward. But until the pope renounces his infallibility and the cardinals their Mariolatry and the priests their masses and confessionals, and until the Roman church officially renounces those dogmas which flatly contradict Scripture, we simply cannot enjoy unhindered fellowship with them; much less can we share the same platform of evangelism, for *they* exalt tradition to equal authority with the Bible and do *not* preach the truly Biblical doctrine of salvation which *we* preach.

Does doctrinal fidelity to God's written Word no longer matter? Are we now to play fast and loose with those liberating truths which were restored to us at the cost of sacrificial blood and tears? Are we now to ignore as irrelevant the red lamp of solemn warning in Galatians 1:8: "Though we, or an angel from heaven, preach any other gospel unto you than that which we have preached unto you, let him be *accursed*" (emphasis mine)? Let my earnest prayer be "Lord, fill me with true love for *all*, for Roman Catholics, for Liberalists, for heretics and extremists, and for all others who differ from me. But may it *never* be in a way which betrays the clear truths of Thine inspired Word, for *they* are the truths which alone can save *them* as well as me."

As I see it, one of the most worrying weaknesses of the present Charismatic movement is its foolish turning a blind eye to doctrinal differences between Evangelicals and Roman Catholicism. Far more vital than speaking in tongues or bodily healings, and far more vital than public "fellowship" with leaders of nonevangelical churches, is the preservation of those *saving truths* for which Protestant martyrs suffered rack and torture and death! I here prophesy that unless the modern Charismatic movement makes its position firm and clear as to this, it will decay and disappear: it will prove to be a short bamboo blaze instead of a continuing fire.

Anyway, at this time of writing I am neither *pro* nor *anti* charismatic, though I confess to some disturbing suspicions as I observe excesses in the Charismatic movement. Viewing it cautiously but openly, I pray God's best for it; as for myself, I want all that the gracious Holy Spirit is wanting to give. And that brings me back to what I was saying about the need for a revived experience of the Holy Spirit's healing ministry in our local evangelical churches. However much some of us may dislike features in the Charismatic movement, may it not be that our Lord is trying to say something to *us* through it? In thinking others are *wrong*, let us be careful lest we be *blind*.

I ask my brethren in the evangelical ministry, Are *you* living in the experience of the Holy Spirit's *infilling?* Are your public services of worship and witness evidently in the "demonstration and power" of the Spirit? Is the seal of the Spirit manifest in continual conversions and in a continual soul-winning outreach of your church members? If so, should you not be asking for heavenly guidance in the matter of the Holy Spirit's "gifts of healings"? What a blessing it could be to your dear flock! Have you half-a-dozen elders or deacons or spiritual seniors who are Spirit-taught brethren and who wholeheartedly believe in the Scripturalness of "gifts of healings" and who would be willing, under your own pastoral leadership, to give themselves to prayer with a view to becoming available to the sick and afflicted among you? Ought you not to pray and pray and pray again that God will give you such a group, that the Holy Spirit will "clothe" *you* in a new way so that special healings or special intelligence may be communicated through you and your specially consecrated group to your membership?

Think what it might mean if this became operative once again in *all* our evangelical churches. Think what it might mean to the *neighborhoods* where our churches labor. May it not well be that the Spirit of God is calling our attention to this through the Charismatic renewal movement?

Possibly, in the present-day new aliveness to the Holy Spirit's gifts, there is a significance which has been unsuspectedly *latent* but ought now to become *patent*. Let me elucidate. Travel back in thought to the first centuries of our Christian era. Paul and Peter were right, alas, in forewarning that after their demise "wolves" from without and "false prophets" from within would cause doctrinal and spiritual breakdown in the organized church (Acts 20:29-30; 2 Peter 2:1 et. al.). But the historical corruption of early Christianity did not happen suddenly. It was a downgrade process, first slight, then steep, with an eventual slump into Roman ecclesiasticism and totalitarianism—and the Dark Ages.

It is solemnizing to observe the order in which the defection and perversion proceeded. First, the true "gifts" of the *Spirit* were lost, being gradually substituted by imaginary miracles until eventually the simple rite of elders anointing the sick for *healing* degenerated into the last rites of a priest preparing the sick for *dying!* Next we see the disappearance of the Church's true *hope*—the return of Christ and the resurrection of the saints. Death and the grave became the goal; and instead of healings through faith in a living Christ, we find alleged healings through contact with the bones of dead "saints"! Next, the true concept of personal *holiness* died. Instead of a positive holiness in-wrought by the Holy Spirit came a negative, legalistic monasticism! Then, the true doctrine of the *Church* was lost. Instead of the Church as a spiritual organism came the monolithic, institutional, politico-religious hierarchy of Rome. Finally, the cardinal doctrine of personal salvation through Christ, of "justification by faith," was lost in the pathetic debris of a Christendom stifled amid the sacerdotal draperies of the Dark Ages.

Now it is a notable fact that since the Protestant Reformation those great evangelical distinctives have been recovered, or considerably so, but in *inverse order*. First, through Luther's leadership the keystone truth of "justification by grace through faith" was released and shouted from the housetops. That was the first big Reformation issue over which the battle was fought and won. Then, inch by inch, the true doctrine of the *Church* was recaptured. Then, with Marshall and Wesley, a more truly Scriptural doctrine of personal holiness began to be rediscovered. Then, about the middle of the nineteenth century, the long-lost "blessed hope" of the Church began to shine out again in resurrected resplendence. While now, as that rapturous prospect draws discernibly nearer, it would seem as though the Holy Spirit is restoring and reemphasizing the lost *pneumatikoi* (spiritual gifts) or *charismata* (grace gifts) with conspicuous activity in "gifts of *healings.*"

Without any charismatic bias, but with an eager yearning that our local evangelical churches might be more truly accordant with the New Testament original and more vibrant with the life and energy and supernatural doings of the Holy Spirit, I would cordially recommend to my brethren in the evangelical ministry the challenge of Christ: "He that hath an ear, let him hear what the Spirit [is now saying] unto the churches" (Rev. 2:7).

Can any of us who have sifted the evidences doubt that God was saying something significantly timely, for instance, through Kathryn Kuhlman? Many of us conservatives are rigidly skeptical of such heroic-sized public "healers" (as we call them) and rightly so, to a degree, for there have been slick-tongued manipulators and exploiters among them. Kathryn Kuhlman herself was a cynosure by reason of the healing abnormalities which proliferated around her: but those healings were *real*. For any of us conservatives to downplay miracles of healing which were as provenly the work of the Holy Spirit as any which ever happened throughout history is not mere skepticism; it is a dark and risky refusal which I believe deeply grieves the Spirit of grace.

Admittedly, the Kuhlman operation was a one-track testimony, with nothing new theologically or even in evangelistic technique. But it was specially raised up of God as a monumental witness that a new opportunity is knocking. The Holy Spirit is looking for evangelical pastors and groups through whom He can give revived manifestation of His power to heal and unify and energize.

Why should God *need* to raise up a woman like Kathryn Kuhlman and specially work through *her* such numerous miracles of healing? We might just as well ask, Why does God periodically raise up special evangelists like Charles Finney, D. L. Moody, R. A. Torrey, and Billy Graham? It is because of evangelizing failure on the part of our Protestant churches in general. If all our local churches were red-hot evangelizing centers, there would be little if any need for God to raise up outstanding "specials" to do the job. Similarly, in the case of Kathryn Kuhlman, perhaps there would be no need for such if all our churches today were living in the freshness and vigor of the first century Christian assemblies. Surely God is now calling us back to that first century pattern, to a new experience of the Holy Spirit with a new release of His supernatural activities among us.

Note That Double Plural

Perhaps at this point I should draw attention to a circumstance which we have not mentioned earlier in these studies, a circumstance connected with the Holy Spirit's healing ministry among Christian believers *inside* local churches. Let me refer again to 1 Corinthians 12 and what it says about the "gifts" of the Spirit. Note verses 8 and 9.

> For to one is given by the Spirit the word of wisdom; to another the word of knowledge by the same Spirit; to another faith by the same Spirit; to another the *gifts of healing* by the same Spirit.

Look again at that phrase "gifts of healing." Observe that the noun is plural, i.e., *"gifts"*; that plural is important. It becomes the more meaningful when we note that the word "healing" should also be pluralized (as in the English Revised and American Standard Version). In the Greek there is a double plural: "gifts of healings." It is notable because it does not occur with any other gift of the Spirit. Nor is it accidental, for it occurs three times—always that double plural:

> "gifts of healings" (v. 9)
> "gifts of healings" (v. 28)
> "gifts of healings" (v. 30)

So the double plural is evidently used precisely, which means that there is a reason for it; and indeed there *is* a reason which we do well to ponder.

The other gifts of the Spirit, having been imparted to different members of the assembly, become *resident* in them. For instance, when the gift of "tongues" has been imparted, it *remains* with a believer—even when not being used—and can be called into exercise from time to time, whenever spiritual impulse may kindle it. So is it with the gift of "prophecy." Even when dormant, the gift, having been once imparted, remains. Indeed it is so definitely a resident gift that he who has it may become distinctively known as a "prophet" (Acts 11:27; 13:1; 15:32; 21:10; 1 Cor. 12:28; 14:29, 32; Eph. 4:11).

Now healing power, apparently, is *never* given in that way. There is no such thing as a "gift" (singular) of healing which *remains* in anyone. Each miracle of healing, even though effected by the Holy Spirit *through* a human intermediary, is a gift all by itself. It comes *through* some believer but never *from* that believer. Each separate healing is a "gift" (singular) from the Holy Spirit. *Many* such healings are "gifts" (plural) of healings.

But *why* cannot there be a resident gift of healing, after the pattern of the Spirit's other gifts? It is because the communicating of *healing* is the communicating of renewing *life*. With none of the other gifts is there any such biotic communication from one believer to another. Only the Holy Spirit can communicate life; therefore, *each healing comes freshly from Himself*, even though He may use a human transmitter.

Let it sink in: no Christian, however otherwise gifted or consecrated, has in himself or in herself a continuing *gift* of healing. The Phillips translation of 1 Corinthians 12:9 is miles off course when it says, "The same Spirit gives to another man faith, to another the *ability* to heal" (emphasis mine). No! None of us is given any resident ability to heal. Only the Spirit imparts life and health. Even though He may use a certain brother or sister *repeatedly* as His healing conductor, each new healing is a separate "gift" from Himself. A Christian brother or sister may *use* any other "gift" of the Spirit; and each is meant to be used for the edifying of the assembly as a whole (1 Cor. 14:12), but no man can "use" the Holy Spirit. In this matter of healing, it is *HE* who breaks in and uses *us* each time there is a healing.

But why should the word "healings" also be in the plural? Is it not because there are so many different kinds of sickness and disease? Thank God, the Spirit's "gifts of *healings*" cover them all!

I believe that today the Holy Spirit is looking in our local evangelical churches for "vessels unto honour, sanctified, and meet for the Master's use" through whom He may restore the gracious activity of supernatural healing. He never leaves truly yielded vessels unfilled. Brother pastor and fellow-believers all, what about *you* and *your* church?

Healings in Relation to Faith

Let me underline again here the importance of distinguishing between the Holy Spirit's healing "gifts" (in local Christian churches) and His healing nowadays in connection with large public evangelizing. Not only does that shed light on why some are healed and others not in public healing missions, but it may be the key, also, as to why in some cases healing comes in answer to *faith* while in others it seems to have little or nothing to do with faith.

Plainly, those supernatural cures which the Holy Spirit is working among the *public*, in big healing campaigns, cannot be on the principle found in Matthew 9:29 of "according to your *faith* be it unto you"; for many are healed who have formerly been indifferent to Christian truth. It has taken sickness to interrupt their irreligion and give them a concern about God. Even then, in not a few cases their concern has been far more for bodily healing than for soul salvation. If God were to wait for *faith* before healing such, they would *never* be healed. But God does not wait for faith in those cases; for the healing is meant to be a "sign," a proof, a demonstration, an unanswerable "evidence" that the Gospel is the saving truth of God. Sometimes the convincing impressiveness is all the greater, especially among the nonreligious, *because* the miraculously healed person was hitherto similarly careless about spiritual realities.

But among Christians, members of our local evangelical churches, God's method is understandably different. *There,* in His dealings with the born-again (who, reflect, are His eternally "elect"), God is primarily concerned with their spiritual *education.* It is with that in mind that sickness itself is often permitted; and it is with that in mind that in their case God also requires *faith* to be exercised for healing—albeit, not alone the faith of the sick one but the sympathetic, vicarious faith also of the praying and anointing elders (see our earlier comments on James 5:14-15). The heart searchings occasioned by the sickness and the strugglings through to where faith can really *believe* for healing are all part of the educative and sanctifying process.

SOME FINAL TOUCHES

Since this book has been throughout a consideration of healing *miracles,* perhaps it is wise, now, to add a balancing reflection as to their value and limitations. There is no doubt that such miracles *get the crowd.* If you want to pack the building, announce miracle-healing services! You will have more patients and sightseers than you can handle! In John 2:23 we read, "Now when he [Jesus] was in Jerusalem at the passover . . . many believed in his name when they saw the miracles which he did." A few verses later we find Nicodemus saying to Jesus, "Rabbi, we know that thou art a teacher come from God; for no man can do these miracles that thou doest, except God be with him" (John 3:2). See, then, the twofold value of miracles: their power to attract the "many" and their evidential power to convince the Nicodemuses.

Yet now go right to the end of our Lord's public ministry and get John's final comment on the miracles. In 12:37 of his Gospel, John says, "But though he had done so many miracles before them, yet they *believed not on him"!* As the old proverb says, You may lead a horse to water, but you cannot make him drink. Even so, no one was ever yet born again by seeing a miracle. No, miracles may convince the head but they cannot convert the heart. Paul wrought so many miracles in the name of Jesus that "all they which dwelt in Asia" were stirred (Acts 19:10-11, 17-20). There was no getting over those mighty miracles. They were sure proof of God. Thousands were impressed. But now read 2 Timothy 1:15, written some time later: "All they which are in Asia be *turned away from me.*"

So we are under no delusion as to the value and the limitations of miracles. They have an important place; but to preach divine truth under such enduement by the Holy Spirit that *souls* are truly saved and regenerated is a far bigger thing than the miraculous healing of a mortal *body.*

Miracles and Maturity

It will be our spiritual wisdom, also, to realize that miracle healings are not necessarily a proof of spiritual superquality in those through whom the Holy Spirit effects them. I regret to say this, but Jamie Buckingham's biography of Kathryn Kuhlman leaves no doubt that she was far from a spiritual model in some respects. Indiscretion, impulsiveness, extravagance, and thinly disguised egotism—all symptoms of spiritual immaturity—appeared in her from time to time, dear servant of God though she was. Only recently I was chatting with two brethren who have been signally used in the ministry of miracle healing, who, nevertheless, evinced far less grasp of deep spiritual truth than others I have known who never experienced "gifts of healings." This is one reason why Paul says that "prophecy" (not necessarily prediction but the expounding of divine truth in the power of the Spirit) is the greatest of the gifts, for "prophecy" more than any other gift *is* a sign of rich maturity.

Handkerchief Healings

I hope these studies have successfully shown that although the New Testament promises healing for Christians, and although "gifts of healings" are included among the Holy Spirit's *charismata* in the churches, we have no warrant to insist that supernatural healings and other miracles are meant for today in the way they occurred during the Acts of the Apostles. The New Testament Epistles nowhere vouchsafe *that.* Those Apostolic miracles were *peculiar* to the Apostolic interval. That people were healed by Peter's shadow and Paul's handkerchiefs *then* is no reason in itself why they should be *now*. Let us not try to wrench things into present operation which are not promised. Let there be no vain pressuring of the Holy Spirit, as though we could "twist the arm" of the Lord! If the Holy Spirit starts healing again through shadows and handkerchiefs, well and good; but it will *not* be in fulfillment of any promise to the *Church:* it will be an independent "repeat performance." Meanwhile, therefore, let us not try to *force* the past into the present, or we shall mix up the dispensations!

An Appeal: A Suggestion

As I come to the close of these studies and reflections, I am back again at that vexing question: Why are some healed but not others? In that connection I want to make an appeal to those brethren who believe they are called to public healing missions. With all my heart I wish them the blessing of God, but that only makes me the more anxious to address this appeal to them. Is it not time we stopped preaching that divine healing is promised to *all?*—for it is *not*. Is it not time we stopped offering to people in general what is promised to born-again believers *only?* Is it not time we stopped preaching that because Jesus healed all the sick who came to Him long ago He does the same today?—for He does *not*. Is it not time we stopped preaching that all sickness is directly from Satan?—for it is *not*. Is it not time we stopped preaching that it is *always* the will of God to heal?—for it is *not*.

As long as preachers of divine healing keep preaching *that*, there will be needless heartburning and souring disillusionment. People will keep getting badly hurt, the cause of our dear Savior will correspondingly suffer, and the question, "Why only some and not others?" will keep cutting with raw edge. To all mixed audiences let the preaching be first that *the salvation of the soul is far more important than the healing of the body*. Let the unconverted be urged to receive Christ as Savior before seeking Him as Healer. Let it be said plainly that the New Testament promises of divine healing are made to Christians only, not to others. Then let it be affirmed that in these last days, in addition to the New Testament promises to Christian believers, God is plainly doing "a new thing"; He is healing many by miracles for the twofold purpose of expressing His wide *compassion* and of giving new *evidence* that Christianity is of God.

That leads me to make a further recommendation, namely, that those who minister by way of public healing missions or gatherings should align themselves as far as possible to the Kathryn Kuhlman pattern: no coming to the platform for anointing and laying on of hands in the *hope* of getting healed but a praying down of the Holy Spirit upon the whole audience so that the healings break out *there.* Undoubtedly there is something much more moving and convincing in *that* kind of divine manifestation, and it takes away all charges of hypnotism or artificiality from the lips of would-be critics. Oh, for more such thrilling outbreaks of the divine presence and power in our meetings!

Charismatic Characteristics

Apropos of that, is it not time that our charismatic brethren improved the *style* and *quality* of their public gatherings? In all of those which I myself have attended, there has been a disappointing superficiality and jauntiness. In emphasizing liberty, friendliness, and informality, they have slidden into an unrestrained freeness which sometimes seems to border on levity. I am seldom if ever aware of the "hush" of the divine presence in their conducting of a gathering. There is a lot of hand clapping, arm waving, and chorus singing; but the spiritual quality and atmosphere are poor, along with the lack of orderliness. I, too, believe there should be the "liberty of the Spirit" in our Christian convocations; but I believe that it should be liberty with orderliness, not liberty with slovenliness.

Where has the Bible got to in many charismatic gatherings? To my own way of thinking, in every such meeting the Word of God should be heard. Where has the hymnbook gone? The people are not given hymnbooks; so none of the richer-quality hymns can be sung (such hymns have much to do with the spiritual tone or level of Christian gatherings). The hymnbook is forsaken in favor of lilting choruses—chorus after chorus, with repetition after repetition, meeting after meeting. Where has Bible teaching gone? Instead of enriching, challenging, edifying Bible exposition and application there is a platform-engineered stir up of emotion. There is a place, of course, for stirred emotions; but emotional*ism* is bad, and there is far too much of it.

I used to think that meetings in which supernatural healings take place *must* by reason of that be most deeply spiritual; but I have been in healing meetings where I have felt sadly sure that although the Holy Spirit was honoring the witness given to divine healing, it was *despite* the poor type of meeting.

These remarks are just as charitable as they are frank. The longing of my heart is that a deeper, richer quality of meetings and fellowship might take the place of much that is modern fashion; for I believe that then we might see *far more* wonderful activity of the "power from on high" in the healing of suffering humanity.

A Cautionary Postscript

And now let me add this parting counsel. When we have said the first and the last about divine healing of the body, it still remains that God purposely does *not* heal all His people of their sicknesses; and it still remains that there is often a blessed *ministry* in suffering.

It is because we fail to recognize this that seeming enigmas hit us with such depressing force. How could it be that Paul, the greatest of all our Lord's miracle healers, should himself have an unhealed malady year after year until his martyrdom? Why should it be that Kathryn Kuhlman, the most remarkable of all present-time ministers of healing, should have a slowly developing trouble with enlarged heart for twenty years, eventually causing damage to the mitral valve and causing continual pain for several years before she died so that for some time before her decease she "never went anywhere without her medicine"? Although she ministered healing to thousands, she herself never experienced it!

Yes, there are still strange enigmas—at least seemingly so to us human onlookers. Meanwhile both Scripture and Christian experience through the centuries unite to tell us that sickness is often divinely permitted with gracious purpose, that healing is sometimes withheld for the sake of even richer benefit, and that there are higher levels of blessing than miraculous physical healings. Therefore, in Peter's words we counsel, "Let them that suffer according to the will of God commit the keeping of their souls to him in well doing, as unto a faithful Creator" (1 Peter 4:19).

And as a parting addendum to that let me here register disapproval of those who still persist in preaching that divine healing is in opposition to human medical skill. Heaven be praised for all the healing knowledge gradually acquired by the medical profession through the centuries, often through much sacrifice, and especially for therapeutic and surgical triumphs achieved in our more scientific modern world.

Some time ago a preacher of divine healing went to a certain town in England to hold special meetings. On the first Saturday evening he was asked whether he would give his testimony at an open-air meeting. As he stood forward to speak, one of the supporting workers thoughtfully offered him a megaphone which had been found very useful; but it was disdained with the remark, "In this kind of God's work I do not use such merely human aids." With unpardonable naughtiness his would-be helper replied, "Then had you not better take out your artificial teeth?"

Yes, we are all forgetfully vulnerable! We may take it as settled that even our infinite God never does the superfluous. He will not intervene to work a miracle where human medication or contrivance can effectively meet the need. I believe that Christian praying for healing should go hand in hand with the human physician or surgeon when the required answer can come *that* way just as much as we should pray when healing is sought from some malady which is *beyond* human skill to heal.

Does someone happen to have traveled through these chapters who now comes to the end saying, "*I* am one of those with a disease which *no* merely human skill can cure"? What is my parting word to you? I would offer five comments. (1) Do not think that because God has not said yes, you are strangely peculiar or that God dislikes you. (2) Although so far God has not given you the healing for which you long, He may yet do so. (3) Try not to murmur, for God dearly loves you even though His permissive will seems shrouded in mystery. The God who so suffered on Calvary for you can never mock you or turn a deaf ear to your pleading. (4) Do not struggle or wrestle or argue with God because of the seeming no answer. Many have testified afterward that the *greatest* blessing came, not through a healing, but through the weary, hanging-on-to-God process. That is my own testimony, dear reader. In my deepest abyss of suffering and of seeming repulse from God, I made my gladdest discovery of Him and have been different ever since. (5) Jesus is risen, alive, ever present, almighty; and He loves you. Today again, and to a degree scarcely known before, He is healing people. Surrender your whole being to Him. Then, so yielded to Him that you would sooner be in His dear will *without* healing than have healing *apart* from His will, ask Him to do it for you, to His own praise and glory. Do not weary yourself with plaintive begging. Let your asking be part of a loving *communing* with Him. Who knows?—perhaps even yet you may find yourself singing with David,

> Bless the Lord, O my soul,
> And forget not all his benefits:
> Who forgiveth all thine iniquities;

Who healeth all thy diseases;
Who redeemeth thy life from destruction;
Who crowneth thee with lovingkindness
And tender mercies.

(Psalm 103:2-3)

NOTES

[1]Jamie Buckingham, *Daughter of Destiny* (Plainfield, N.J.: Logos International 1977), p. 207.
[2]Ibid.
[3]Ibid.

Subject Index

Scripture Index

Old Testament

New Testament